*Principles of Hotel*

Fro...ration

ORT LOAN CO

This book is **due** for ret
TIME STAMPED BEL

2nd Edition

*Please note that fines will be charged*

**Also available from Thomson Learning:**

*Principles of Hospitality Law*, 2nd Edition: Boella and Pannett

*Sales and Service for the Wine Professional*: Julyan

*HRM in Tourism and Hospitality*: Lee-Ross (ed)

*Fundamentals of Hospitality Marketing*: Mawson

*Using Computers in Hospitality*, 2nd Edition: O'Connor

*Supervision and Leadership in Tourism and Hospitality*: Van der Wagen and Davies

*Environmental Management for Hospitality*: Webster

# Principles of Hotel Front Office Operations

## 2nd Edition

**Sue Baker, Pam Bradley and Jeremy Huyton**

Australia • Canada • Mexico • Singapore • Spain • United Kingdom • United States

THOMSON

**Principles of Hotel Front Office Operations**

**Copyright © 2000 Sue Baker, Pam Bradley and Jeremy Huyton**

The Thomson logo is a registered trademark used herein under licence.

For more information, contact Thomson Learning, High Holborn House, 50-51 Bedford Row, London WC1R 4LR or visit us on the World Wide Web at:
http://www.thomsonlearning.co.uk

*British Library Cataloguing-in-Publication Data*
A catalogue record for this book is available from the British Library

**ISBN 1-84480-090-3**

**First edition published 1994 by Continuum**
**Second edition published 2000 by Continuum**
**Reprinted 2001 by Continuum**
**Reprinted 2003 by Thomson Learning**

Typeset by Fakenham Photosetting Ltd, Fakenham, Norfolk

Printed in the UK by TJ International, Padstow, Cornwall

# Contents

# *Preface*

In countries throughout the world the steady and continual increase in size of the tourist and hospitality industries continues. In order to accommodate, both literally and figuratively, the world's travellers, the hotel industry is also expanding to keep up with the demand.

For many people it is the façade, design or even location that creates the important, lasting first impression. However, the hotel industry, more so than almost any other, is highly people orientated. It is the effectiveness, efficiency and warmth of these people which is what really creates that lasting impression and it is these same people who, by their attitudes and friendliness, subconsciously attract guests back to the hotel.

Very often the first and last place in which the guest comes into direct contact with the hotel staff is the front desk. This book is an introduction to the vibrant world of front office operations.

The chapters tend to follow the chronological order of this hotel department, with the taking and handling of reservations being followed by the guest's check-in, subsequent billing and eventual check-out. However, as with life, nothing is quite so cut and dried, and throughout the book we will make small detours into other areas and departments. The book has been written under the assumption that its readers are new to the hotel industry and especially to the front office. Consequently, some of you may find certain aspects familiar or well known to you; if this is the case then simply move through the book more quickly. However, please do remember to use your lecturer in order to gain better clarification and comprehension. Not only will this help to give more understanding of the subject, but it will also help to make the topic come alive.

In many cases throughout the book we have used the example of large and computerized hotels. This is not because we want to ignore smaller hotels, but simply because we feel that the trend is inexorably towards a computerized hotel regardless of size. However, it must be remembered that the principles of the operation of a front office are basically the same whatever the hotel's size, and once you have mastered them with understanding and imagination you can adapt them to suit any property.

The activities throughout the book should always be attempted. They are structured to help you to get a better grasp of what is being said. They are also there to stimulate you into thinking like a front office person. No book on its own can make you a receptionist or reservations clerk. There are many systems and procedures to be understood and mastered, as well as many customer and social skills to be learned; all of these take time and most of all practice. Consequently, what we want is for you to have not only the chance to read and practise theoretical exercises, but more importantly the opportunity to gain the ability to think like a front office person. With a sound knowledge of the basics, and an understanding as to how and why the front office operates in the way that it does, plus the capacity to think as a front-of-house person, there is no reason why you should not readily become a competent member of the front office team.

Once you have progressed through the book you will have a good grounding in the principles of front office operations. With this knowledge, and the understanding that these same principles need to be flexible so as to suit the various styles of hotel property, you are able to enter employment in any hotel regardless of size.

The teaching and training of students in front office operations is difficult, for, unlike other aspects of hotel service such as food and beverage, there are inherent difficulties in enabling students and trainees to obtain 'hands-on' practice. Hotels are reluctant to permit students to train using real customers and real problems. Because the front office is the first and often the most vital impression of the hotel, it is understandable that hotels are somewhat reluctant to allow students and inexperienced staff members to 'practise' in this important area. Consequently, the use of case studies, in place of real-life experience, is a useful and practical method of imparting knowledge without compromising the function and reputation of an operating establishment. In order to give you an opportunity to practise your skills, to try to reach solutions that require lateral thinking, and to get you to realize that every action has a cause and an effect, we have included a number of case studies throughout the book.

Finally, we would like to wish you well on your journey along the path to becoming a competent and successful front office person, and hope that you will find it as interesting and exciting as we have done.

# 1

# *Introduction to the hospitality industry*

## Introduction

The hotel sector is a vital part of the hospitality industry. In order to understand the operations of hotels, you therefore have to know about the nature of the hospitality industry. This chapter will begin by briefly describing the nature of the hospitality industry and its relationship with the closely related tourist industry. We will then describe some factors which have affected the development of the hospitality industry in recent years. Finally, we will look at the different types of businesses in the hospitality industry, in particular the different types of hotels.

## THE HOSPITALITY INDUSTRY

To most people, the hospitality industry consists only of hotels and restaurants. However, the *Oxford English Dictionary* defines hospitality as the 'reception and entertainment of guests, visitors or strangers with liberality and goodwill'. Therefore, the hospitality industry can be broadly defined as the collection of businesses providing accommodation and/or food and beverages to people who are away from home. In other words, the hospitality industry includes not only famous hotels or restaurants, but also a wide range of businesses, such as small guest houses, snack bars and fast-food outlets.

---

**Activity 1**   Indicate which of the following businesses are part of the hospitality industry:

McDonald's

A student restaurant

Your local supermarket

A movie theatre

A night club

The YMCA

A wine merchant's

A residential home

---

## THE NATURE OF THE HOSPITALITY INDUSTRY

The hospitality industry provides services for people who are away from home regardless of whether it is for long or short periods of time. These services can vary according to the specific needs of both the person away from home and the organization operating those services. For example, the needs of a person in a residential home differ dramatically from those of an executive business person in a deluxe hotel. Similarly, a student staying in a hall of residence would expect to be treated and accommodated differently from someone on a cruise-liner. Therefore, it is important that staff in the hospitality industry must be able to identify the various needs of their customers and be able to act and provide the services expected.

## PROFIT-MAKING AND NON-PROFIT-MAKING BUSINESSES

Not all hospitality businesses are profit orientated; as a consequence they can be categorized into either profit-making or non-profit-making businesses.

A profit-making business is one which is set up with the intention to earn a profit. Examples include commercial restaurants and hotels.

A non-profit-making business is one which is not run specifically to make a profit. It is usually operated with the intention of promoting the benefits and welfare of its members. If there is any excess income, it is usually reinvested in the business (e.g. in purchasing new equipment or refurbishing premises). Examples include private clubs, industrial catering for offices and factories, institutional or welfare catering, and accommodation and provision of food in state hospitals, universities and other institutions.

---

**Activity 2**  (a)  Name three profit-making businesses in the hospitality industry in your local area.

(b)  Name three non-profit-making businesses in the hospitality industry in your local area.

---

## THE HOSPITALITY INDUSTRY AND TOURISM

The hospitality industry is a part of a wider group of economic activities called tourism.

Tourism refers to a collection of industries providing necessary and essential services to the travelling public. These services may include:

- transportation (e.g. car rental, and travel agents)

- specialist shops (e.g. gift shops, souvenir shops, shops selling local products)

- food and beverage operations (e.g. restaurants, bars and fast-food outlets)

- accommodation (e.g. hotels, guest houses, conference and exhibition venues)

- leisure activities (e.g. sports events and festivals)

The relationship between the hospitality industry and tourism is illustrated in Figure 1.1.

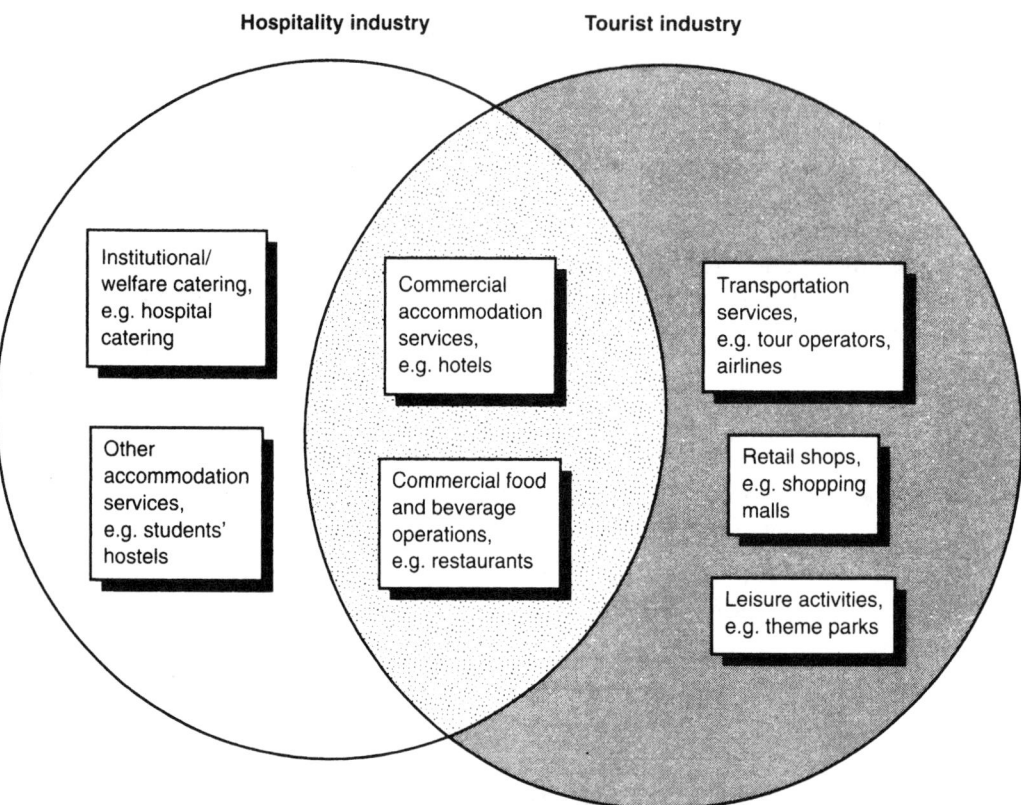

**Figure 1.1** The relationship between the hospitality industry and tourism

---

**Activity 3**  Study Figure 1.1 again carefully, and then answer the following questions.

(a) Name three types of business which are part of the tourist industry, but which are not considered as part of the hospitality industry.

(b) Name three types of business in the hospitality industry which are not usually considered as being part of the tourist industry.

---

## THE IMPORTANCE OF TOURISM

Tourism is important to the economic development of many parts of the world. In some regions, income from tourism is the one of the main sources of foreign exchange (e.g. Fiji, the Caribbean and Hong Kong).

**Figure 1.2** The importance of tourism

Tourism is important because it contributes to the growth of an economy by:

- *Providing a lot of employment opportunities for local people.* This could be in the form of lodging employees, who cater for those travellers staying in hotels, motels and guest houses, tour operator, transportation staff, e.g. airline caterers and crews, rail and coach operators, as well as restaurant and fast-food outlets and retail shops.

- *Funding a large percentage of a country's gross domestic product (GDP), thereby helping to raise the national income.* The GDP is the name of the total monetary value given to all of the goods and services produced by a country over a set period of time. A healthy tourism industry helps to increase the volume of sales of these goods and services. This in turn helps to raise the country's national income and as a consequence helps to lower unemployment and inflation.

- *Earning foreign currency through the goods and services provided to foreign visitors, thus improving the balance of payments.* The currency of a foreign country is often needed for the buying of goods imported from foreign countries. For example, the greater the number of American tourists, the greater the amount of US dollars which enter the economy. Japan, which has a balance of payments surplus, actually encourages Japanese people to travel overseas, to help reduce the balance of payments.

## THE PROMOTION OF TOURISM

Because of its important contribution to economic development, tourism is encouraged by the governments of most nations. Governments have established tourist organizations and authorities to advertise their countries overseas. These organizations may also study the development and improvement of local tourist facilities.

---

**Activity 4**  Investigate a local or national tourist association in your area.

(a) Explain why your region or government is willing to subsidize its activities.

(b) State three ways in which this association promotes your region.

---

## THE DEVELOPMENT OF THE HOSPITALITY INDUSTRY

To become effective in your job, you should be aware of what has been happening in the hotel sector of the hospitality industry over the past few years. In this section, we shall briefly look at some of the recent developments in the hospitality industry worldwide.

The hospitality industry is a rapidly growing business in many parts of the world, particularly in regions where tourism is newly developed. In addition, there has been a tremendous growth in business travel.

The rapid growth of the industry can be attributed to:

- increasing internationalization of business which has led to more travel

- increasing economic prosperity which means people now earn more, and are able to spend more on travel

- improvements in transportation, particularly air travel

## HOTELS AND THEIR CLASSIFICATION

The Hotel Proprietors Act 1956 provides a clear definition of a hotel:

> An establishment held out by the proprietor as offering food, drink and, if so required, sleeping accommodation, without special contract, to any traveller presenting himself who appears able and willing to pay a reasonable sum for the services and facilities provided and who is in a fit state to be received.

As a consequence, while there are other types of establishments which also provide accommodation services (e.g. hospitals, university hostels, apartments, prisons or even private hotels), they do not come under the definition of hotels because they do not cater for the specific needs of travellers.

Hotels can be classified into different types according to their target market, size, location, facilities or ownership. Different types of hotels will provide different kinds of services for their guests and will, therefore, be run differently. The main ways of classifying hotels are described below.

### Target market

One way of classifying a hotel is according to the type of guest it caters for. Hotels can be divided into commercial, tourist and resort properties.

Hotels which offer drink and accommodation to travelling business people are called commercial hotels. Tourist hotels, on the other hand, offer services to people travelling for pleasure. Resort hotels also provide services to people travelling for pleasure, and are more likely to be found at scenic spots (such as in the country or on the coast).

Hotels can also be divided into residential hotels and transient hotels on the basis of the expected length of stay of their guests. Residential hotels provide accommodation for guests staying for a long time, while transient hotels are used by guests who stay only for one or two nights.

Transient hotels are very often found near airports, railway terminals or ports.

### Location

Hotels can be classified according to where they are located (e.g. city centre hotels, suburban hotels, or resort hotels).

---

**Activity 5**   (a) Name three commercial, tourist and resort hotels in your region.

(b) Can you name any residential and transient hotels in your region?

(c) Where are they located?

---

### Size

Some hotels may be classified with respect to their size. Small hotels have fewer than 100 rooms, medium-sized hotels normally have between 100 and 200 rooms, while large hotels usually have more than 200 rooms. However, this categorization by size alters from country to country. For example, in Asia a small hotel may be 200 rooms and a large property 700 to 1000 rooms.

The size of a hotel will affect its organization and operation. For example, large hotels are usually divided into distinct departments which specialize in providing one type of service to guests (e.g. room service waiters only serve food in the guest-rooms). In medium-sized and small hotels, departments are less specialized and the staff have a wider range of duties (e.g. the coffee shops may serve meals not only in the coffee shop, but also in guest-rooms).

### Facilities

Hotels also differ in their standards of services and in the facilities which they offer. Because of this, establishments can be divided into full-service hotels, budget hotels, and self-catering hotels.

A *full-service* hotel provides a wide selection of guest services in addition to accommodation, such as food and beverage service, room service, laundry services, health, sports and business facilities.

*Budget* hotels tend to provide cheaper and more basic guest-rooms with limited food and beverage services.

*Self-catering* hotels provide no other service besides basic accommodation. Guests are expected to prepare their own food, clean and tidy their rooms, and do their own laundry. However, some establishments offer a weekly cleaning service.

Self-catering hotels are popular in North America and Australia.

Such hotels may provide food shops in their foyers and microwave ovens in their guest-rooms. Most of these hotels are situated close to expressways, and are often called *motels* (where the accommodation is in individual chalets). These hotels are sufficiently large to provide one car-parking space for every room.

---

**Activity 6**   What standard of service is most likely to be offered in the following classes of hotels? Why?

(a)   a well-known commercial hotel

(b)   a motel

---

### Ownership

Another way to classify hotels is by their ownership. Hotel ownership can be:

- private (i.e. an independent hotel owned by a person, a partnership, or a private company)

- a local group (i.e. several hotels owned by a local company)

- an international group (i.e. a hotel which is part of an international chain of hotels)

---

**Activity 7**   Identify which hotels in your area are as follows:

private

local group

international group

---

### Management contracts and franchises

In many cases, hotels are managed by the owner(s), but in some hotels, the management is carried out by a different group of people. The reason for this is that some owners may not have the necessary expertise, or they may not have the desire, to become involved in the operation of the hotel. In such cases they may arrange for a management contract with a company which specializes in managing hotel properties. Some of the large hotel chains also manage properties in this way, e.g. Hilton or Thistle Hotels.

In other cases hotels are said to be franchised. This means that the property may be owned by one company and run by another hotel company of international repute, e.g. the Holiday Inn corporation. In such cases the hotel owner buys into the name of the reputable company. This will require the owner to pay a sum of money to the franchisor for the use of its name and expertise in setting up the hotel. It will also have to pay the franchisor an agreed percentage of either the profits or turnover. In return for this expenditure, the owner of the hotel will get:

- the use of the name of a well-known hotel group
- the benefits of bulk purchasing
- the benefits of group marketing
- initial and possible subsequent assistance in the setting up and management of operational systems

So far, we have discussed the main ways of classifying hotels. In fact, many hotels can be described by using several of the above classifications. For example, it is possible to describe the Birmingham Copthorne hotel as a large, city centre, transient, full-service hotel, operated under a management contract with the Copthorne group.

---

## Activity 8

Read the newspaper article below, and then answer the questions that follow.

Europa International Hotels is due to take over management of the Portland Hotel in Birmingham, England on 1 April, replacing the existing group. The 250-room hotel will retain its name, but it will be billed as 'a Europa International Hotel'.

Europa currently has four hotels in Europe with over 1400 rooms: the 200-room Europa Lodge, Ireland; the 298-room Carlton, Lisbon; the 543-room Europa Lodge, Paris; and the 187-room Europa Lodge, Switzerland.

With good-quality exhibition centres in both Birmingham and London, the Portland Hotel is strongly positioned to dominate this sector of the English market.

With the opening of the Portland Hotel, Europa International Hotels' room count will be almost in line with that of Holiday Inn, the hotel management chain with the largest number of rooms in Europe at present.

(a) Who will be responsible for the management of the Portland Hotel?

(b) Suggest two possible reasons why the owners have arranged a management contract for the hotel with another company.

(c) What benefits will the Europa enjoy by expanding its share of the market in England?

---

## SUMMARY

This chapter has introduced the hospitality industry to the future professional. It began with a description of the nature of the hospitality industry and its development, giving examples of its various aspects. The close interrelationship between the hospitality industry and tourism was examined, showing how the two areas overlap, especially in the provision of commercial establishments which offer food, drink and accommodation to the travelling public.

The effects of tourism, both local and national, on a country's gross domestic product, and its influence in the creation of jobs, were explained. A clear definition was given of what constitutes a hotel. Finally, hotel classifications were identified: target market, location, size, facilities and ownership.

---

# Review and discussion questions

1 Explain how the international hotel industry has changed in recent years.

2 How does the economic environment affect the hotel industry?

3 Explain the relationships between the following:
   hotel industry;
   hospitality industry;
   tourism.

4 Study the information on the location, facilities and services of the King's Hotel overleaf, then classify the King's Hotel according to the classifications explained in this chapter. Provide justification for your answer.

**KING'S HOTEL**

| Location |
| --- |

Harbour City
South Coast Road
Dover
Kent

| Introduction |
| --- |

The King's Hotel is privately owned by Natotel (Holdings) Ltd and has been in operation since June, 1989.

The hotel is located in part of the Harbour City Complex, adjacent to the busy waterfront. It has easy access to the Channel and the Continent and is well placed for both business and holiday clientele.

The hotel has 188 guest-rooms of the following categories: standard, superior, deluxe, adjoining suites, and presidential suites.

| Facilities |
| --- |

The hotel is well served with facilities. These include: a shopping arcade containing the latest designer shops; a restaurant; steak bar; coffee shop, lobby lounge and bar; swimming pool; health centre; beauty parlour; business centre; and car-parking facilities.

| Services |
| --- |

The following services are available to our guest:
- room service
- baby-sitting
- video hire
- laundry/dry cleaning
- complimentary daily newspapers
- money exchange
- car hire
- cable/in-room computer/fax facilities
- secretarial/translation services

# 2
# *Organization of a hotel*

## Introduction

In order to provide a wide range of services efficiently to its guests, a hotel is usually divided into different departments, each being responsible for certain functions and duties. For a hotel to operate effectively and harmoniously it is vital that the various departments understand each other's work.

This chapter examines the organization of a hotel, and the roles and functions of the various departments. The need for interdepartmental cooperation is explored, with particular attention being given to the work of the front office.

## ORGANIZATION

An organization can be defined as a system of coordinated activities of a group of people working cooperatively towards a common goal under authority and leadership.

A hotel can be regarded as an organization because it:

- is set up to achieve certain goals which may include the production of accommodation and food and beverage services for its customers in order to make a profit

- plans and coordinates the activities of its staff in order to achieve its goals

- divides personnel into functional departments, each with their own areas of authority and responsibility

## ORGANIZATIONAL CHART

As a hotel comprises a large number of staff responsible for different areas of work, there is a need to coordinate the activities of the different staff and departments. Each worker has to clearly understand their duties and responsibilities, as well as how their work fits in with that of the other staff or departments of the hotel.

The relationships between the different positions within a hotel can be represented by means of an organizational chart or hierarchical chart. This gives a pictorial display of the relationships and how they interlink with each other. The organizational chart enables the manager to know the positions of staff within the hotel, as well as who is responsible for whom. It also gives the employee a clear picture of who is their 'boss'. Figure 2.1 shows the organizational chart of a small hotel.

As you can see from Figure 2.1, this organizational chart shows where and how each department fits into the overall organization of a hotel. In addition, it illustrates the division of responsibilities and lines of authority. For example, the hotel in Figure 2.1 is divided into six major sections, each with a distinct area of responsibility. The front office, for instance, may well be responsible for the selling and marketing of rooms, the handling of bookings, guest accounts, wages and suppliers' invoices, and many other clerical duties. The storekeeper can also be responsible for the purchasing of all food and beverage items, housekeeping supplies and very often stationery. The chart also shows that in this small hotel each department is directly responsible to the manager or owner.

Because of its complexity, a hotel's organizational structure will vary according to the size and style of operation. Figure 2.2 illustrates

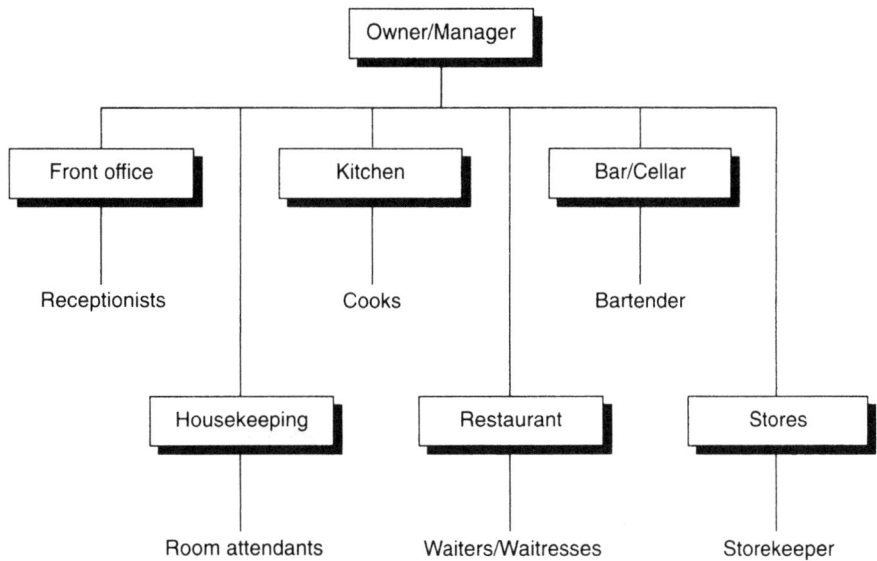

**Figure 2.1** Organization of a small hotel

the organizational chart of a large international hotel. If you compare it with that of a small hotel (Figure 2.1), you will see that the structures of the two are quite different. The increase in size of the hotel means that very often there is a corporate level of management, which makes all the long-term future plans for the hotel. These plans and strategies are then passed down to the hotel manager (or general manager) for implementation. Again because of the size of the property, there are more, very specialist departments, such as human resources, purchasing, accounts and training.

A major difference between a small hotel and a large hotel is that, in a small hotel, the manager may also be the owner, while in a large international hotel, the owner may be on the board of directors. In this case it is the board of directors which is responsible for formulating the goals of the company and carrying out long-term planning. In such hotels, it is rare for the manager to be the owner. However, it is the manager who is responsible for the implementation of the goals set by the board of directors.

**Activity 1**   Compare Figures 2.1 and 2.2 carefully and then answer the following questions.

(a) What are the main differences in the organization and structure between a small and a large hotel?

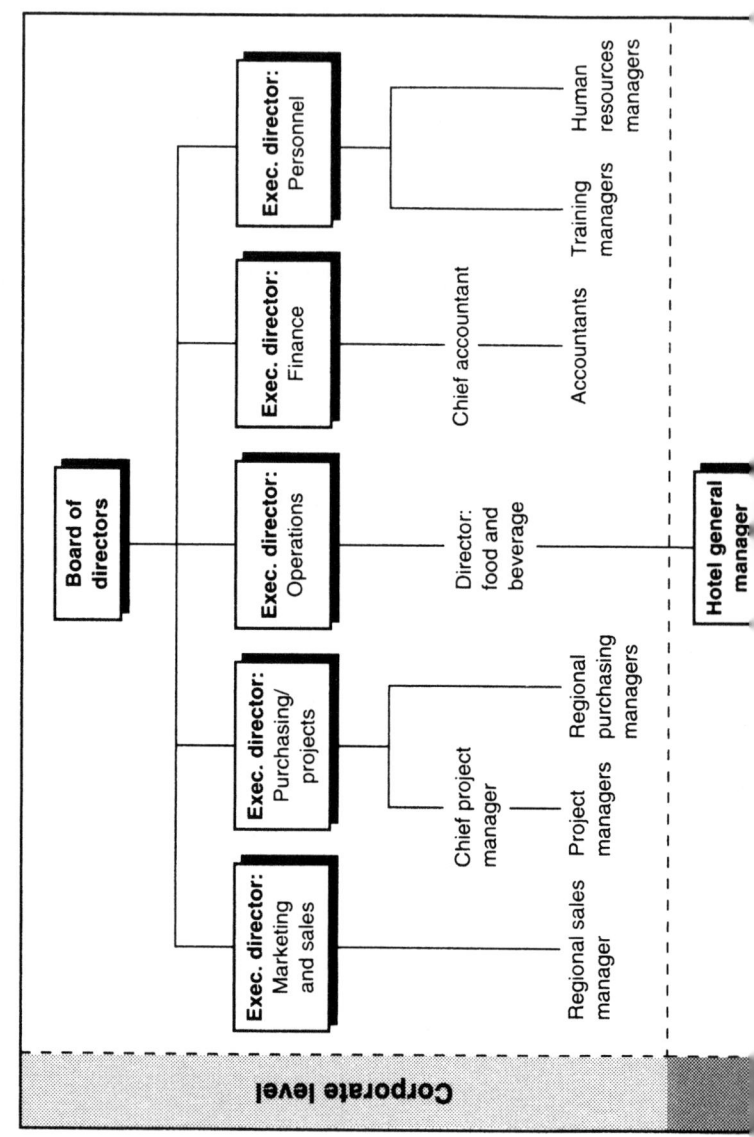

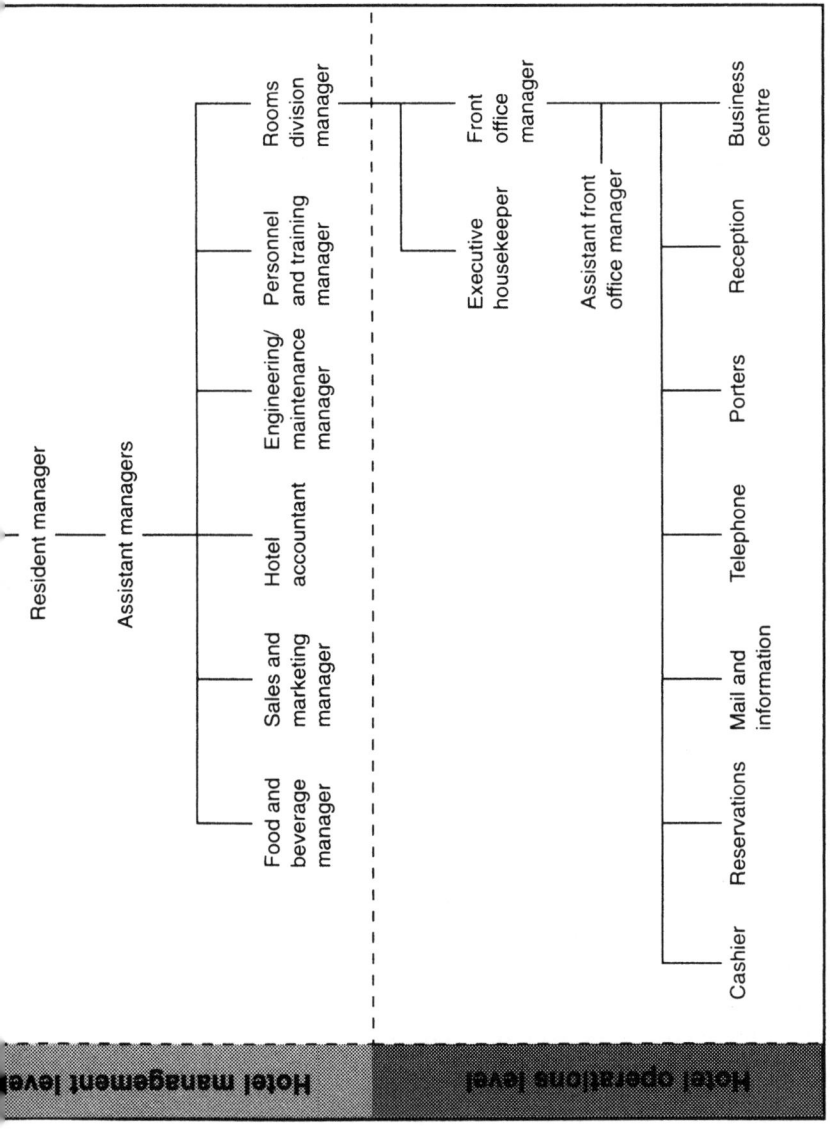

**Figure 2.2** Organization of a large international hotel

(b) In what way may the organizational chart of a hotel change over a long period of time?

## MAJOR DEPARTMENTS OF A HOTEL

Because of the variety of food, beverage and accommodation services provided by a hotel and in order to give an efficient service to the customer, it is necessary to divide the hotel operation into distinct departments. Figure 2.3 shows the principal divisions/departments of a full-service hotel.

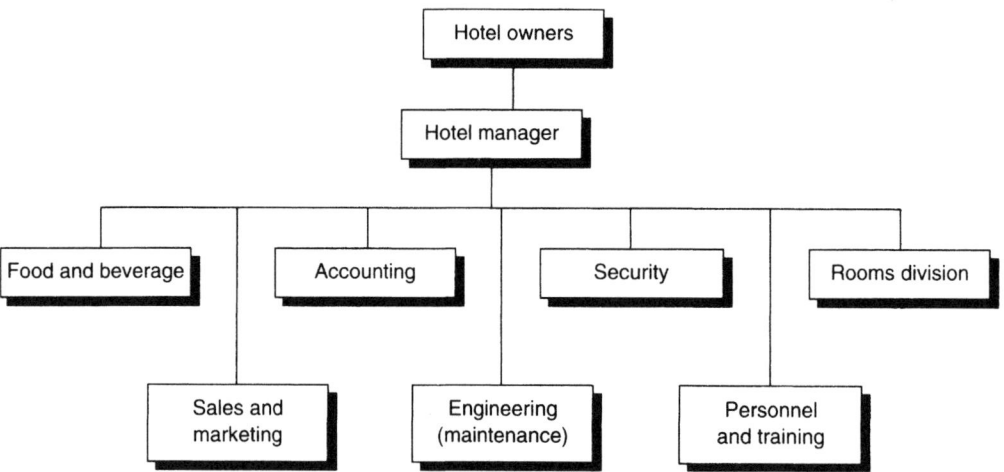

**Figure 2.3** Major departments of a full-service hotel

The larger the hotel and the more facilities offered, the more specialized each of the departments will become. This means that there will be an increasing number of sections within that department. Look again at Figure 2.2. In this example, the front office is under the control of the rooms division manager. At the same time, reservations, reception, cashiering, etc. are subdivided into their own particular sections, normally with a manager or supervisor in charge of each (e.g. the reservations manager, front office manager and chief cashier).

### Revenue and support centres

The classification of the departments or divisions of a hotel can be done in a number of ways, such as by the service offered (food, beverage, rooms, recreation, etc.) or more broadly by grouping them as either a revenue centre or a support centre.

*Revenue centres* (or operational departments) sell goods or services to guests and thereby generate revenue for the hotel.

Examples of major, or primary, revenue centres are:

- rooms division

- food and beverage

Examples of minor, or ancillary, revenue centres are:

- guest telephones

- guest laundry/dry cleaning

- recreational facilities

- business centre

*Support centres* (or service support departments) provide a supporting role to the operations departments. These departments usually do not provide direct services to the guest and so do not generate revenue directly (Figure 2.4).

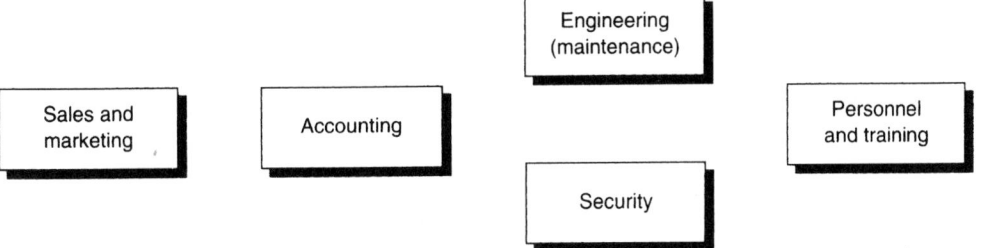

**Figure 2.4** Examples of support centres

### Front-of-the-house and back-of-the-house departments

An alternative method of classifying hotel departments or divisions is by the extent to which they are involved in customer contact. In this respect, hotel departments may be divided into the front-of-the-house and the back-of-the-house departments.

Front-of-the-house departments are those in which employees have extensive guest contact, such as reception, cashiers, concierge, restaurants, room service, bars, recreational areas, etc.

Back-of-the-house departments are those in which the staff have little or no direct guest contact, such as personnel, accounting, and the engineering and purchasing departments.

# Activity 2

(a) Decide (by indicating with the letter R or S) whether the following departments (or divisions) are revenue or support centres:

Food and beverage      Rooms division
Engineering (maintenance)      Accounting
Front office      Personnel and training

(b) Decide (by indicating with the letter F or B) whether the following departments are front-of-the-house or back-of-the-house departments:

Kitchen      Front office
Restaurant      Purchasing
Laundry      Housekeeping

## RESPONSIBILITIES OF MAJOR HOTEL DEPARTMENTS

In the previous section, we listed the major departments of a hotel and explained how they can be classified. These departments are usually set up to carry out specific duties. In this section, we shall describe the main areas of responsibility of the various departments.

### Food and beverage

The food and beverage (F&B) department offers a variety of facilities to guests but concentrates mainly on the provision of food and drink. These services may be provided by coffee shops, bars, lounges and speciality restaurants, and also by the banqueting and room-service departments.

### Sales and marketing

The sales and marketing department is responsible for generating new business for the hotel. This could be the sales of rooms for groups/tours, functions, conventions or even restaurants and bars. It also handles the advertising of the hotel as well as sales promotions and publicity and often takes on the role of public relations.

### Accounting

Accounting is responsible for monitoring of all the financial activities of a hotel. Such accounting activities may include: cash receipts and banking; the processing of payrolls; accumulating operating data; and the preparing of internal reports, audits and financial statements. Because of the importance of financial data and statistics, it is necessary for the accounting department to coordinate closely with the front office.

### Engineering (maintenance)

Engineering (maintenance) is responsible for the maintenance and the operation of all machinery and equipment (including heating, air-conditioning and lighting). It is also responsible for carrying out all carpentry, upholstery and small building, plumbing and other works, both inside and outside a hotel. Not all engineering and maintenance work, however, can be handled by a hotel's staff. Sometimes problems or projects may arise which require outside contracting.

### Security

Security is mainly responsible for the safety and security of hotel guests, visitors and hotel employees. This may include: patrolling the hotel premises; monitoring surveillance equipment; and, in general, ensuring the security of guests, visitors and employees and their property.

### Personnel and training (human resources)

Personnel and training is responsible for the employment of staff (including internal and external recruitment and selection), as well as: induction programmes; training; employee relations; compensation; labour relations; and staff development.

In recent years this division has gained in importance because of the need to contend with legislation, labour shortages, and the growing pressures of competition. Hotels nowadays tend to put more effort into the training and development of their staff, and into revising their recruitment policies in order to retain their existing workforce.

---

**Activity 3**   (a)  List six facilities provided for the guests by the food and beverage departments of a hotel.

(b)  Explain the main responsibilities of security.

(c)  Explain the main duties of personnel and training.

---

### Rooms division

In the rooms division most departments or sections are involved in the sales of rooms as well as the provision of services and facilities for guests. Such departments may be: the front desk; housekeeping; reservations; telephone; and the concierge.

In general, hotel room sales are the largest source of hotel revenue and, in many cases, more sales are generated by rooms than by all the other services combined. Room sales also yield the highest profit margins.

The rooms division is composed of two major departments: the front office department and the housekeeping department, as shown in Figure 2.5.

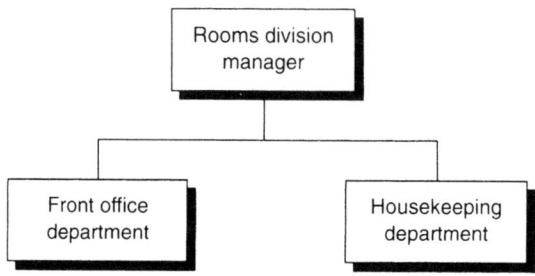

**Figure 2.5** Organization of the rooms division

### The front office department

The front office department is the most visible department in a hotel. The focal point of activity within the front office is the reception desk. The reception desk is usually the place at which guests form their first important impressions of the hotel. It is also the communication centre for the hotel's operation.

The reception desk may comprise: cashiering; mail and information; registration; and room assignment. There may be separate desks, or all tasks could be performed at one counter (sometimes known as multiskill). The reception desk is located in the busiest area of a hotel's lobby. The main financial tasks which are handled by front office staff include: receiving cash payments; handling guest folios; verifying cheques; and handling foreign currency and credit cards. (Note: the front office department will be discussed in greater detail in Chapter 4.)

### Housekeeping department

The housekeeping department is responsible for the management of guest-rooms and the cleanliness of all public areas of a hotel.

A close liaison between housekeeping and front office is essential so that the information about guest-rooms is kept accurately up to date: for example, which rooms are available for letting, which are occupied, those which are out of order and those which are vacant but dirty.

The housekeeping and front office usually have a department head or supervisor who reports to the rooms division manager. Each of the two departments is responsible for its own specific operation. Since these two departments have to work very closely together, teamwork is essential.

Note that the organization and staffing of the rooms division will vary from one hotel to another, depending on factors such as the number of rooms available, the type and standard of rooms, the sources of business and the facilities offered.

**Activity 4** You are the rooms division manager of a hotel. One day, a group of visitors arrive and you are asked to explain to them the work of your division. Write a short paragraph stating: the importance of the rooms division to a hotel; the role of the division; and how the division is organized.

## MANAGEMENT STRUCTURE OF A HOTEL

The management structure of a hotel comprises all positions of responsibility and authority below the level of corporate management (i.e. the head office).

Figure 2.6 shows the management structure of a hotel. In general the positions at the top of the management tree, 'executive', and including department 'heads (A)', are considered to be a part of the management structure of a hotel.

Department 'heads (B)' are involved in the management of their departments but to a lesser extent. They are normally responsible for the discipline and welfare of their staff and for carrying out any instructions given to them.

As with the rooms division of a hotel, the number and type of management staff required depends on the size of the hotel and its particular arrangement of operations, or management style.

In a small hotel, the hotel manager may be responsible for almost every aspect of the operation (e.g. the planning of budgets, recruitment of staff and ordering of goods). As the hotel increases in size and facilities, the management structure also increases in its complexity. In larger hotels the manager has a more administrative function and is accountable to the corporate managers. A deputy or resident manager will then be wholly responsible for the day-to-day operations within the

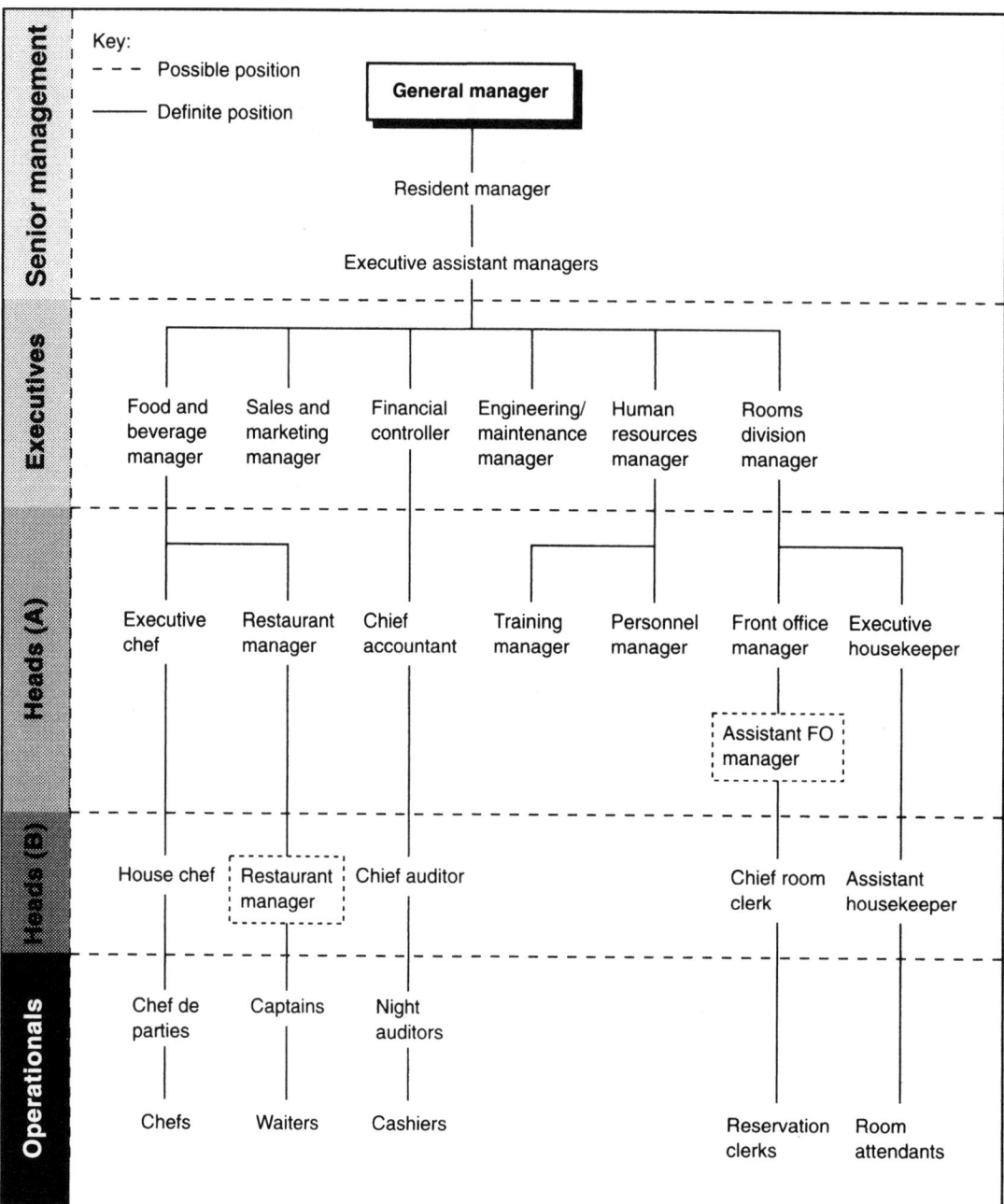

**Figure 2.6** Management structure of a hotel

hotel. At the same time, there will be a greater specialization of responsibility among departmental managers.

The roles and responsibilities of the various management positions will now be explained.

### General manager

The main responsibilities of the general manager (GM) are as follows:

- Participates in the formulation of hotel policies and strategies
- Implements hotel policies and strategies
- Responsible for the overall performance of the hotel
- Accountable to corporate management and ultimately to the board of directors
- Coordinates the work of all departments

### Resident manager or executive assistant manager

The main areas of responsibilities of the resident manager (RM) or executive assistant manager (EAM) are as follows:

- Responsible for the day-to-day management of hotel activities
- Deals with emergencies, complaints or special events
- Responsible for the welfare and safety of the staff, property and guests

### Executives

The persons in this area of management report directly to senior management and are responsible for the short- and long-term planning of the finance, marketing and staff development in their particular areas of specialization.

### Heads of department (A)

It must be remembered that the titles of the managers mentioned above are general, rather than being specific to their roles and responsibilities. Effective hotel management needs a clear definition of responsibility and authority, especially in the cases of heads of department. The roles of the heads of department are usually described by their titles, which also indicate their main areas of responsibility. For example, the executive housekeeper is in charge of housekeeping, the chief accountant is in charge of finance, and so on.

Hotel department heads may be categorized into two main groups:

***Line managers.*** Line managers are heads of operating departments. These heads have direct lines of responsibility both up to their own superiors and down to their staff. One example is the front office manager, who reports up to the rooms division manager and down to the supervisors of the various sections of the front office.

*Service specialists*. Service specialists are heads of service support departments who give advice and service to the line managers. However, despite giving this help and advice, they have no authority over employees in departments other than their own. An example is the hotel controller, who assists line managers with their budgets, control systems and staffing costs but has no direct authority in the operation of that operating department.

---

## Activity 5

Indicate whether the following personnel are line managers or servicing specialists, and explain your reasoning.

| Executive housekeeper | Personnel manager |
|---|---|
| Hotel accountant | Executive chef |
| Purchasing manager | Front office manager |
| Chief engineer | Security manager |

---

## SUMMARY

This chapter has shown how organizational structures are important to any business, and has shown that the hotel industry is no exception.

For the effective management and operation of a hotel, a business which by its very nature is totally customer orientated, it must be broken down into different departments. The type of work and number of departments in a hotel vary according to the size of the property. In order to better group these departments on an organization chart, they can be classified in two ways: firstly, on a purely financial basis, i.e. whether or not the department is revenue earning, in other words an operational department; or according to whether it is a department which offers help, guidance and assistance to an operational department. Such sections are known as service support departments.

Departments may also be broken down into two groups according to their location. Departments which are in the 'front line', i.e. deal directly with guests, are said to be front of house, whilst those that have little or no customer contact are back of house.

Despite all of the different departments in a hotel, it is the rooms division which is the nerve centre of the operation, and as such is very important to a hotel for both financial and communication reasons.

The chapter went on to explain in general the duties of the various departments within a hotel and looked more briefly at the functions and areas of work of the front office and housekeeping section. It then went on to identify the management structure of both a large and small hotel, and listed some of the responsibilities of the different members of the management team.

A hotel is (usually) a single building, either large or small, but inside that building is a team of people who make it work. For anyone to control and make a financial success of that hotel it requires teamwork, organization and a sound management and staff structure.

## Review and discussion questions

1   (a)  Explain briefly what is meant by the term organization.

    (b)  To what extent is a hotel an organization?

2   Explain the differences between a revenue centre and a support centre in a hotel. Give two examples of each.

3   (a)  Using Figure 2.6 as a guide, draw up an organization chart of a hotel of your choice in your local area.

    (b)  Briefly explain the relationship between each of the department heads, as shown on your organization chart.

## Case Study: *'Mismanage or Mrs Manage'*

The King's Hotel caters mainly for the business and conference market. Occupancy levels can vary considerably from week to week and day to day and are difficult to predict exactly.

The executive housekeeper is in her fifties. She has worked in the hotel for ten years and been in her present job for five. She has no vocational qualifications and has never worked in any department other than housekeeping. The aspects of her work that she likes the most are 'looking after her staff and dealing with staff problems'. She is less confident about the budgeting, control and paperwork aspects of her job.

All the room attendants work full time. They are expected to clean 16 rooms each day and are paid per room. A supervisor who is responsible for returning rooms to reception checks each room. If the hotel is full or one or two maids ring in sick, supervisors have to clean rooms. On the other hand, if occupancy levels are lower than forecast and the department is overstaffed, the executive housekeeper will try to meet her staffing budget by encouraging staff to take holidays or go on training courses. At these times room attendants may only be required to clean 14 rooms, but even though this means losing money, they don't seem to mind, as they find it extremely tiring to clean 16.

It is difficult to attract and retain room attendants because the hotel is situated close to an airport where much better paid cleaning jobs are available. Staff working in other areas of the hotel are unwilling to help out if the department is short staffed and are not sufficiently trained to do so as it takes one month to train a room attendant to the required standard.

The Prince Hotel is in the same chain as the King's. It is slightly smaller but has a similar market. The executive housekeeper is in her twenties, has catering college qualifications and is ambitious to become a general manager.

Here only eight of the room attendants in the hotel are full time. The rest are part time; they work two days a week and agree to wait by the phone on other days up to 10a.m. in case they are required. Labour turnover is low. Staff and supervisors do not mind changing jobs and opportunities are provided for those interested to move to other jobs for variety and to improve their long-term job prospects.

As an experiment, the room attendants have been given more control and responsibility for their work. They now check their own rooms and return them to reception. The full-time room attendants have been allocated a block of rooms on a particular floor as 'their' rooms. Supervisors now carry out rigorous inspections against a detailed checklist on a random sample basis.

## Question

**As the executive rooms division manager responsible for the King's Hotel and Prince Hotel, what would you do to encourage standardization within the housekeeping departments of the two hotels, taking into account each hotel's strengths and weaknesses?**

**Evaluate your answers taking into account the cause and effect as it applies to the housekeepers, the room attendants and the floor supervisors.**

# 3

# *The accommodation product and hotel guest*

## Introduction

In Chapter 1 we established that a hotel sells a combination of accommodation, food, beverage and other services to the guest. In order to provide a quality service to guests, the hotel staff, especially the front office staff, have to have a full knowledge of the products which the hotel sells; the way these products can be offered for sale; and the clients to whom these products will be sold.

In this chapter we shall examine the accommodation product and the particular needs or wants of different types of hotel guest.

We shall start by explaining the accommodation product which is offered by hotels, and then we will examine the various types of accommodation products commonly provided by hotels and the different systems of room rates. Finally, we will identify the different types of hotel guests and look at their needs.

## THE ACCOMMODATION PRODUCT

As mentioned before, the sale of rooms is one of the main products to be provided by a hotel; it is also very often the principal source of hotel revenue.

It must be noted, however, that the accommodation product consists of more than a room with a bed. A guest purchasing accommodation also receives other facilities and benefits, such as ambience, decor and security. While all hotels provide accommodation services for their guests, the type of facilities and benefits associated with that service can often differ greatly, even within the same hotel.

The accommodation product, therefore, does not just consist of a guest-room – single or double – but also the additional facilities and services which are applicable to that room. For example, does the room have a sea view? Is there a mini-bar? Are there in-house movies? Can a guest dial direct from the room? Is there room service? Can the guest have access to the Internet? All these services, facilities and amenities may be included in the accommodation product of a hotel.

Since the accommodation product normally cannot be examined before purchase, guests are reliant upon the front office staff to be able to describe the product to them accurately. It is, therefore, particularly important for the front office staff to have full knowledge of what is included in the accommodation package of a hotel.

---

**Activity 1**  (a) What may the accommodation product of a hotel include? Use a local hotel in your area as an example.

(b) Study the information about the King's Hotel in Figure 3.1, and then list the main aspects of the accommodation package in the table at the top of p. 31.

---

## TYPES OF GUEST-ROOMS

To cater for the different needs of their customers, hotels usually provide a variety of accommodation products. In other words, a hotel offers different types of guest-rooms for sale, which may have different room sizes, decor, views, facilities and services.

Hotel guest-rooms can be classified in a number of ways. For example, one way is according to the number or size of beds in the room; others are by the decor, the room size or the view. In addition, some

**KING'S HOTEL**

| Accommodation | | |
| --- | --- | --- |

| Room type | Number | Room rate |
| --- | --- | --- |
| Standard single | 22 | £100 |
| Standard double | 7 | £100 |
| Standard twin | 18 | £100 |
| Standard suites | 14 | £165 |
| | | |
| Superior single | 30 | £120 |
| Superior double | 8 | £120 |
| Superior twin | 37 | £120 |
| Superior suites | 14 | £220 |
| | | |
| Deluxe single | 17 | £150 |
| Deluxe twin | 19 | £150 |
| | | |
| Presidential suites (Dover and Calais) | 2 | £500 |

### Number and types of rooms

The hotel has 188 rooms.
The rooms are located on 8 floors with a standard 24 rooms on each floor, except for the top floor which contains 20 rooms and two presidential suites.

Each guest-room is well appointed with its own individually controlled air-conditioning system, refrigerator, mini-bar, colour television, radio, alarm clock, IDD, STD, a private safe and a hairdryer. Other electrical items such as adaptors and shavers are available on request. A selection of in-house movies is available.

### Services

The following services are available to our guest:

- room service
- baby-sitting
- laundry/dry cleaning
- secretarial/translation services and business services
- foreign exchange
- car hire
- in-room Internet/email/tele-shopping/fax facilities
- complimentary daily newspapers

- Service charge = 10%
- VAT 17.5%
- Discounts: 15% for group bookings. Discounts available on request for airline crew, tour groups and business travellers.

**Figure 3.1** Guest information

hotels may even offer special types of accommodation for particular types of guest, e.g. the executive floor for business people, non-smoking rooms, and presidential suites for VIPs.

## Number and size of beds per room

Guest-rooms can be classified according to the number and size of beds in a room. These are commonly known as:

- single rooms (with a single bed)

| Accommodation, e.g. deluxe single, standard single |
| --- |
| Facilities: |
| Services: |

- twin rooms (with two single beds)
- double rooms (with one large bed)
- suites, i.e. two distinct areas, one for sleeping and one a lounge area

The types of room according to the number and size of beds in the room are illustrated in Table 3.1. These are European bed sizes. In the United States, bed sizes are normally larger.

**Table 3.1** Number and sizes of beds

| Types of room | No. of beds per room | Size of bed | No. of people per room |
| --- | --- | --- | --- |
| Single | 1 | 3′0″ | 1 |
| Twin | 2 | 3′0″ | 2 |
| Double | 1 | 4′6″ | 2 |
| Queen | 1 | 5′0″ | 2 |
| King | 1 | 6′0″ | 2 |

Suites differ considerably from one hotel to another and from one suite to another in the same hotel. Sometimes the lounges and bedrooms may be separated, whereas in the case of studio suites, the bedroom is screened or partitioned from the living area. Very often suites have a king-size double bed.

## Decor, room size and view

Hotel guest-rooms may be grouped into standard, superior or deluxe rooms according to their decor, i.e. the furniture and fittings, as well as by size and situation.

Table 3.2 is an example of how such a categorization of guest-rooms may be made.

**Table 3.2** Categories of guest-rooms

| Type | View | Decor |
| --- | --- | --- |
| Standard single | Town view | Pine furniture |
| Superior single | Sea view | Pine furniture |
| Deluxe single | Sea view | Rosewood furniture |
| Deluxe double | Sea view | Rosewood furniture |
| Suite | Sea view | Antique furniture |

Some hotels have guest-rooms which are connected to each other (communicating rooms). This means that two or more rooms are joined together by a private interleading door, which permits access between the rooms without passing through a public corridor. These rooms are particularly popular with families. The studio room is another type of guest-room; this type of room has beds which fold away into the wall so that the room can be used for meetings during the day.

## Executive floors and presidential suites

In some hotels, special types of accommodation may be provided for a particular type of customer. For instance, if the market of a hotel is mainly business travellers, then a section of the accommodation may be used exclusively as executive floors. The standard and style of the rooms and the facilities offered, as well as services provided, are suited to the special needs of the business clientele. For example, executive floors may provide separate check-in desks, meeting-room space and in-room fax facilities, cellular phones and sometimes separate lounge and bar areas.

To accommodate the wishes of the growing numbers of people who do not smoke, most hotels now have non-smoking floors; this prevents furnishings from absorbing any tobacco smells, causing a staleness of odour in the room. Similarly, to look after the special needs of female executives, a number of hotels have rooms specifically designed for women.

The 'presidential' type of suite is a special form of accommodation geared to the needs of VIPs and wealthy people. It is usual for the rooms to be very much larger than a normal room. The furnishings and fixtures are both exotic and expensive and the services offered are often unique to that suite of rooms.

---

**Activity 2** Look again at the King's Hotel accommodation information (Figure 3.1), and then answer the questions below.

(a) Explain what may be the difference between a standard single room and a presidential suite.

(b) Imagine that you are a receptionist. While you are on duty, a number of customers come up to you with different requests. State in each case which type of guest-room you would recommend to the guest, and why you made that recommendation:

– Two female travellers want cheap overnight accommodation.

– A married couple want a very nice room with two beds and a sea view.

– A couple, travelling with their elderly parents, want two rooms which are very close to each other.

---

## ROOM RATES

The room rate refers to the price at which a hotel sells its rooms. As can be seen from the example of the King's Hotel, the type of accommodation, size, decor, and view from the room will influence the room rate charged to the guest.

As the guest's needs for accommodation become more sophisticated, there is an increase in the variation of room rates. Many hotels have room rate tariffs which fluctuate according to the class of business, time of year, and services included. Some commonly used room tariffs are illustrated in Table 3.3.

The purpose of room rate variancing and price discounting is to tailor the product as closely as possible to the needs of the market. If, for example, a hotel caters for a high proportion of corporate and company

**Table 3.3** Some commonly used room tariffs

| | |
|---|---|
| Standard room rack rate | The standard rate for the room, with no meals, discounts or reductions |
| Corporate rate | The standard rate charged for executive personnel from businesses and industrial corporations, who are regular guests |
| Commercial rate | The rate which is agreed upon by a company and hotel for all individual room reservations |
| Airline rate | The rate negotiated between the individual airline and the hotel, based on the volume of business the hotel gets from the airline |
| Children's rate | As either free of charge, or at a nominal rate if they share the same room as their parents. Each hotel has an agreed age limit for the child up to which this rate applies |
| Flat or group rate | Specific room rate for group, agreed by hotel and group in advance |
| Series rate: back to back | Where a company or travel agent books a series of rooms. As one group checks out of their rooms, another group will check into them after cleaning |

personnel, it may offer a 10 or 20 per cent discount on the normal room rack rate in order to attract more corporations or companies to use the hotel. Alternatively, for group bookings, a tourist hotel may offer a 20 or 25 per cent discount of the normal room rack rate when it quotes a rate. If the hotel has a limited guest market segment, i.e. limited types of guest, it may offer two or three rates. However, many big hotels offer a large variety of rates for their many different guests. It is important for front office staff to be aware of the different room rates and who is entitled to what, in order that they are able to offer sound and accurate advice to guests. Front office staff also have to know what is included in the room rate and what is an extra charge. A much practised technique to help hotels maximize both their occupancy and revenue is called 'yield' or 'revenue' management. This technique is explained in greater detail in Chapter 15.

## HOTEL BROCHURES AND TARIFFS

The information on the room rate charged, the facilities and services provided is usually found in a hotel's brochure and tariff.

Hotel brochures and tariffs are sales and marketing tools which help to sell the accommodation, the food and beverage, the facilities and services of a hotel. A brochure with a photograph of a room can be useful to the front office staff when they are selling rooms. Tariffs are normally printed separately, as an insert, so that any price change does not make the brochures out of date.

Rates which are quoted on the hotel tariff can show a variety of pricing options (Table 3.4).

**Table 3.4** Pricing options

| Rate (UK terminology) | Rate (US terminology) | Rate (French terminology) | Explanation |
|---|---|---|---|
| Room only | European plan | | The rate quoted is for the room only. This can be on a per person or per room basis |
| Room and breakfast | Continental plan | | This rate includes breakfast as well as the accommodation |
| Half board | Modified American plan | Demi-pension | The rate includes room, breakfast and one meal, usually dinner |
| Full board | American plan | En pension | All meals are included with the accommodation, i.e. breakfast, lunch and dinner. Sometimes afternoon tea is also included |

**Activity 3** Visit a hotel in your area and obtain a brochure and tariff. Use the brochure and tariff to help you answer the following questions.

(a) What is the room rack rate for each type of room quoted?

(b) Is there a rate quoted for group or tour bookings?

(c) Is the rate inclusive or are there any extra charges quoted?

(d) What type of rate does the hotel quote? Is it per person, per room, per day, per week?

(e) Does the hotel offer discounts to special types of guest? If so, who is entitled to the discounts?

---

## TYPES OF HOTEL GUEST

Previously we explained what the accommodation product of a hotel was, the variance in types of guest-room, and the types of room rates and tariffs which may be offered to guests. Different guests have different preferences in their selection of accommodation. In the following sections, we shall investigate how hotel guests are categorized.

It is always beneficial to understand the needs and wants of the guests who use your accommodation. The more information a hotel can gain about its guests, the better it can anticipate what they want, and so be able to offer quality service.

This information is also of special value when: analysing and trying to satisfy guest requirements; determining the facilities and service expected; and evaluating the hotel's pricing policy.

In general, hotel guests can be classified according to: their purpose of visit (pleasure or business travellers); numbers (independent or group travellers); and their origin (local or travellers from overseas).

### Purpose of visit

Pleasure travellers (otherwise known as tourists) are people who travel for pleasure (e.g. sightseeing or entertainment). Their arrivals are highly seasonal and are attracted by special festivals, sports or other cultural events. Pleasure travellers are generally price sensitive. Their personal income is an important factor in determining their particular needs.

Pleasure travellers may include:

- Domestic tourists (local people who stay at a hotel for weekends, special functions and activities).

- Free (also known as foreign) independent travellers (FITs); international tourists, who make their own travel arrangements and purchase their accommodation independently. This type of group is not usually looking for an accommodation package (i.e. full board or half board); they normally require accommodation only.

- Group inclusive tours (GITs); groups of tourists who travel together on package tours. Their expenditure is very often lower because they tend to budget their spending allowance. Accommodation and sometimes meals are usually booked well in advance, by the tour agency.

● Special interest tours (SITs); groups of people who visit a place once, usually with a special interest in mind (e.g. the castles of Europe, the game parks of Africa).

Business travellers are people who travel for the sole purpose of conducting business. Business travellers are the largest source of demand for accommodation. This demand exists all the year round, with the exception of public holidays, but can also decrease during summer holiday months.

Business travellers often require accommodation at short notice and, for this reason, they prefer to establish close ties with a particular hotel so that they can use the accommodation services on a regular basis and not be inconvenienced by lengthy reservation procedures. Examples of types of business travellers are shown in Figure 3.2.

**Figure 3.2** Types of business traveller

### Group size

An independent traveller is someone who travels alone, for either business or pleasure. Whatever the purpose, the guest travels independently and, for this reason, unlike groups or tours, a set timetable is not normally followed.

A group booking tends to be seen as a booking in which five or more people travel together, or when ten or more rooms are pre-booked. The booking is normally done through a travel agent and is paid in full to the travel agent before the group embarks on the tour. The travel agent acts as a representative of the guest and usually receives a commission of some 10 per cent of the cost of the accommodation from the hotel. The purpose of the tour is, in most cases, for pleasure, but the incentive tours business is responsible for an increasing part of hotel occupancy, particularly tours from the USA.

### Origin

Travellers may generally be divided into local or foreign travellers. This means that any hotel resident whose permanent address is in the same country as the hotel is deemed to be a local. Anyone whose home is in another country will be classified as a foreign or overseas traveller.

---

**Activity 4**    (a)  Explain the differences between FITs and GITs. Give two examples of each.

(b)  Explain the differences between local or foreign travellers.

---

## SELECTION OF A HOTEL

To provide a high standard of service, front office staff have to understand the wants and needs of their guests. One way of looking at this is to find out how a guest chooses a hotel. In general, it is found that if a guest has stayed in a city before, then there is a strong possibility that they will choose the same hotel again to stay in, provided that they were satisfied with its services. However, if a guest has not previously visited the city, they are more likely to select a hotel which is well known or is easy to find and get checked into.

It is for these reasons that large international hotel chains very often attract guests. If the guest has previously stayed in one of their other hotels and was satisfied with the service, they can easily reserve a room through the hotel chain's central reservation office.

Other factors which can influence a guest to stay in a hotel may include advertisements, personal recommendations, the location of a hotel, its price, and preconceptions about a hotel based on its name and affiliation. In some cases the guest may use hotel guidebooks or the Internet. These publications are written by independent organizations which recommend hotels according to different criteria (e.g. cleanliness and comfort, facilities, service, price and recreation facilities). Examples are the AA and RAC guides. Alternatively, hotel companies will advertise through their own website.

When customers make decisions to purchase certain goods or services, their decisions may be either deliberate or impulsive (Figure 3.3).

A business person who asks their secretary to book accommodation on a business trip (deliberate)

The family who select a hotel after scrutinizing of hotel guides (deliberate)

A conference organizer who makes several inquiries before selecting a final choice (deliberate)

After a wedding reception in a hotel, a local guest decides to stay in the hotel overnight (impulsive)

A tourist arriving at the airport with no previous booking made (impulsive)

A business person who has to attend a sudden emergency meeting away from home (impulsive)

**Figure 3.3** Impulsive versus deliberate purchase of the accommodation product

A deliberate buying decision means that the buyer plans their buying very carefully; they will look into all possibilities or alternatives before making a decision. An impulsive buying decision is where the buying is unprepared and is usually done quickly. Impulsive buying usually results in making last-minute bookings.

---

**Activity 5**   Suggest three ways in which a hotel can attract more guests.

---

### GUESTS AND THEIR NEEDS

Different types of guests usually have different needs. For example, an FIT travelling on business would have different needs from those of a GIT travelling for pleasure, in terms of both facilities and services required from a hotel (Figure 3.4).

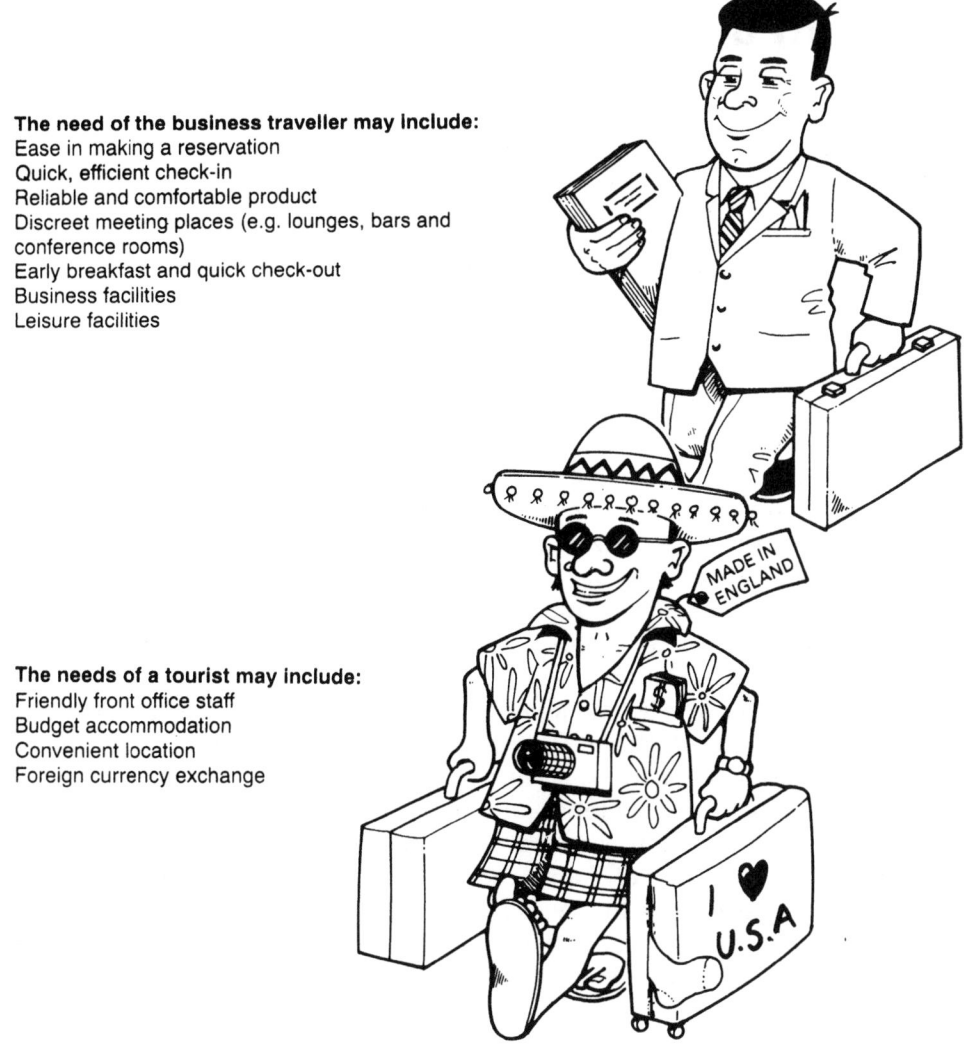

**The need of the business traveller may include:**
Ease in making a reservation
Quick, efficient check-in
Reliable and comfortable product
Discreet meeting places (e.g. lounges, bars and
conference rooms)
Early breakfast and quick check-out
Business facilities
Leisure facilities

**The needs of a tourist may include:**
Friendly front office staff
Budget accommodation
Convenient location
Foreign currency exchange

**Figure 3.4** The needs of different types of guests

Because of the keen competition in the hotel industry, some hotels may target their hotel facilities and services to satisfy only certain types of guests. For example, in Chapter 1 we mentioned three different types of hotels, commercial, tourist and resort, each of which caters for a specific target market.

**Activity 6** Explain how a business traveller and a tourist would differ in their respective wants and needs from a hotel.

(Hint: You may compare their needs in terms of location, special facilities and services of a hotel. You may also examine whether the two types of guests would differ in terms of the priorities of their needs.)

## SUMMARY

In this chapter we have identified the main products of a hotel as being food, beverages and accommodation. We then looked at how the guest-room may be classified according to size, location, ambience and decor and then further categorized by the number of beds in each room.

An example of a hotel's room tariff was given, with the options of full board, half board, bed and breakfast and room-only rates being explained. Like rooms, guests can be typified, and the needs and wants of the business person and tourist were explored.

The chapter as a whole showed that hotels offer considerably more than just a room with a bed. There are many other services and facilities which, combined, form the accommodation product. In order to offer a quality product, every hotelier, and their staff, must be aware of the differences in expectations brought to a hotel by the variety of customers who wish to stay there. Tours and groups want a far simpler product than does an executive business person.

The skill of a front desk clerk is to pick up on and tune in to these expectations as soon after meeting a guest as possible, and, as with all skills, it becomes better with practice.

# Review and discussion questions

1 A hotel guest wants to know why your hotel charges a higher rate for a deluxe twin room than a standard twin room, even though the two are more or less the same size. Write a reply to his inquiry.

2 Who do hotels offer discounts to?

3 You work in a large hotel of 250 rooms. The hotel can expect to be full most nights. However, you must accept business from each section of your

business mix. You have no airline crew contracts. Thinking in purely overall financial terms, list in order of importance your business mix categories and give in each case the most important reason for your choice.

4 Explain what is meant by executive floors.

5 You are the front office supervisor and your manager has asked you to give him some suggestions on how the hotel may improve its facilities and services to attract more business travellers. Make four suggestions in response to this request, and explain why you think that they are useful.

6 Which type of guests should a hotel attract in order to increase the average room rate received? Explain why.

7 Explain how the receptionist's role would alter when working in different styles of hotel, using budget hotels, transient, business, resort and country house hotels as examples.

8a If you were a frequent business traveller staying in a hotel, which of the following aspects would you see as being most important to you, and what would be least important? Rank your selection from 1 (most important) to 10 (least important).

| Important factors | Ranking 1–10 |
| --- | --- |
| Convenient business location | |
| Room prices | |
| Non-smoking room | |
| Good reputation of the hotel | |
| Cleanliness | |
| Friendly staff and service | |
| Safety and security | |
| Restaurant facilities | |
| Business centre facilities | |
| Express check-out | |

**b** Discuss and compare your answer with your lecturer and your classmates.

**c** Now answer this question again, as if you were a frequent tourist.

# 4

# *The front office department*

## Introduction

The purpose of this chapter is to give you an overview of the duties and organization of the front office department. A more detailed explanation of the operations of the various sections within the front office will be given in later chapters.

We begin by explaining the four phases of the guest cycle and the various transactions and services within each phase. The different sections of the front office involved in these transactions are then identified, and the job titles and duties of staff in each section are explained. Finally, we shall look into the front office workshift system as practised by most hotels.

## THE GUEST CYCLE

The main function of the front office department is to support and facilitate guest transactions and services. Therefore, the operation of the front office department is largely determined by the type and number of guest transactions which take place during the different stages of a guest's stay.

A typical hotel stay can be divided into four distinct phases, namely:

- pre-arrival
- arrival
- occupancy
- departure

These four phases constitute the guest cycle, as shown in Figure 4.1. In each phase of the cycle there are certain standard transactions which occur between the guest and the hotel.

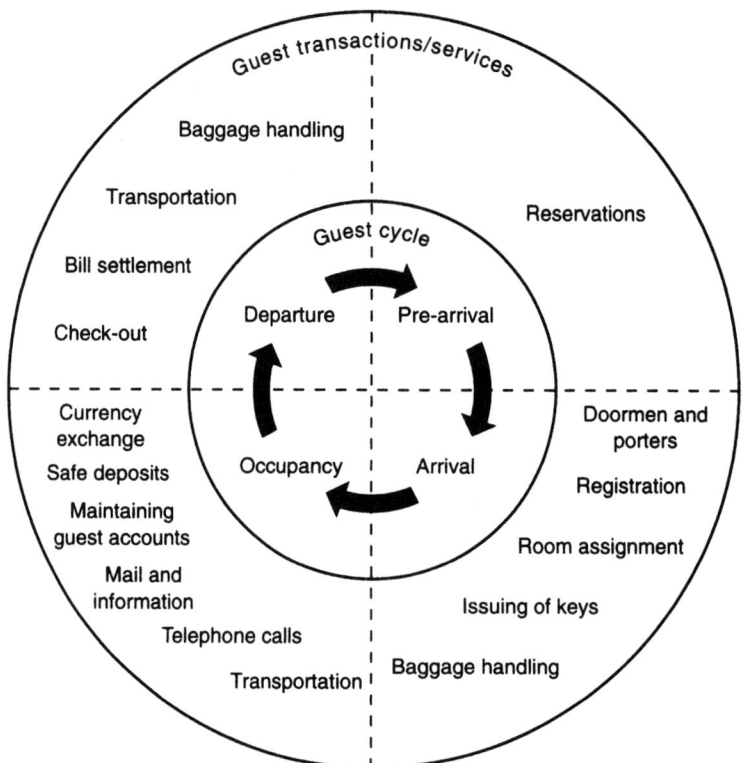

**Figure 4.1** The guest cycle

As we can see from Figure 4.1, there are different types of guest transactions and services which are involved in the different phases of the guest cycle. These are listed below:

- reservations
- check-in and registration
- mail and information
- uniformed service and baggage handling
- telephone calls and messages
- handling guest accounts
- check-out and bill settlement

Most of these services and transactions are handled by the front office department. In the following sections, we shall explain how the front office is organized to handle them.

## ORGANIZATION OF THE FRONT OFFICE

In Chapter 2, we showed how an organizational chart can be used to illustrate the hierarchical structure of a hotel. Similarly, an organizational chart can show the structure and lines of communication which operate in the front office. The example given in Figure 4.2 shows the organizational chart for a very large hotel. What has to be remembered is that the same jobs have to be performed in smaller hotels. However, because in smaller hotels there is a reduction in the number of requests for many of the services offered, many of the jobs shown as individual sections in a large hotel are combined. That means that just a few people do a great variety of tasks. For example, a receptionist could also function as a telephone operator and the reservations clerk, and staff the information desk. The porters could act as mail and information clerks, and drivers, as well as performing their main role, portering. In fact, in most hotels the function of the mail and information department has been totally absorbed by either the concierge or reception.

From Figure 4.2 we can see that the front office of a hotel is organized into different functional sections, each responsible for a particular area of work. For example, the reservations office is responsible for dealing with all advanced bookings. Within the reservations department there is a further hierarchical chain. The reservations office is headed by the reservations manager or reservations supervisor, to whom the reservations clerks are directly accountable. It should also be noted that there is a broken line from front office manager to the

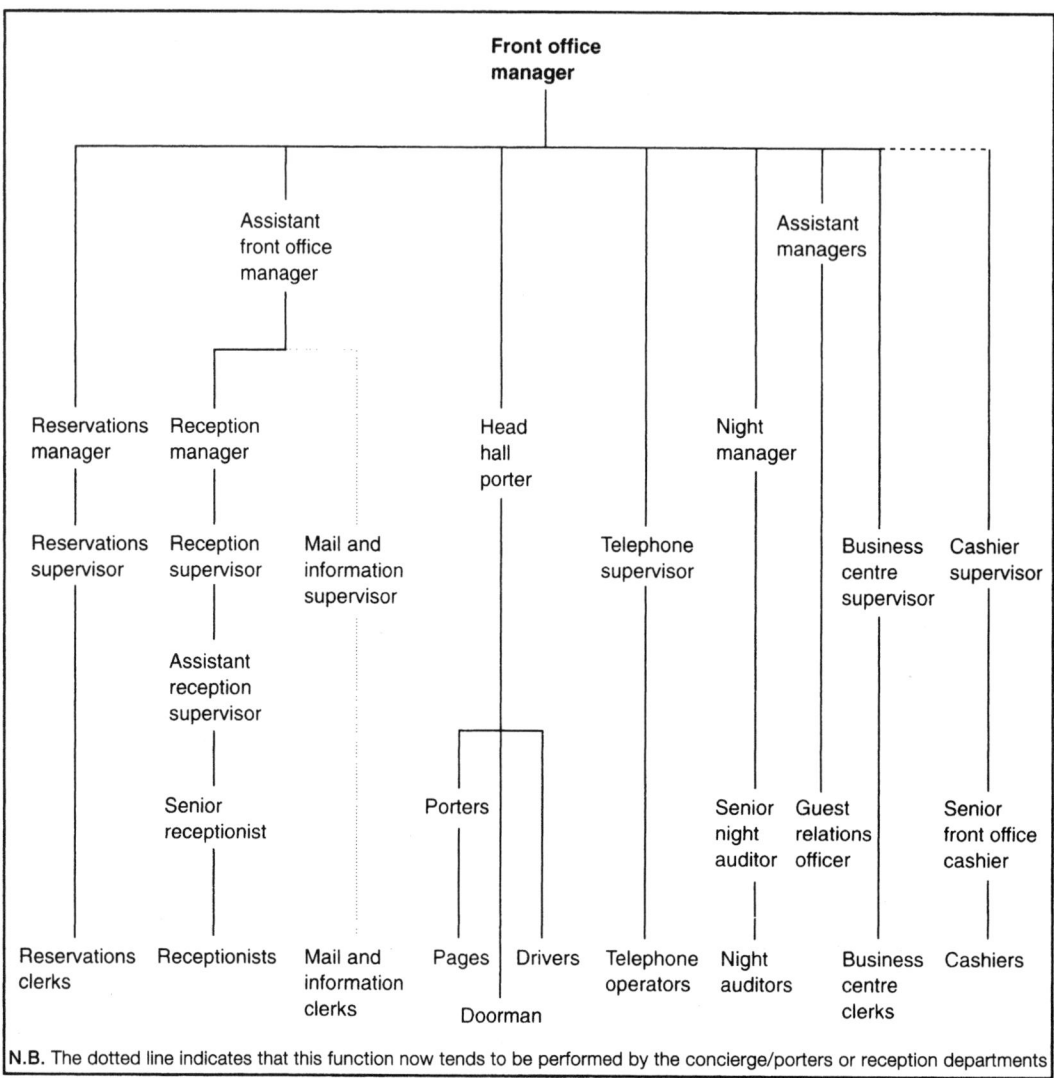

**N.B.** The dotted line indicates that this function now tends to be performed by the concierge/porters or reception departments

**Figure 4.2** Organizational chart of the front office

cashiering section. This is because in large hotels the cashier's department reports directly to the accounts department, with the financial controller taking overall responsibility. This is also sometimes the case for the night auditor and their staff.

You will remember from Chapter 2 that the organization of a hotel depends on a number of factors. In the case of the front office, these may include:

- *Size of the hotel*. Large hotels employ more staff and tend to have greater specialization among sections and staff. In small hotels, one member of staff may have a wide range of duties.

- *Standard of service.* High-class hotels usually provide more personal services for guests, so they expect greater specialization.

- *Type of guests.* Business people expect efficient check-in and check-out services but may be prepared to carry their own bags. Consequently, a commercial hotel may need more staff in the front desk section but fewer at the concierge. Tourists usually require information on local attractions, but their accounts may be simple to prepare. A tourist hotel, therefore, needs greater emphasis on giving information and assistance and less on clerical and cashiering duties. In airport hotels, guests may check in or check out of a hotel at any time during the 24 hours of a day, a fact that may well require a full front desk team to be on duty at all times.

## Activity 1

Study Figure 4.2 again, then answer the following questions.

(a) Name the major functional sections of the front office, as illustrated on the chart.

(b) List the different categories of staff involved in the reception section of the front office.

(c) For each of the guest transaction services listed below, state the section of the front office which would be directly responsible, and give your reasons.

- a guest wanting to make a telephone call

- taking a reservation

- checking in a guest

- baggage handling

- issuing a key to a guest

- settling a guest's bill

- arranging transportation for a guest

- a guest wanting to collect mail

- a guest wanting directions to the coffee shop

- a guest who needs to call in a doctor

# INTERACTION BETWEEN GUESTS AND THE FRONT OFFICE

During a hotel stay, guests may require certain services from, and engage in various transactions with, a hotel. These are mostly handled by the front office. (Note: each section of the front office has an area of task responsibility.) An example of the interaction between the guest and the different sections of the front office department is shown in Figure 4.3.

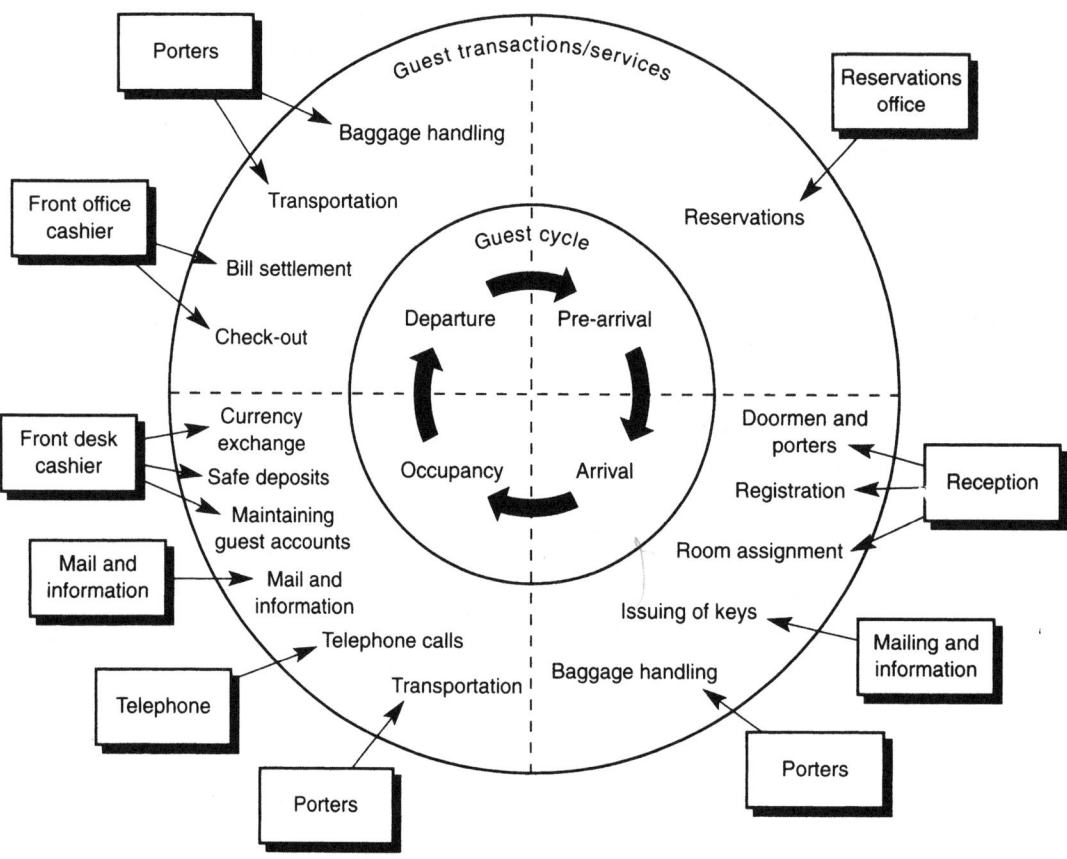

**Figure 4.3** Interactions between guest and the front office

**Activity 2**  Study Figure 4.3 again, and then answer the following questions, giving the reasons for your answer:

(a) Which section(s) of the front office will a guest first make contact with when wishing to stay in a hotel?

(b) Which section(s) will have the opportunity to give guests a good lasting impression of a hotel?

(c) Which section(s) of the front office will be involved when a guest arrives at a hotel?

(d) Which section(s) will be involved in providing occupancy services to guests?

---

## DUTIES OF FRONT OFFICE PERSONNEL

In this section we shall examine more closely the duties of each section of the front office, by looking into the titles and roles of staff involved.

### *The reservations office*

Staff in the reservations office include:

- the reservations manager (or reservations supervisor)
- the reservations clerks

The reservations manager would be in control of the section, and would organize the staff duty rotas, establish and maintain high standards of work, and make decisions on whether bookings should be accepted or not. For example, if a hotel is fully booked, the reservations manager would decide whether to stop taking bookings, or to continue and become overbooked. (Overbooking refers to the situation where a hotel takes more reservations for rooms than it has rooms available.) The reasons why overbooking is sometimes an option are discussed in Chapter 5.

In some medium-sized hotels this section may not have a manager, and the reservations supervisor would then report directly to the front office manager. In many hotels the task of dealing with reservations is performed by the receptionist.

The reservations supervisor, apart from taking reservations, will also closely monitor all the bookings taken, perhaps referring to the manager when important decisions are to be made, e.g. when the hotel is full, or when someone requests a booking which might not be accepted.

The reservations clerks (or reservations agents) take the bookings, which may be made by telephone, fax, mail or e-mail. They keep records of the number of bookings taken for each night, and record all the relevant details of each booking. They will try to 'up sell' accommodation (see Chapter 8) and ask guests to confirm or guarantee their bookings. Each day they will give reception all the booking details of the guests who are due to arrive on that day. (Note: a guaranteed booking must always be held for a guest because payment is guaranteed whether or not they arrive.)

The operations of the reservations office are covered in Chapters 5 and 6.

## Reception (the front desk)

Staff in the reception section (or front desk) may include:

- the reception manager (or front desk manager)

- the reception supervisor (or front desk supervisor)

- senior receptionists and receptionists (or reception clerks/agents)

The front desk is controlled by the reception manager (sometimes called the front desk manager). It is their duty to see that a hotel achieves the maximum revenue and the highest level of room occupancy possible. It is also the responsibility of the front desk manager to monitor and motivate their staff, as well as to maintain a high profile with the guests. This helps to ensure that a quality service is being given by the front office departments in particular and the hotel in general.

The specific responsibility of the reception supervisor is to guarantee the smooth running of the front desk. Apart from this overall duty, they would organize duty rotas, and handle complaints or difficult customers which a receptionist may not be able to deal with. The notification and greeting of important guests (VIPs) would also be the duty of the reception supervisor.

The senior receptionist is in charge of each shift of staff. The senior receptionist will take responsibility for assigning rooms to guests, dealing with group arrivals and handling guests' immediate problems or queries. For example, guests may wish to change rooms or may have a special request.

The receptionists (or front desk clerks/agents) prepare for the guests' arrival, greet the guests when they arrive, check the guests into the hotel, assign suitable rooms and check the guests' method of payment. They also keep a record of the status of each room in the hotel, i.e. whether it is occupied, vacant, clean or dirty or out of order, give out information to guests, and in many cases take charge of guest-room keys.

The operational procedures of the front desk will be further discussed in Chapters 7 and 8.

## Activity 3
Distinguish between the duties of a reservations clerk and a receptionist.

### Porters (concierge/lobby services)

The porter's department comprises a large group of uniformed staff, including:

- head hall porter (bell captain/lobby services manager)
- doorman
- porters or pages (bellboys)

The head hall porter is in charge of all of the uniformed staff in the front office, and normally works from a desk in the main lobby. The following are some of the duties and services which they conduct:

- control of the uniformed staff
- close liaison with the front office manager and other departments
- giving of information to guests concerning hotel services and local directions
- message taking and issuing room keys (note that mail and information or reception is sometimes responsible for this)
- the booking of theatre tickets and the confirmation of airline passages
- arranging the hire of hotel cars
- the solving of guests' problems and queries about the locale and recreational facilities

(Note: the head hall porter, traditionally, is the person who arranges anything a guest requires, even such things as a private aeroplane trip.)

Other services provided by the staff of this section are shown in Table 4.1.

In hotels which do not employ separate security staff, the security of the hotel lobby may become a duty of the uniformed staff.

**Table 4.1** Services provided by the porter's section

| Uniform staff | Duties |
| --- | --- |
| Doormen | The organization of baggage handling for both arriving and departing guests<br>Open car doors |
| Head hall porters | Greet all new arrivals<br>Give directions<br>Call taxis |
| Driver (car jockeys) | Take guests to and from airport or railway station<br>Park guests' cars |
| Porters/pages | Run errands and take messages for both the hotel staff and the guests, carry bags to and from rooms, generally keep the lobby are clear, neat and tidy. |

### Mail and information

A mail and information counter is normally found only in very large hotels and as was mentioned earlier has now generally been incorporated into the concierge/porters or reception departments.

The mail and information section comprises:

- the mail and information supervisor
- mail and information clerks

The mail and information supervisor is responsible for a team of mail and information clerks who give out guest keys and deliver guests' mail and messages. They are also responsible for dealing with guests' visitors, and providing information on the hotel or local attractions. They would also carry a supply of local postage stamps and stationery.

Many hotels now have business centres which provide secretarial services, fax and computer facilities for the guests. These centres relieve the mail and information desk of some of the specialist information and requests made by business people.

The hotel kiosk or shop, which sells books, magazines, toiletries, etc., is generally not part of the front office. However, in medium-sized hotels, a selection of small items for sale may be carried by front desk staff.

### Telephone

Staff in this section include the telephone supervisor and telephone operators for both day and night operation.

The telephone supervisor and telephone operators process all incoming and outgoing calls through the hotel switchboard. These staff need good language and communication skills. They frequently give out general information over the telephone on subjects as diverse as the weather or the time in another country through to attractions within the hotel. They will place international calls and give wake-up calls as required by guests. They also operate a hotel's paging system, which provides a communication service to certain members of hotel staff and management who, by the nature of their jobs, are not always in their offices. A vital role of the telephone department is to act as the communications centre in the event of emergency (e.g. a bomb scare, fire alarm).

We will discuss the services provided by the portering, mail and information, and telephone sections in greater detail in Chapter 12.

### Guest relations officers

In large hotels, it is quite possible that guests will only meet the receptionists and porters, and will have very little contact with other members of the hotel staff. In such hotels, guest relations officers are sometimes employed to try to create a more caring and personal hotel atmosphere.

Guest relations officers (GROs) usually have a desk in the main lobby. Their main responsibility is to make guests feel welcome and provide a more personal service, very often by simply talking to guests who are travelling on their own and perhaps feel lonely staying in a strange new town or city. GROs also handle guests' problems and complaints, and always become involved should a guest need a doctor, or simply feel unwell.

In addition, it is the GRO's responsibility to care for VIPs and frequent guests: checking that their rooms are prepared and escorting them on arrival.

### Front office cashier

Staff in the front office cashier section include:

- the cashier supervisor
- cashiers

The cashier supervisor has full responsibility for all of the cash and methods of payment by guests as well as the supervision of the work of the front office cashiers. As mentioned before, in some hotels the front office cashiers report directly to the accounts manager, rather than to the front office manager.

The front office cashiers are responsible for the opening preparation and settlement of resident guests' accounts. They check to ensure that all charges are added to guests' bills and that the settlements are properly processed. Front office cashiers also administer the safe deposit system of the hotel. In hotels which have overseas visitors they also provide a foreign currency exchange service.

We will further discuss the work of the front office cashier (i.e. preparing and settling bills and maintaining credit control) in Chapters 9, 10 and 11. As with the mail and information staff, this function has tended to be combined with reception

### Business centre

In recent years business people have come to expect hotels to provide a wide range of facilities and services to meet their specific needs. Such a range of services may include fax, photocopying and secretarial work. There may also be a demand for translation and interpreting services as well as the hire of equipment, such as lap-top computers, portable telephones and dictaphones. The organization of private meeting rooms is also one of the duties of business centre staff. If a hotel has many non-English-speaking guests, then bilingual secretaries may be required. Similarly, most properties now have full e-mail and Internet facilities for guests.

### Night auditor

The front desk may be staffed by a separate team of staff at night, or, less commonly, it may be covered by staff who are scheduled to work a night shift.

The front desk is fairly quiet during the night, and night has traditionally been a time when duties involving paperwork and the checking of figures are performed; these are called the audit duties. Audit duties include the checking and completion of guest and hotel accounts, the balancing of hotel revenue figures, as well as producing statistics and summaries of hotel revenue for management.

In the past, most cashier billing systems audit duties were done either manually, or by using simple mechanical or electronic machines. However, with the arrival of computerized systems, most of the work is now performed automatically by the computer throughout the day. The need for billing and audit staff is therefore greatly reduced, and the night audit duties have become much simpler, usually only requiring running off and collation of computer print-outs of the hotel's revenue and statistical information. Occasionally, staff may complete manual summary sheets and undertake special checks.

One of the most important tasks which night auditors supervise is the back-up of the computer system. This involves making copies of all the important files in the computer. In the event of a system failure, another copy of all the files and records is then available. More detail of this department is given in Chapter 9.

---

**Activity 4**   (a)   Which of the following is the main task of a front office cashier?

- processing guests' accounts

- recording the number of bookings

- processing payrolls

- supervising the work of other staff in the cashier section

(b)   Indicate which one of the following front office supervisors is in charge of the uniformed staff:

- the head hall porter

- the mail and information supervisor

- the front desk manager

(c)   When guests check out, which members of the front office staff will they meet? What duties will they perform?

(d)   Why is the telephone department the centre of communication during an emergency?

(e)   Name two members of the front office staff whom a guest may speak to but never see.

(f)   If a hotel has a business centre, what services may it provide for overseas guests?

---

## FRONT OFFICE WORKSHIFTS

It is normal practice for staff in the front office to work a 40-hour week over five days and the staff to work five days out of seven. This means that a front office worker cannot expect to have every weekend off. A typical shift pattern could be:

- day shift, 7a.m. to 3p.m.

- evening shift, 3p.m. to 11p.m.

- night shift, 11p.m. to 7a.m.

However, an allowance of 15 minutes usually has to be made for the changeover of shifts so that any problems can be explained and passed on.

Most front office sections have shifts similar to those shown above. However, reservations is different in that they may well start at 9.00a.m. and finish at 6.00p.m., and they also tend to have weekends off duty. That is because most companies and businesses operate on a 9.00a.m. to 5.00p.m. basis. Reservations outside these hours would be handled by the front desk.

It is common for most hotels to operate on a standard check-out time of 12 noon. This means that guests are expected to vacate their rooms by 12 noon on the day of their departure. If they wish to keep their room for longer (e.g. until 6.00p.m.), they may be charged a half-day room rate charge but this is usually at the discretion of the reception manager. In the case where guests vacate their rooms but do not wish to leave the hotel until later in the afternoon or evening, they may deposit their bags with the porter for storage.

---

**Activity 5**  The Dudley Hotel is a busy hotel during the week and quiet at weekends. It has six receptionists, all of whom have two days off per week and work an early shift of 7a.m. to 3p.m. and a late shift of 3p.m. to 11p.m. Two night receptionists are permanently employed from 11p.m. to 7a.m. Draw up a two-week rota for the reception desk which would be fair and equitable to all of the staff.

---

## SUMMARY

Chapter 4 has explained how the front office department of a hotel comes into contact with a guest, in chronological order. There are four distinct phases.

Phase 1 is the pre-arrival of the guest, where they make the room reservation, phase 2 is the point of arrival, phase 3 is the period during which the guest is resident, and phase 4 is when the guest checks out. During all of these phases the guest deals with one or more sections of the front office.

The chapter then went on to explain the roles, responsibilities and duties of the reservations, reception, cashiers, head hall porter, night audit, telephone, guest relations, business centre and mail and information departments and the staff who work in them.

Finally, we explained the 'shift' system of working, which is common to the hotel industry, and how all front office department employees tend to work on the basis of early and late shifts with an occasional overnight (graveyard) shift.

## Review and discussion questions

1   Explain the duties of the head hall porter.

2   Explain what is meant by the term 'shift', and how it relates to a front office clerk.

3   What factors influence the organization of the front office department?

4   At what time of the day will the front office staff be busiest with the following transactions? Why?

- checking in new arrivals

- settling guest accounts

- handling reservations

5   Explain the necessity of having different categories of staff involved in the front office of a hotel.

## Case Study: 'Accommodation Management: You must be joking!'

One morning, Mrs Chubb, the King's Hotel executive housekeeper, was having a serious debate with her assistant Jill on career opportunities, especially in the field of rooms division and general management.

Mrs Chubb has been working in the hotel industry for the last 34 years, entering the industry at a very early age with little formal qualification. However, two years previously Jill had completed her degree in hotel management at the local university. Jill was commenting to Mrs Chubb that her ambition in life was to become a rooms division manager and then, later, general manager of an up-market hotel.

'I know that I won't be the first female general manager,' remarked Jill, 'but I will definitely be one within the next ten years.'

'Ten years! Interesting, but you have forgotten one main point,' said Mrs Chubb, 'housekeeping is the wrong career path to rooms division manager let alone general manager.'

'Why? What do you mean by wrong career path?' exclaimed Jill with some surprise.

'Okay, I will pose a question to you. How many rooms division managers do you know, who are females?'

'Er . . . er . . . er . . . One I think, Royal Park,' replied Jill.

'Next question,' challenged Mrs Chubb. 'How many rooms division managers and even possibly general managers are promoted from a housekeeping background?'

'A few I think?'

'Wrong! None,' exclaimed Mrs Chubb. 'And why? Because we are the poor relations. Given low priority and even worse, low status.'

'Rubbish! We have status,' replied Jill. 'Possibly in your day and age, traditional prejudices existed and housekeeping was only about servicing bedrooms. But today, housekeepers are professionals, with extensive managerial and technological knowledge and more.'

'Please continue.'

'Okay, look at your own job. Responsible for repairs, maintenance, furniture, linen, laundry, equipment, supplies, wages, budgets etc. etc. etc.' Jill was running out of breath. 'I would say that is more than just servicing a room.'

'Jill, you are right, we have more responsibilities today, than even ten years ago, but not necessarily, status,' said Mrs Chubb.

'Well, you sit on the department heads meeting every week. Wouldn't you say that is acknowledging your status?'

'No, Jill. the rooms division manager and resident manager are telling me what to do, not asking for my opinion,' Mrs Chubb remarked tiredly. 'And, I will tell you something else, sometimes I feel out of my depth. Save costs! Prepare budgets! Maintain standards! Maintain morale! I think I am too old for the job. Change doesn't suit me.'

Mrs Chubb was really looking quite dejected at this stage.

'Remember, Jill, you are young. It is people like you who can change the image of accommodation. Mops and Buckets we are not.'

Jill reached over and put her hand on Mrs Chubb's shoulder. 'What do you mean change the image?'

'Accommodation management, whether it be housekeeping or front office, is an important and complex function. Top management in the hotel can play an important role, to improve the image. But, Jill, so can you, especially you,' Mrs Chubb replied.

'How?'

'Education, knowledge, compete, Jill, with other departmental managers. Remember, running a cost effective and well motivated department is the answer, and you have the knowledge, skills and attributes to give accommodation management the respectability and credibility it deserves.'

'Respectability and credibility,' nodded Jill intensely. 'Why should food and beverages have all the status, high salaries and opportunities? I remember, when I was at the university, reading an article written by Val. Paul, where it said that F & B and accommodation should have equal importance. But that is not true in reality, is it?'

'No, Jill. But it can be,' remarked Mrs Chubb. 'Go on dear, let's change the perception of housekeeping. You and others like you can develop and increase the priority of accommodation management. A more positive attitude is needed. And then my dear, maybe one day, you will be a general manager with a housekeeping background. How proud that would make me.'

'Jill Pitman, general manager of the Hilton. Yes, that sounds good,' Jill proudly stated. 'Oh, goodness Mrs Chubb, it is 2 o'clock, time for the department heads meeting.'

At that moment Mrs Chubb got up from her chair and tiredly left the office.

## Questions

1. **What is your perception of accommodation management?**

2. **Is Jill on the wrong career path?**

3. **Explain why you think Mrs Chubb refers to housekeeping as the poor relation, with low priority and status?**

4. **How would you improve the image of accommodation management?**

5. **In your region how many rooms division managers, front office managers and housekeepers are men and how many are women?**

# 5

# *Basic reservation activities*

## Introduction

In Chapter 4, we explained the four phases of the guest cycle and the various types of transactions and services involved in each phase. Reservation is the major activity at the pre-arrival phase and is usually the first occasion when the guest and the hotel interact. In this chapter, we shall examine the reservation process in detail.

During the course of this book you may come across some terms that are used specifically in the hotel industry. If you are in any doubt about their meaning, refer to the glossary at the back.

## MEANING OF RESERVATION

A reservation in the context of the front office of a hotel means the booking or reserving of a bedroom (accommodation) by a guest, and involves a particular type of guest-room being reserved for a particular person or persons, for a certain period of time.

When a reservation or room booking is made at a hotel, it is expected that the hotel will honour its commitment in accepting that reservation and guarantee that a room will be available when a guest arrives.

## CONTRACT OF BOOKING

A contract of booking is an agreement which is entered into every time a reservations clerk offers a prospective guest a room and that guest accepts the room. However, the guest must be informed of all relevant details relating to the booking, i.e. type of room, the cost, dates, VAT and service charges involved.

This contract of booking means that

- The hotel ensures there will be a room as specified, available for the guest upon their arrival.

- The guest will arrive to use the room which they have booked, on the specified day.

However, a 'release time clause' may be added to an agreement. (This is explained under 'Non-guaranteed reservation'.)

It must be remembered that a contract of booking is legally binding between both parties, regardless of whether it is made in writing or verbally. If either a hotel or a guest wishes to alter or cancel the reservation, they can do so only by mutual agreement (i.e. when both parties agree to the amendment or cancellation). If either the hotel or the guest does not agree to the change, then the injured party can sue for compensation. For example, if a guest does not notify the hotel of a cancellation, the hotel is entitled to charge the guest for the loss of accommodation revenue, or may retain any deposit paid. Alternatively, if a hotel cancels the accommodation without prior notice to the guest, the hotel should provide alternative accommodation of similar standard in another hotel, and pay for any differences in room rates and additional expenses the guest may have to incur (e.g. taxi fares).

## THE IMPORTANCE OF THE RESERVATION PROCESS

The reservation process is of vital importance to a hotel because it:

- gives the first impression of the hotel to guests

- sells the main product of a hotel, i.e. accommodation

- generates customers for other departments

- provides important management information to other departments

As you saw in Chapter 4, the reservation process is often the first contact between a guest and a hotel. It is, therefore, essential for the reservations clerk to provide prompt and accurate service in order to present a good first impression to the guest. In the hotel industry, strong competition exists for the selling of accommodation; a guest who experiences problems or slow service from the reservations section will think carefully before confirming a reservation or returning to that hotel. An efficient reservations system is, therefore, very important.

The reservations department sells accommodation and helps to generate income for other departments of a hotel, e.g. the food and beverage department. A hotel can have a large number of guest-rooms available to let each day, but unless rooms are sold, they will not generate revenue. Hotel rooms are a saleable commodity and are strictly limited by factors of time and quantity. Therefore, if a room is not sold on a particular night, the revenue from that room is lost forever. Reservations contribute to the three main objectives of a front office department, i.e. to maximize *rooms*, *beds/sleepers* and *average room rate*, thereby achieving the highest possible revenue and profitability for the hotel.

In addition, other departments often benefit from the reservation details collected by the reservations department. Such details may include an accurate estimate of the number of guests staying in the hotel, or an indication of when the hotel is expected to be full.

Reservation information can be used by the hotel and by individual departments to:

- prepare sales forecasts

- prepare weekly or monthly staff schedules, menus, and purchase requirements

- relate sales forecasts to expenditure budgets (e.g. money available for staff wages and purchases)

- control costs, including materials, labour and overheads

- carry out long-term planning (e.g. renovation of rooms and expansion programmes)

---

**Activity 1**   In what ways are advanced reservation details important
to:

    – a guest?

    – a hotel?

---

## THE IMPORTANCE OF RESERVATION CLERKS

As mentioned previously, the reservation process is the first important
contact between a guest and a hotel. The social skills of the reservations
clerk and the way in which the reservation is handled largely determine
a guest's impressions of a hotel.

Imagine that you are a guest telephoning a hotel from long distance
to reserve a room. In what way would you like the hotel to deal with
you? You would probably like the hotel to:

- give a quick reply to your request or enquiry

- give you a firm 'yes' or 'no' reply

- record your reservation details accurately, in a manner which
  inspires your trust

- treat you politely

In summary, one might state that to meet the expectations of the guest,
it is essential that staff in the reservations department should respond
to any requests by being a SAP, i.e. dealing with reservations speedily
(S), accurately (A) and politely (P).

For a reservations system to function effectively, set procedures
should be established for the handling of requests, the updating and
amending of information, and the generation of confirmations. These
procedures help to ensure that any request from a guest will be dealt
with quickly and accurately, and require that, consequently, a reservations clerk be well-trained in a number of areas:

- reservation procedures

- social skills (personal quality and interpersonal communication
  skills)

- salesmanship (product knowledge and the ability to know how
  and what to sell)

**Activity 2**   You are the reservations supervisor of a hotel and you have been asked to plan a training course for a newly appointed reservations clerk in your department. Indicate and explain the items which you would include in your training course, by completing a table like the one below. Some examples have been provided.

| Skills | Training items |
|---|---|
| Social skills | Telephone manners |
| Salesmanship | Knowing the accommodation product |
| Hotel procedures | Set procedures for handling inquiries |

## SOURCES OF RESERVATIONS

Requests for reservations may come from a number of sources. The most common are:

- a direct reservation
- reservation network systems
- agencies

### Direct reservations

Direct reservations are reservations which are handled directly by a hotel. These requests may come to the hotel in a number of ways (Figure 5.1).

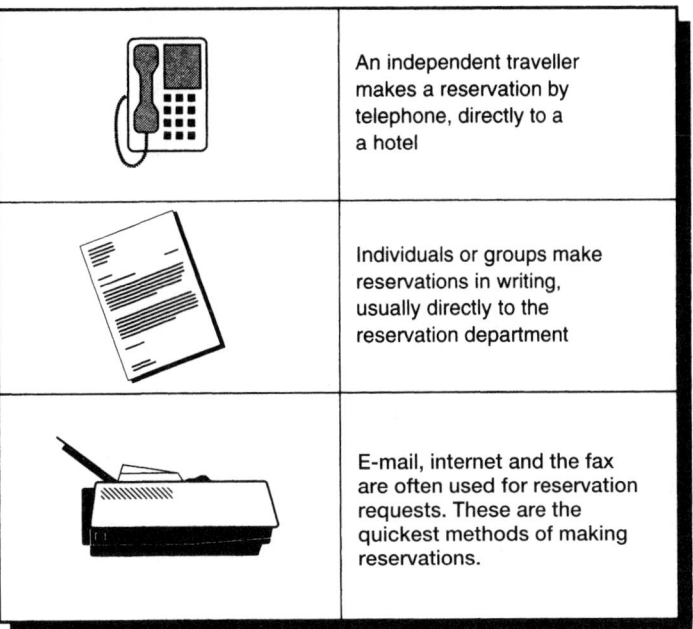

| | |
|---|---|
| | An independent traveller makes a reservation by telephone, directly to a a hotel |
| | Individuals or groups make reservations in writing, usually directly to the reservation department |
| | E-mail, internet and the fax are often used for reservation requests. These are the quickest methods of making reservations. |

**Figure 5.1** Making direct reservations

### Reservation network systems

Today, a growing number of hotel reservations are from guests who have been referred to the hotel by another hotel in the same chain or marketing group, via affiliate or non-affiliate reservation network systems. Similarly, many hotel guests make their reservations through the central reservation office (CRO).

An affiliate reservation system is a hotel reservation system in which all hotels within the same hotel chain participate. This means that guests can make reservations for future or onward accommodation at any hotel within the same group. In this way, group hotels can streamline the processing of reservations, thereby reducing costs and at the same time increasing the service facilities to guests as well as encouraging brand loyalty. Holidex (operated by the Holiday Inn group) and Hyadvantage (operated by the Hyatt group) are two examples of affiliate reservation systems.

A non-affiliate reservation network is a subscription system which is designed to connect independently operated hotels. Guests can make future reservations at any hotel within the network. Examples include the Leading Hotels of the World (LHW) and the Steigenberger Reservation Service (SRS).

Central reservation systems can deal either directly with the customer or with the hotel. When a customer contacts the CRO with specific details of their proposed stay, the agent in the CRO will check the room availability of the nearest hotel to where the customer wishes to be. If accommodation is available, all relevant details will be recorded directly into the computer terminal at the CRO, which is interfaced to the hotel's system. In some cases, this is followed by a telephone call or a voucher to the designated hotel. However, for this system to function well, it is vital that individual hotels should provide the CRO with accurate and regularly updated room availability information.

Most CRO systems demand a 'freesale' agreement with a hotel, i.e. an agreed pre-set number of rooms are sold by the CRO without reference to the hotel's room availability. This can create occasional problems for the hotel, and freesale agreements must be borne in mind when the hotel is getting close to a 'full house'.

If a particular hotel is going to be a 'full house', i.e. if all the rooms are sold, the reservations department should immediately inform the CRO that that date has been 'closed off'.

The CRO system is further investigated in relation to computerization in Chapter 16.

### Agencies

Guests may also make reservations through a travel agent. The agent will normally take a prepayment from the guest, send the confirmation to the hotel, and issue an accommodation voucher on its behalf. Travel agents will receive a commission from the hotel for their services and recommendation.

Many airlines also offer a hotel booking service for their passengers and this works in a similar way to those of a travel agent. Often accommodation may be booked whilst in flight.

---

**Activity 3**  Explain the differences between a direct reservation and a booking through a central reservations office.

---

## GUARANTEED AS OPPOSED TO NON-GUARANTEED RESERVATIONS

Reservations can be divided into two main types: guaranteed and non-guaranteed. The type of reservation depends on whether a guest agrees to guarantee the booking by a certain method of payment, or by contractual agreement.

### Guaranteed reservation

A guaranteed reservation means that a guest will guarantee to pay for the room even if it is not used, unless the guest has followed the hotel's prearranged cancellation procedure. In return, the hotel promises to hold the room until the check-out time of the day following the date of arrival.

Guaranteed reservations protect the hotel from 'no-shows' (guests who make a room booking but do not arrive or cancel it). In this way the hotel will not lose the revenue from room sales, should the guest not turn up. This system also protects the guest because the hotel agrees to ensure that a room will be kept for the guest, even if that guest arrives later than expected. Reservations may be guaranteed in one of the following ways:

- *Prepayment*. The guest sends full payment for the room in advance.

- *Credit card*. The credit card number of the guest is recorded and if the guest fails to turn up, the hotel will bill the card holder in the normal way. This is the most common form of guaranteed reservation.

- *Advance deposit (or partial prepayment)*. The guest sends a specified amount of money in advance (normally to cover one night's accommodation). This form of deposit is usually required for group booking or long-stay guests. If the guest fails to show or cancels their booking on the actual day of arrival, the hotel may retain the deposit as compensation. However, in some hotels, the deposit may be returned to the guest or company, depending on the hotel policy.

- *Contractual agreement*. This normally involves a corporation where the company has agreed with the hotel to pay for an agreed number of rooms regardless of whether or not they are used.

### Non-guaranteed reservation

A non-guaranteed reservation is a reservation in which the guest has simply agreed and confirmed that they will arrive. It is normal with this type of reservation for the hotel to agree to hold a non-guaranteed room until a stated cancellation time, normally to 6.00p.m. on the day of arrival. If the guest does not arrive by the cancellation time, the room is then released. The hotel can then freely sell the released room to another guest, or to the original guest if they arrive late and if the room is still available. This cancellation time is sometimes called the release time. The purpose of stating a release time is, again, to avoid revenue losses for the hotel due to guests who fail to arrive. It is quite usual to have 6p.m. as the release time; however, it can be at any time that is appropriate to an individual hotel. For example, in Hong Kong most people arrive by air at around 4p.m. So hotels could have a 4p.m. release time.

---

## Activity 4

You are a reservations clerk of a hotel. A customer telephoned your department to make a reservation but she had some queries concerning whether or not she should guarantee her booking.

(a) Briefly explain to the guest the benefits she could obtain by guaranteeing her booking.

(b) Explain the different methods by which she could guarantee her booking.

(c) In the eyes of the law, is it necessary for her to guarantee a booking? Why?

---

## BASIC RESERVATIONS ACTIVITIES

Different hotels may adopt different systems and documents for receiving reservations. However, the basic procedure involved in the reservation process is similar for all hotels, as illustrated in Figure 5.2.

In the following sections, the procedures that need to be followed in each of the activities described in Figure 5.2 will be explained. The systems and documents used in the process will be further discussed in Chapter 6.

### Receiving reservation inquiries

As previously stated, a reservation request can be received through a variety of methods. The first step in the reservation process is to obtain information about a guest's proposed stay, to check whether a room is available.

The information a reservations clerk needs to obtain from the guest in order to give a speedy response, whether yes or no, is as follows:

- date of arrival

- length of proposed stay

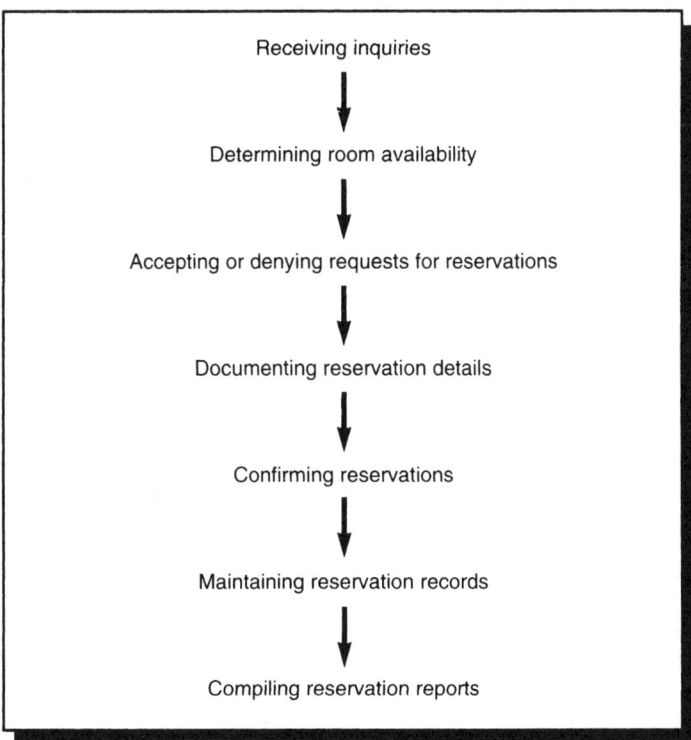

**Figure 5.2** Basic reservation activities

- type and number of room(s) required
- number of persons

### Determining room availability

After obtaining the information about the proposed stay from the customer, the next step in the reservation process is to check whether the type of accommodation asked for is available for the requested date(s). In any reservation system, it is essential to keep a close check on the number of reservations taken so as to avoid excessive overbooking.

Overbooking occurs when a hotel accepts more bookings than the number of rooms which are available. By overbooking, the hotel may find that major problems and loss of goodwill occur if a guest who has made a booking arrives at the hotel only to find that the hotel has no accommodation for them.

However, it is common in many hotels for the reservations department to overbook intentionally in order to ensure that a full house, i.e. 100 per cent occupancy, will be achieved. For example, when a hotel expects a lot of GIT bookings, which normally operate on a long lead time (the time between making the booking and actually arriving), there may be a large number of cancellations prior to arrival. The practice of overbooking helps to reduce the loss in revenue due to no-shows and late cancellations.

Whether hotels intentionally overbook or not, an effective system has to be used to check on room availability. This can be accomplished through the use of:

- forecast boards
- reservation charts
- computerized systems

The operational details of the systems will be explained in Chapter 6. (Note that each of these methods of indicating room availability can be called an availability chart or a room status availability.)

### Accepting or denying requests for reservations

Having checked that a room is available, the reservations clerk will either accept or deny the booking.

If a room is available, the request will normally be accepted. The reservations clerk will then record the details onto a reservation form or a computer terminal.

The reservations department may choose not to accept a booking (this is called denying the booking). Denying the booking happens when:

- A hotel may not have the specified accommodation available on the requested date(s).
- A hotel is fully booked.
- A guest is known to be on the blacklist. (A blacklist is a record authorized by the hotel management of the names of persons not welcome in the hotel for various reasons.)

When denying a specific reservation request, the reservations clerk should always be polite and helpful, and should follow the procedures below.

he specific accommodation requested is not available, gize and explain to the customer that the particular modation requested is not available. Try to help by g alternative accommodation or dates at the hotel, or if unacceptable the accommodation of the guest's choice in hotel.

tel is fully booked, apologize and explain that the

el Front Office Operations

hotel is fully booked. Offer alternative dates or accommodation at the hotel or in another hotel of the group. NB. For yield management and rooms maximization purposes, cumulative historical data of all denied bookings should be kept.

- **If the guest is blacklisted**, the actions to follow will depend on the reasons why the guest was blacklisted. For example, the reservation clerk may refuse the request completely if the guest has previously been a nuisance, or accept the request but on a cash-only basis if the guest is known to be bad about paying bills. Complicated cases should be referred to the reception manager.

---

**Activity 5**
(a) Why do hotels sometimes deny bookings from customers?

(b) Explain how a reservations clerk should handle a reservation request if the hotel has been overbooked on the requested date.

(c) How would you explain to a 'blacklisted' guest that they are unwanted in the hotel?

---

### Documenting reservation details

If the request for a reservation is accepted, the reservations clerk will then complete a reservation form, recording all the necessary details concerning the guest and their stay. It must be remembered that in many cases the enquiry may not come from the potential guest, but from a third party.

The *reservation form* is the only document which contains all the relevant information about the prospective guest and their accommodation request. It is therefore important that the form is fully and accurately completed. The reservation form can generate important information which is essential to other sections or departments of the hotel. The details of a reservation form and the things to consider when completing the form are explained in Chapter 6.

If a computer system is being used, then the details are normally typed directly into the system. Whether the system is manual or computerized, the principles of recording the information are similar, the only difference being that the reservations clerk may either type the information into the computer, or manually write the information down on a form.

When obtaining the reservation details from the guest, the reservations clerk should also explain the differences between a guaranteed and a non-guaranteed booking. Should a guest decide to guarantee their booking, the reservations clerk has then to obtain additional information concerning the method of guarantee (e.g. credit card, prepayment or deposit).

Once a request has been accepted and the details of the reservation recorded, the reservations clerk must immediately update the room availability chart. This ensures that the room availability record is accurate and thereby helps to avoid overbookings or omissions.

### The hotel diary

Immediately after updating the accommodation availability chart, the reservations clerk must enter all of the booking details into a hotel diary. However, if the hotel operates a computerized reservations system, this will be done automatically.

The details recorded in the diary are placed in order under date of arrival; this helps in the preparation of an arrivals list. The hotel diary should include the following:

- guest's name
- type of accommodation requested
- length of stay
- rate and terms quoted
- how and when booked
- contact telephone number
- reservations clerk's signature
- remarks

In many smaller hotels the number of the room to be given to the guest is sometimes recorded, along with the other information. However, this can only be done when the diary is used in conjunction with the conventional charting system, or for VIPs in larger properties.

If confirmation is given or received then this too may be entered into the hotel diary. A major advantage of the diary is that it acts as a backup for the information on guests who are due to arrive, especially should the original reservation form become misplaced. On a computerized reservations system this information is hyperlinked from the initial reservations details.

| Room no. | Name | Room type | Date of arrival | | | | | |
|---|---|---|---|---|---|---|---|---|
| | | | Nights | Rate and terms | How and when booked | Signed | Remarks |
| | | | | | | | |

**Figure 5.3** A hotel diary

### Confirming reservations

Confirmation of a reservation is a written acknowledgement sent either by the hotel to the guest or vice versa, depending on the hotel's policy regarding the room reservation details. It confirms that a request for a room or rooms has been made with the hotel, and is written evidence that a contract has been made between a hotel and a prospective guest. Examples of confirmations will be shown in Chapter 6, and will illustrate the types of manual and computerized form or letter which can be sent to the guest.

As a part of the confirmation process, the reservations clerk, or the central reservations office, may assign a reservation confirmation number to each booking; again, this may be done using either a manual or a computerized system. This assures the guest that a booking has been made. This reservation confirmation number should subsequently be quoted in the cases of cancellation of or amendment to the original booking.

Because large hotels very often have a large number of transient guests whose bookings are on short lead times, they do not attempt to confirm any bookings, except in the cases of a guaranteed reservation from a local company or agent.

### Maintaining reservation records

The maintenance of reservation records consists of two main types of activity: the filing of the original booking, and the modification of the bookings because of changes to reservation details.

### Filing bookings

After recording the reservation details onto the reservation form or into the computer and updating the room availability chart, it is necessary to have an efficient method of filing the booking details so that the documents relating to each particular booking are easily retrieved when needed.

In a manual reservation system, the reservation forms or cards and relevant correspondence are usually filed in chronological order, i.e. according to the date of arrival, and then in alphabetical order according to the guest's surname.

Correspondence and reservation forms are often filed according to the categories described below:

Today's Arrivals:
Documents relating to guests who are due to arrive and check in on a particular date.

Sub-section A, Provisional Bookings and Inquiries: Documents relating to reservations which have not been confirmed or guaranteed. These bookings could possibly turn out to be cancellations or no-shows.

Sub-section B, Confirmed Bookings: Documents relating to bookings for which the guests have physically acknowledged in writing and are due to arrive at the hotel.

Past Bookings:
Documents relating to guests who have stayed in the hotel and have now departed. These documents are kept for any future inquiries and are stored separately from current bookings.

Such a system of filing is useful to the reservation department because it provides easy access to important information, essential to subsequent operations.

Each category in the filing system has its own purpose in the process of reservation. For example, the Today's Arrivals correspondence can be transferred from the reservations department to the front desk on a particular day. This allows the front office staff to have all the relevant details about the guests prior to their arrival. Similarly, all past correspondence is filed after the guest has checked out and can be referred to easily.

Letters, memos, reservation forms or tour operators' lists (which relate to reservations) must also be filed appropriately for quick access. If a booking needs amending, the reservations clerk must be able to access the correct record quickly.

### Modifying bookings

Occasionally a change to or cancellation of a booking is requested. In these cases, an amendment or cancellation form is completed by the reservations clerk and attached to the original reservation form and correspondence. At the same time, the room availability chart should be amended accordingly.

In the case of a booking cancellation, various details are recorded to ensure that the correct booking is cancelled. It is also necessary to show who is responsible for cancelling the booking, i.e. who in the hotel received the cancellation and who on behalf of the guest made the cancellation. If any discrepancies should occur, the reservations clerk will be able to spot the error right away. The cancellation details should include:

- date of original booking
- guest's name
- date when the booking is cancelled
- name of person who cancelled the booking
- cancellation number
- name of reservations clerk who received the cancellation. As with denied bookings all the details of cancelled bookings must be kept for historical data.

**Activity 6**    What consequences may there be for the operation of a hotel should a reservations clerk fail to adjust the room availability chart after dealing with a cancellation of booking?

### *Compiling reservation reports*

The final step in the reservation process is the compilation of reservation reports. Information from these reports can help a hotel to maximize its room sales by the accurate control of room availability and the forecasting of potential room sales. Other departments may also make use of this information to assist in the planning of their budgets or forecasts.

Management reports available through a reservation system can vary depending on the needs of the hotel and the capability of the reservation system. Figure 5.4 shows the most common types of reservation reports prepared by the reservations department.

Reservation reports are just one kind of report which may be prepared and distributed to the management, as well as to other departments of a hotel. Some types of report are prepared daily (e.g. the arrivals and departure list, which is essential for the smooth operation of the front desk and the housekeeping department), while others are prepared on a weekly or monthly basis (e.g. reports on the number of guests, number of rooms occupied, number of reservations from different sources, no-shows, or walk-ins).

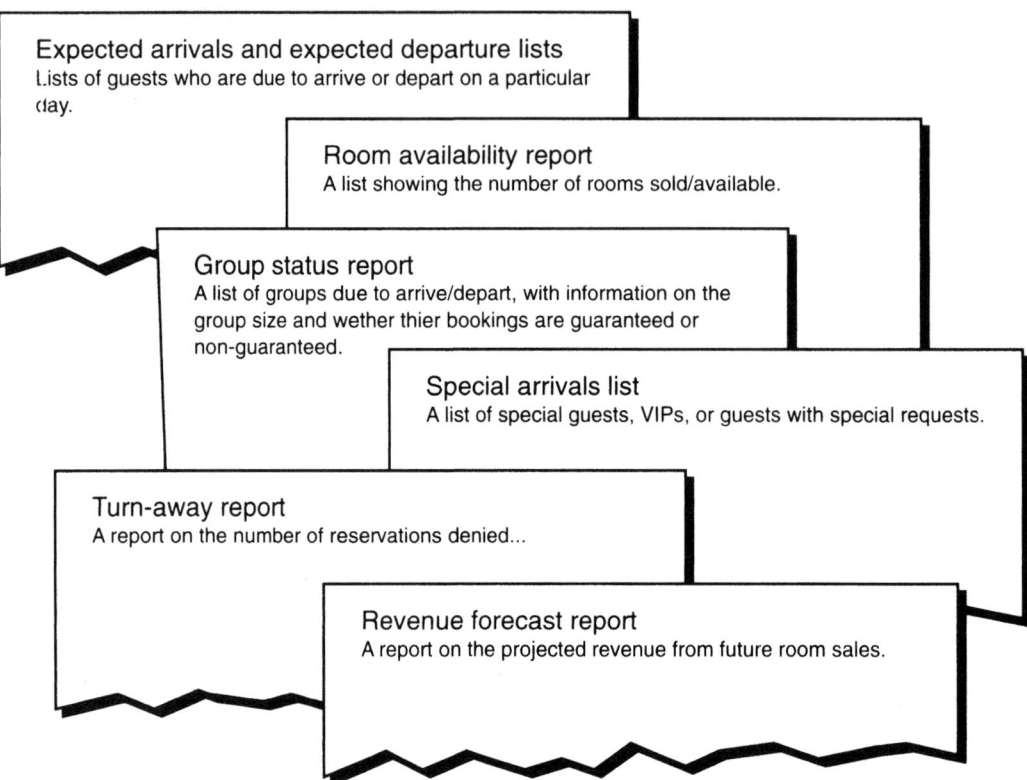

**Figure 5.4** Types of reports

These reports give management data and information to enable them to forecast better the occupancy, future revenue potential and market mix of the hotel.

The task of gathering and collating all of this information has been greatly reduced, while at the same time speeded up, by the highly efficient computer systems which are extensively used in today's hotel industry.

**Activity 7** For each of the following types of report produced by the reservations department, identify the sections or departments of the hotel which would be most interested in the information. Explain your reasons.

- special arrivals list
- turn-away report
- revenue forecast report

**SUMMARY**

Chapter 5 has explained at some length the operations of the reservations department. It also looked at the terms in common use when talking about reservations.

Initially we looked at the definition of the meaning of reservation, and then explained the implications of the law of contract for room bookings.

The importance of reservations to the hotel industry was explained, as was the role of the reservations clerk. The sequence of actions which are usually carried out by most hotels was covered, and reasons were given for these actions. The terms guaranteed and non-guaranteed bookings, no-show, lead time and release time were dealt with, and the relevance of these terms when related to the reservations department.

Finally, a list of some of the reservation reports was given, as well as a description of their use to the management of the hotel.

It is hoped that this chapter has given you an insight into the special role the reservations department plays in a hotel's operation. As with many jobs, its effectiveness and efficiency generally go unnoticed and to some extent not fully rewarded – that is until something goes wrong, when everyone in the hotel becomes aware of the pressures under which a reservationist works, and the skills they need to possess.

As the role of reservations department becomes more widely acknowledged, there is a greater and greater tendency for the department to be linked with the department of sales and marketing rather than with rooms. We shall have to wait and see what its eventual resting place will turn out to be.

# Review and discussion questions

1   Explain the difference between an affiliate reservation system and a non-affiliate reservation system.

2   Why do hotels sometimes deny bookings from customers?

3   Explain the meaning of a hotel reservation.

4   Why is the recording of advance reservation details important to a hotel?

5   Explain the meanings of the following terms:

    – release time

- no-show

- overbooking

- full house

6   Why is it necessary for hotels to adopt a release time policy?

7   Why do some hotel reservations offices intentionally overbook?

8   With the aid of a computer, explain how a customer can make a reservation through the Internet/email.

## Case Study: *Reservations: Systems or Systematic Chaos?*

Mr Roberts, the Hibiscus Gardens Hotel reservations manager, is concerned that his reservations clerks do not seem capable of accurately maintaining room availability. He also realizes that any amendments to an existing reservations record seem to cause confusion. Consequently he decides to investigate the operations of the reservations department.

He decides to play the part of a local travel agent and telephones the hotel requesting ten single rooms and five double rooms to be booked for four nights in the name of Sunlight Travel. The reservations clerk records the date of arrival and all other relevant information concerning the group booking. Mr Roberts waits a few minutes and then redials the hotel, this time making a reservation of one double room for two nights for the Tuesday and Wednesday of the next week. The reservations clerk asks for the necessary details, which are duly completed on a reservation form.

Later that afternoon, Mr Roberts decides to check on the two bookings that he had placed earlier that day with the reservations department. He goes to the reservations department and looks in the booking diary, under the appropriate date of arrival, to see whether his Sunlight Travel group booking has been recorded. Instead of finding the name Sunlight Travel, he finds that the group booking has been recorded under the name of Mr Walker, the name he used when he placed the booking. He then decides to check the density chart and notes that the 15 rooms have been deducted for the nights concerned and assigned to Mr Walker. Mr Roberts wonders about the reservations procedure, but then decides that the transaction had been handled correctly and if something had to be changed with the reservation it would probably be Mr Walker who would be the caller.

When checking on his second booking, the double room for the following week, he has a problem in locating the booking. He checks the booking diary and reservations file but no booking can be found. He returns to his office and decides to call the reservations department to alter his booking. The reservations clerk records the amendments and completes the telephone call. Mr Roberts, knowing that the hotel's policy requires the reservations clerk to confirm changes, including a confirmation number, whilst the guest is still on the line, begins to get upset with his department's procedures.

Mr Roberts waits about 20 minutes and then approaches Liz, the reservations clerk who handled his double room booking for the following week.

He explains to Liz that a Mr Walker had called his office, complaining that a reservation change had been requested but was not confirmed by the reservations clerk. Mr Roberts then asks Liz for Mr Walker's reservation details. Liz pulls the reservation form from one of the drawers in her desk. Mr Roberts asks Liz why the reservation form was stored in her desk and she says, 'it makes the job easier'. Mr Roberts asks Liz to explain this matter of fact statement. She tells him that her temporary files minimize the number of trips she needs to make to the office files and density chart. Mr Roberts asks how the other reservations clerks would know of the booking, and she replies, 'that's why we don't confirm changes over the phone, we notify the guest later'.

## Questions

1. **If you were Mr Roberts, explain what procedures the reservations clerk should have followed when handling the group booking, and can you foresee any problems?**

2. **Explain, with the present procedures in place, how controlling room inventory would be difficult and the consequences of this.**

3. **What suggestions can you make to improve the present reservations system?**

# 6

# *Reservation systems and documents*

## Introduction

In Chapter 5, we were concerned with the basic activities of the reservation process. In this chapter, we will look at the operational details involved at each stage of the process.

The first part of this chapter focuses on developing your skills in the receiving of reservations. The systems and documents used at each stage of the reservation process will then be explained.

Illustrations of the various forms and charts used in the reservation process have been included in this chapter. The actual format of these forms will vary from hotel to hotel.

## RECEIVING RESERVATIONS

In Chapter 5, we pointed out the importance of speedy, accurate and polite responses to reservation requests. To be able to do this, staff in the reservations department must have a good understanding of the reservation system and the operational procedures involved in receiving reservations. Furthermore, they should possess good communication skills.

The main objective of this section is to help you develop skills required for receiving reservations by giving you some examples of dialogue between a guest and a reservations clerk over the telephone.

The following conversation is an example of the correct procedures to follow when receiving reservation requests.

| | |
|---|---|
| *Reservations clerk*: | Good morning. Reservations. Sue speaking. |
| *Customer*: | Good morning, I'd like to reserve a room for next Tuesday the 16th. |
| *Reservations clerk*: | Yes, how many nights will you require the room? |
| *Customer*: | Two nights. |
| *Reservations clerk*: | Two nights . . . and what type of room do you require? |
| *Customer*: | A twin-bedded room please. |
| *Reservations clerk*: | I can do a standard twin bedroom for £75 per night, or a deluxe twin at the special rate of £95 per night. |
| *Customer*: | I'll take the deluxe twin please. |
| *Reservations clerk*: | May I have your surname and initial, please? |
| *Customer*: | Yes, my name is Mrs A. Freeman. |
| *Reservations clerk*: | Is the room for you and your husband? |
| *Customer*: | No, I'm booking on behalf of someone else. |
| *Reservations clerk*: | May I have the name of the guest, please? |
| *Customer*: | Yes, it's Mr and Mrs D. Carter. |
| *Reservations clerk*: | Can you spell the surname, please? |
| *Customer*: | Yes, it's C for Charlie, A for Alpha, R for Ronald, T for Tommy, E for Edward, R for Ronald, and the initial is D for David. |
| *Reservations clerk*: | May I have your telephone number please, Mrs Freeman? |
| *Customer*: | Yes, it's 5833842, a local number. |
| *Reservations clerk*: | Is this a company booking, Mrs Freeman? |
| *Customer*: | No, the guests are personal friends of mine. |
| *Reservations clerk*: | How are they arriving? |
| *Customer*: | By air. |
| *Reservations clerk*: | Do you have the flight number and arrival time for Mr and Mrs Carter? |

| | |
|---|---|
| *Customer*: | No, not yet. |
| *Reservations clerk*: | Can you inform us of the flight details when you know, please? |
| *Customer*: | Yes, I will do that. |
| *Reservations clerk*: | Let me confirm the details with you, Mrs Freeman. You have reserved one deluxe twin, check-in date Tuesday the 16th, check-out date the 18th, in the names Mr and Mrs D for David Carter. The room rate will be £95 plus VAT. Your local contact telephone number is 5833842. |
| *Customer*: | Yes, that's correct and I will call you when I know the flight details. |
| *Reservations clerk*: | Yes please, Mrs Freeman. Thank you for your reservation. |
| *Customer*: | Thank you. Goodbye. |
| *Reservations clerk*: | Goodbye, Mrs Freeman. |

### Key points

1. The reservations clerk answered the call with a positive, warm tone of voice. To do this, always smile before you speak on the telephone; it makes your voice more friendly and cheerful.
2. The reservations clerk was polite, she used courteous phrases (e.g. 'please' and 'thank you'), and she personalized the conversation by using the customer's name.
3. When using the telephone always speak clearly, and use an appropriate manner. For this private booking the reservations clerk used an unhurried, polite manner. The manner would be adapted for a telephone conversation with a business client or travel agent, when a brisker, more efficient approach would be more appropriate.
4. The reservations clerk took the opportunity to sell a more expensive type of room to the customer, by informing her of an interesting and attractive alternative.
5. During the conversation the reservations clerk ensured that she was clear about the number of guests who will stay (i.e. by stressing 'Mr and Mrs Carter?', she knows that two guests will occupy the room). She also asked the customer to spell the surname of the guests.
6. It is essential to inform the customer of the room rate.
7. Always record the name and telephone number of the local contact, and note the type or source of the booking; this call is

a personal (or private) booking, and not from a company or a travel agent.

8. The reservations clerk asked for the flight details. This detail will help the hotel to judge the time when the guests will arrive. If the guests do not arrive at the stated time, the hotel can telephone the airport to find out if the flight has been delayed. If the flight has landed and the guests are very late, then the reservation may be classified as a no-show.

9. Always repeat the details back to the customer, so that both parties (the hotel and the customer) know the reservation is correct.

10. The reservations clerk ended the conversation pleasantly, using the customer's name and thanking her for the reservation.

## Activity 1

(a) Practise repeating the details of the following booking to improve your technique, pronunciation and manner: You have reserved one standard single room arriving on Tuesday 16 February, and departing on Wednesday 17 February, in the name of Mr T for Tommy Ellsworth. The rate for the room will be £75 per night plus VAT. This is a guaranteed reservation and will be held for the guest. The account will be sent to you for settlement. Your company name and address is Cassell Publishing Limited, 145 Hennessy Road, Bedworth and your telephone number is Area Code 0527 5387484 Extension 232.

(b) Find a partner and practise the telephone conversation between a reservations clerk and Mrs Freeman. After you have read the conversation once, change roles and repeat the exercise. Pay attention to the fluency and tone of your voice.

## DETERMINING ROOM AVAILABILITY FROM AVAILABILITY CHARTS

Before accepting a reservation, it is essential that the reservations clerk checks the room availability to see whether accommodation is available to meet the request.

Room availability is usually shown on an availability chart, which can be in the form of:

- a forecast board
- a reservation chart
- a computerized system

## Forecast boards

A forecast board (Figure 6.1) is similar in appearance to a calendar. It is usually situated on a wall near to the reservations clerks so that they

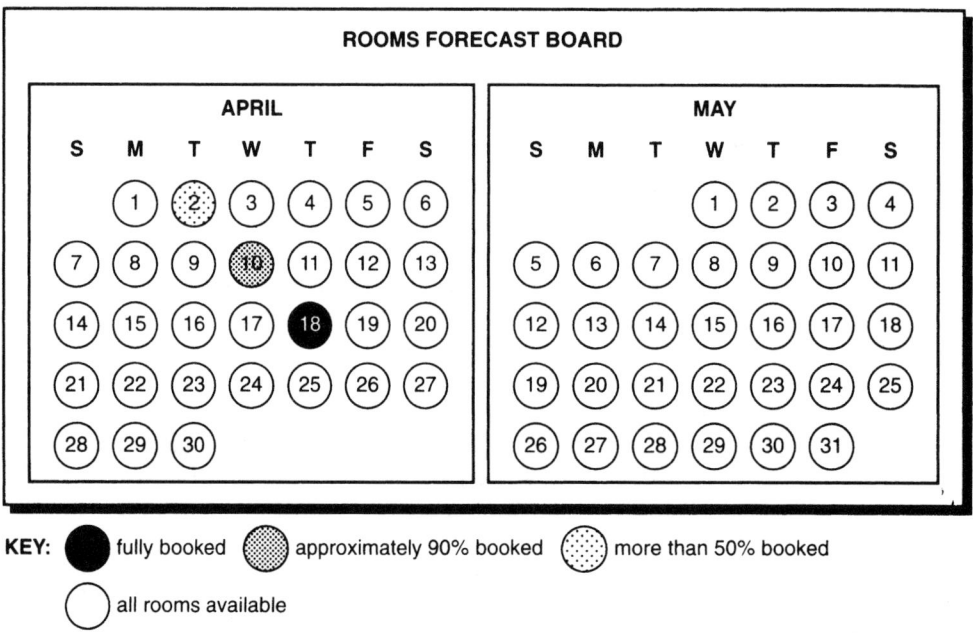

**Figure 6.1** A forecast board

have quick access to the room status information when they have to check for room availability. The board normally indicates a period of four months, and the dates represent specific room status information. For example:

No tag = all rooms available

To maintain updated information, the room availability displayed on the forecast board should be adjusted regularly, according to the reservation conditions of the hotel. This is usually done under the supervision of the reservations manager.

### Reservation charts

Many hotels use reservation charts to display and record room availability. Reservation charts can be of two different types: conventional or density charts. The actual method of charting reservations in a hotel depends on the actual number, types and turnover of rooms in a hotel.

*Conventional charts.* Conventional charts display the availability of each room in the hotel by room number. An example is illustrated in Figure 6.2.

| Month: February | | | | | | | | | | | Key: S = single | T = twin | D = double | |
|---|---|---|---|---|---|---|---|---|---|---|---|---|---|---|
| Room no. & type \ Date | 1 | 2 | 3 | 4 | 5 | 6 | 7 | 8 | 9 | 10 | 11 | 12 | 13 | 14 |
| 101 S | | | | | | | | | | | | | | |
| 102 S | | | | | | | | | | | | | | |
| 103 S | | | | | | | | | | | | | | |
| 104 D | | | | | | | | | | | | | | |
| 105 D | | | | | | | | | | | | | | |
| 106 D | | | | | | | | | | | | | | |
| 107 T | | | | | | | | | | | | | | |

**Figure 6.2** A conventional chart

On a conventional chart, reservations are usually marked in pencil to allow for any necessary alterations or cancellations. Each booking is allocated a room number, with the guest's name shown on the chart. The chart is normally shown on a monthly basis, and is displayed on the wall or desk within easy reach of the reservations clerk.

'Folio' numbers are sometimes used when a guest's name will not fit into the space available on the chart. For example, 'Castle Peak Trading Company' will not fit neatly into the appropriate days, and therefore the letter 'F' and the numeral 1 are written on the chart. Similarly, 'Universal Equipment Corporation' does not fit, so we write F2 (see Figure 6.3).

A key showing who the folio numbers represent is kept with the chart.

The advantage of this system is that it gives not only up-to-date

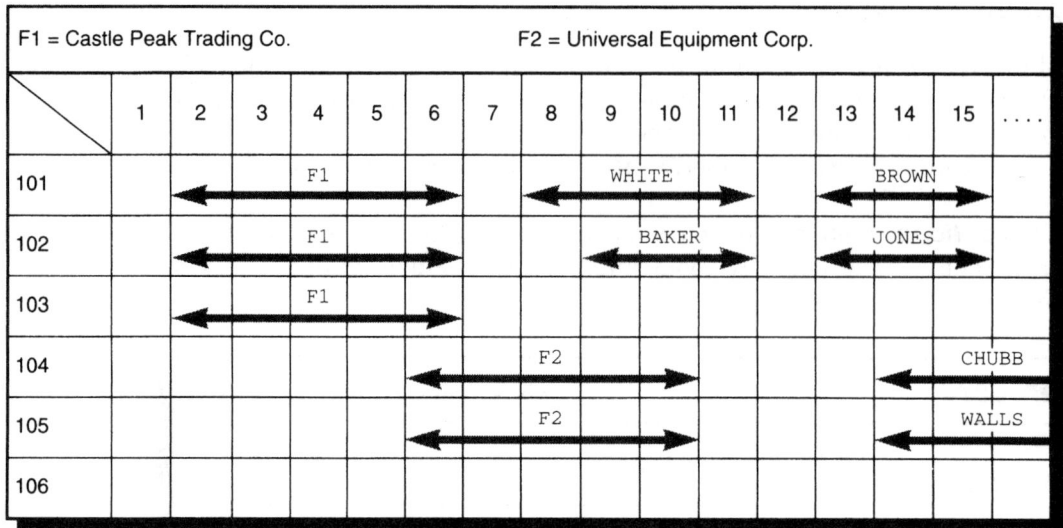

**Figure 6.3** How the conventional chart is used

room status information, but also the details concerning individual bookings. However, this type of chart is normally only suitable for small hotels:

- where the guests usually stay for a long period of time;
- which have a wide variety of room types (i.e. different sizes, decor, features or locations); and
- which offer highly personalized services to their guests (e.g. where guests request specific rooms).

The conventional chart is not suitable for large hotels because it is very time-consuming to record all the individual details. Also, it is very easy for errors to be made when there are a large number of rooms.

***Density charts.*** Density charts show and record the total number of reservations held for each type of room on a specific date. For example, if a hotel has 150 deluxe twin rooms and on one day 105 of them have already been booked, then only 45 deluxe twin rooms are still available for sale.

Figure 6.4 illustrates how a density chart is used. The density chart shows that the hotel has 17 single rooms, of which 10 are superior singles and seven are deluxe singles. All the rooms are available. When a reservation for a superior single for 19 February is received, a line is put through 10, under the superior single category on the actual date of arrival (19 February). From this information, we know that one superior single room for 19 February has been booked, and only nine superior single rooms are still available on that date.

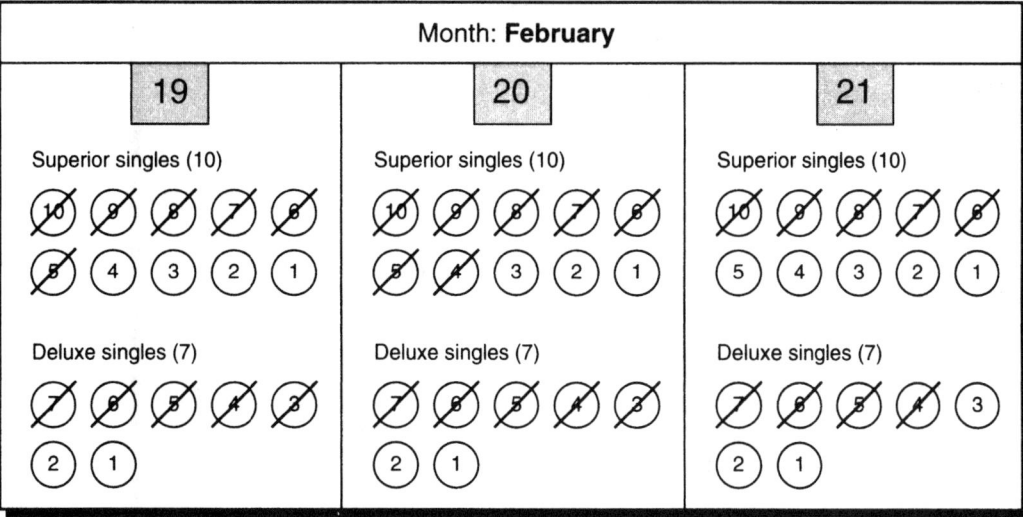

**Figure 6.4** Part of a density chart for February

When the reservation is for more than one night, the subsequent days on the chart should be marked in the same way as described above. For example, a deluxe single is wanted for two nights, arriving on 20 February. A line is drawn through 7 under the deluxe category for both 20 and 21 February, showing that we have only six deluxe singles left to sell.

In general, density charts are suitable for large hotels in which:

- there are a large number of rooms with similar decor, location and price
- the guests will usually stay for a short period
- there is a need for quicker handling of large numbers of bookings

---

**Activity 2**  Study the density chart on p. 90, then answer these questions.

(a) How many deluxe singles are available on 20 February?

(b) How many superior singles have been booked on 21 February?

(c) Should you accept a booking from a guest who requests two superior single rooms on 19 and 20 February? Why? Why not?

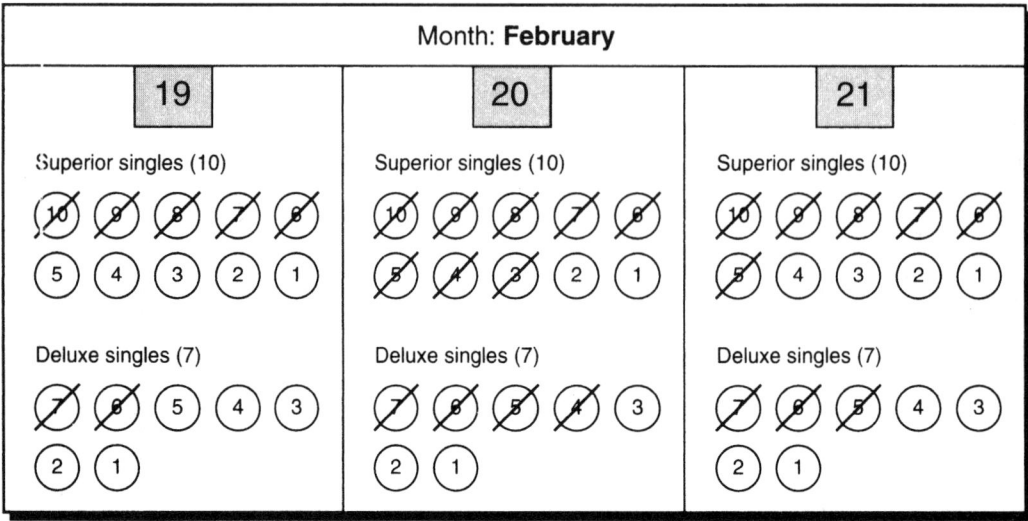

**Activity 2**

(d) Now you have answered question (c), update the density chart. How many superior single rooms are now available on 19 and 20 February?

(e) A request is made for four deluxe singles for three nights starting on 19 February. Should you accept this request? Why? Why not?

(f) What alternatives would you offer the customer in question (e)?

### Computerized reservation systems

A computerized reservation system controls not only room availability but also the whole process of reservations. When a request for a reservation is received, the reservation details are stored in the computer. In this way, it is possible to keep a record of all reservation details, as well as maintain a tight control of the number of rooms available. In some cases, the computer can be programmed to refuse any further bookings when a hotel is fully booked, and create a waiting list for any subsequent reservations. It is also possible to program computer systems to make reservation information available to many reservations clerks at the same time. The general principle of a computerized reservations system is the same as a manual chart, only it is electronically manipulated.

```
Today's date: 1 March

Total Number of Rooms: 105

                    Rooms Available

            SR          DR          TR          ST

  1/3        -3          21          26          5
  2/3        -2          21          11          5
  3/3        -2          22          14          4
  4/3         4          19          12          5
```

**Figure 6.5** A computerized room availability report (density format)

So, if you fully understand how a conventional density chart works you will know what is happening in your computer (Figure 6.5).

In a computerized system, rooms available will appear on the visual display unit (VDU) of the computer terminal or in print, and reservations clerks have easy access to this information whenever they need.

A computerized system has the advantage that it is capable of generating reservation reports in a short period of time. These may include, for example, the daily arrivals, stay-over and departure list, projected estimated revenue, and summary reports on bookings by room type or sleeper forecasts. These reports are essential to the hotel management in the planning of their operations.

**Activity 3**  Complete the exercises which follow:

1. Use the information at the top of p. 92 to complete the conventional chart at the foot of p. 92.

    (a) List which rooms are available for 2 December.

    (b) If the Gould and James booking has been accepted, what is your room status on the nights of 4 and 5 December?

    (c) List the rooms booked for the night of 7 December.

    (d) A group wants to know if you can accommodate nine sleepers on the night of 9 December. What is your reply?

**Today's date:** 30 November

# Future Bookings

| Arrival Date | Type of Room | No. of Nights | Name | Remarks |
|---|---|---|---|---|
| 5/12 | 1s | 3 | Mr Ecker | |
| 9/12 | 1tw | 4 | Mr/s Miller | |
| 2/12 | 1tw/1s | 2 | Mr/s Brooks & son | |
| 3/12 | 2tw | 3 | Castle Peak Trading | |
| 4/12 | 1d/1s | 2 | Mr/s Robins & daughter | |
| 2/12 | 1s | 4 | Mr McNicholl | |
| 7/12 | 2tw | 3 | Mr/s Hung, Mr/s Grey | Adjoining rms |
| 6/12 | 1s | 3 | Mr Patel | |
| 2/12 | 1d | 8 | Mr/s Warner | |
| 4/12 | 1d | 2 | Mr/s Keith | |
| 6/12 | 2d | 4 | Universal Equipment Corp. | names to be supplied |
| 4/12 | 1d | 5 | Mr/s Nirundi | |
| 4/12 | 2d | 2 | Mr/s Gould, Mr/s James | |

## Month: December

Key: S = single    T = twin    D = double

| Room no. & type \ Date | 1 | 2 | 3 | 4 | 5 | 6 | 7 | 8 | 9 | 10 | 11 | 12 | 13 | 14 |
|---|---|---|---|---|---|---|---|---|---|---|---|---|---|---|
| 101 S | | | | | | | | | | | | | | |
| 102 S | | | | | | | | | | | | | | |
| 103 S | | | | | | | | | | | | | | |
| 104 D | | | | | | | | | | | | | | |
| 105 D | | | | | | | | | | | | | | |
| 106 D | | | | | | | | | | | | | | |
| 107 T | | | | | | | | | | | | | | |
| 108 D | | | | | | | | | | | | | | |
| 109 D | | | | | | | | | | | | | | |
| 110 T | | | | | | | | | | | | | | |
| 111 T | | | | | | | | | | | | | | |

2. Use the information below to complete the density chart on p. 94.

   (a) Will there be any overbooking if all the bookings are accepted?

   (b) In what way does your room availability change, after Mr/s Lee cancels their booking?

---

**Today's date:** 30 November

## Existing Residents

| Arrival Date | Type of Room | No. of Nights | Name | Departure Date |
|---|---|---|---|---|
| 24/11 | 1d | 9 | Mr/s Catch | 3/12 |
| 23/11 | 1s | 10 | Mr C. Singh | 3/12 |
| 20/11 | 1s | 13 | Mrs L. Winston | 3/12 |
| 21/11 | 1d | 15 | Mr/s B. Lutherson | 6/12 |
| 26/11 | 1d | 13 | Mr/s F. Des Voeux | 9/12 |

## Forward Bookings

| | | | | |
|---|---|---|---|---|
| 8/12 | 1t | 2 | Mr/s Dupont | |
| 3/12 | 1s | 7 | Mr F. King | |
| 6/12 | 1s | 2 | Miss J. Martinson | |
| 2/12 | 1t | 3 | Mr L. Lord & Mr J. Stevens | |
| 3/12 | 1d | 7 | Mr/s E. Shing | |
| 1/12 | 1d | 4 | Mr/s A. Marks | |
| 8/12 | 1t | 4 | Mr/s T. Millard | |
| 7/12 | 1d | 12 | Mr/s A. Lee | |
| 5/12 | 1t | 5 | Miss Goring & Ms T. Brown | |
| 6/12 | 1t | 3 | Mr/s P. Van Ecke | |
| 6/12 | 1d | 4 | Mr/s G. Arden | |
| 9/12 | 1s | 6 | Mr E. Paris | |
| 5/12 | 1d | 3 | Mr/s C. Carvelho | |
| 8/12 | 1d | 4 | Mr/s G. Erikson | |
| 3/12 | 1s | 3 | Mrs D. Abelman | |

**Activity 3,**
question 2

| Month: **December** | | | | | | |
|---|---|---|---|---|---|---|
| **1** | **2** | **3** | **4** | **5** | **6** | **7** |
| Singles ④③②① | Singles ④③②① | Singles ④③②① | Singles ④③②① | Singles ④③②① | Singles ④③②① | Singles ④③②① |
| Doubles ④③②① | Doubles ④③②① | Doubles ④③②① | Doubles ④③②① | Doubles ④③②① | Doubles ④③②① | Doubles ④③②① |
| Twins ④③②① | Twins ④③②① | Twins ④③②① | Twins ④③②① | Twins ④③②① | Twins ④③②① | Twins ④③②① |
| **8** | **9** | **10** | **11** | **12** | **13** | **14** |
| Singles ④③②① | Singles ④③②① | Singles ④③②① | Singles ④③②① | Singles ④③②① | Singles ④③②① | Singles ④③②① |
| Doubles ④③②① | Doubles ④③②① | Doubles ④③②① | Doubles ④③②① | Doubles ④③②① | Doubles ④③②① | Doubles ④③②① |
| Twins ④③②① | Twins ④③②① | Twins ④③②① | Twins ④③②① | Twins ④③②① | Twins ④③②① | Twins ④③②① |
| **15** | **16** | **17** | **18** | **19** | **20** | **21** |
| Singles ④③②① | Singles ④③②① | Singles ④③②① | Singles ④③②① | Singles ④③②① | Singles ④③②① | Singles ④③②① |
| Doubles ④③②① | Doubles ④③②① | Doubles ④③②① | Doubles ④③②① | Doubles ④③②① | Doubles ④③②① | Doubles ④③②① |
| Twins ④③②① | Twins ④③②① | Twins ④③②① | Twins ④③②① | Twins ④③②① | Twins ④③②① | Twins ④③②① |

**Activity 3,**
question 2

3. You have just received some fax bookings (see top of p. 95); can you accommodate them all? Briefly explain why or why not.

   (a) What room types and how many are available for the nights of 7 and 8 December?

   (b) How many sleepers can you accommodate on the night of 5 and 6 December?

4. Now that you have charted the bookings, explain:

   (a) the differences between the methods used for

```
┌─────────────────────────────────────────────────────────────────┐
│              WORLD TRAVEL AGENCY                                  │
│                    Birmingham                                    │
│                  Fax: 021–476 4111                               │
├─────────────────────────────────────────────────────────────────┤
│                                                                   │
│  To:        King's Hotel, Dover, Kent.                           │
│                                                                   │
│  From:      World Travel Agency, Birmingham.                     │
│                                                                   │
│  Message:   Pls arrange accommodation for the following:         │
│                 one double, for five nights from 1/12            │
│                 one single, for four nights from 2/12            │
│                 one single, for six nights from 7/12             │
│                 one twin, for seven nights from 2/12             │
│                 one single, for four nights from 10/12           │
│                                                                   │
│  Note: Mr/s H. Essex specially requests room 110, which is a     │
│  double, for six nights from 1/12.                               │
│                                                                   │
└─────────────────────────────────────────────────────────────────┘
```

**Activity 3,**
question 2

charting information on a conventional chart and a density chart.

(b) the limitations of the two systems in charting and displaying information on room availability.

---

## RESERVATION RECORDS

When a reservation request is accepted, the details concerning the guest will be recorded on a reservation form. In this section, we shall explain what information is normally required on a reservation form and the things to note when completing the form.

Reservation forms may differ in their layout and design, but they usually ask for similar information about a guest and their stay. An example of a reservation form is illustrated in Figure 6.6 (p. 98).

The following sections summarize the important considerations to be borne in mind when completing each part of the reservation form.

1. *Full name.* Surname, forename and title are to be recorded. Always ensure that names are spelt correctly.

2. *Date of arrival.* Always follow the hotel policy of how dates should be recorded. In most hotels dates are recorded using the day–month–year convention; however, some hotels use the American month–day–year convention. The reservation

department of a hotel should decide on a method and instruct all staff to stick to it. Otherwise, there could be great confusion and misunderstanding.

3. *Date of departure.* Ensure that the date of departure, not the last night of the guest's stay, is recorded. For example, in the case of a guest staying until the night of the 12th and departing on the morning of the 13th, the departure date is the 13th, not the 12th.

4. *Estimated time of arrival (ETA).* This information gives reception an idea as to what time of the day they are going to be busy with check-ins. It also enables the reception staff to check up on a guest should their ETA pass. This is especially important for those guests who are arriving at the town or city by air.

5. *Number of nights.* The number of nights is a further confirmation that the guest's stated arrival and departure dates are correct.

6. *Room type.* This is the specific type of accommodation requested. Many hotels use special codes for the various types of rooms (e.g. DB = double or Sgl = Single).

7. *Number of rooms.* This is the actual number of rooms requested (e.g. two singles or five twins).

8. *Number of persons.* The number of persons refers to the actual number of guests occupying the rooms. This is because it is not uncommon to have a single person sleeping in a double room or a family of four in a twin double-bedded room.

9. *Rate quoted.* Always quote the correct room rate and explain what charges are included, e.g. £75.00 for the room, inclusive of service charge and VAT. As mentioned in Chapter 2, different room rate schedules are offered to different guests. It is, therefore, important that the reservations clerk knows which room rate to quote for a particular guest.

10. *Home address.* The home address is the prospective guest's private address and telephone number, if they will be settling their own accounts.

11. *Caller.* This is the name of the person making the reservation (e.g. the secretary or corporate travel manager). This is usually not the same name as the person using the room.

12. *Company name.* When a reservation is made by a company, the name of the company must be recorded correctly. The name is then checked against a list of credit-approved companies to see if a special rate is applicable.

13. *Company address.* This is the correspondence address of the department of the company which is going to settle the guest's account.

14. *Telephone and fax number.* A local contact telephone or fax number is useful for confirming details (e.g. billing details).

15. *Method of payment.* This is an indication of how the prospective guest intends to finally pay their account. It is important at this stage to remind a guest who wishes to pay by cheque that prior arrangements need to be made, especially if the amount of the bill is in excess of the agreed cheque card limit, as in nearly all instances this will be the case.

16. *Guaranteed or non-guaranteed booking.* When receiving a reservation request, the reservations clerk should ask whether the guest would prefer a guaranteed or non-guaranteed booking (see Chapter 5). If the guest chooses to have a guaranteed booking, the reservations clerk should inform the guest what is required to guarantee the booking (e.g. a credit card number or advance deposit).

   If the guest chooses not to guarantee the booking, the room will be held on a 6 p.m. release. It is important for the reservations clerk to inform the guest that the reservation is not guaranteed and that after 6 p.m. the room may be released.

   Some hotels may ask the guest to inform the hotel if they think that they are going to arrive later than 6 p.m. and the hotel can then avoid releasing the room until a later time (after the guest's stated likely time of arrival).

17. *Card number.* This is the number of the credit card the guest intends to use when he or she eventually checks out. This number enables the hotel to check creditworthiness of the guest, should it be thought necessary, as well as acting as a room guarantee for the guest.

18. *Confirmation.* This is an indication of whether a hotel's confirmation slip has been sent to the guest. (Note: the clerk should answer 'yes' or 'no'.) Alternatively, if the reservation request is for a group booking it is normal for the group leader or travel agent to send a confirmation to the hotel. Very often the abbreviation 'TBC' is used when talking about the confirmation of bookings. This simply stands for 'To be confirmed'.

19. *Taken by, date.* This is the signature of the reservations clerk who takes the booking, and the date when the booking was made.

20. *Remarks.* This is the space where any special request made by the guest is recorded, e.g. transport from airport, extra bed, baby cot, or a quiet room.

   The above details are commonly found on reservation forms for most hotels. However, it must be remembered that these details will vary from hotel to hotel and from place to place. For instance, a particular hotel may not require flight arrival times, but may include booking details for a round of golf should the hotel have its own golf course, or if there is a course nearby.

**Activity 4** Reread the conversation between the reservations clerk and Mrs Freeman (pp. 83–4), and then complete the reservation form below.

## KING'S HOTEL

### Reservation Form

Dr/Mr/Mrs/Miss/Ms 1 ...........................................................................................................

Arr. date: 2 ........................................... Dep. date: 3 ...........................................

ETA: 4 ................................................... No. of nights: 5 ..................................

Room type: 6 .......................................... No. of rooms: 7 ..................................

No. of persons: 8 .................................... Rate quoted: 9 ...................................

Home address: 10 .................................. Contact name: 11 ..............................

Company name: 12 .............................

Phone no.: ............................................ Address: 13 .......................................

....................................................................

Phone/fax no.: 14 ...............................

Method of payment: 15 .......................... Gtd booking: 16 ................................

Cr card no.: 17 ...................................

Remarks: 20 .......................................... Conf: Yes/No 18 ...............................

Taken by: 19 ...............................................

Date: ..........................................................

**Figure 6.6** A reservation form

## RESERVATION CONFIRMATIONS

In Chapter 5, we said that after accepting a reservation request and recording the details on a reservation form, a hotel will normally confirm the booking by sending out a reservation confirmation.

A reservation confirmation can be made by means of:

- a pre-printed confirmation slip or form which includes a registration form for the guest to complete and/or present at reception on arrival (Figure 6.7a)

- a personalized letter, though with a standard wording (Figure

---

**KING'S HOTEL**

Address: South Coast Road, Dover, Kent.
Telephone: (0527) 723 6788
Fax : (0527) 745 6345
E-mail: kingsotel@hotemail.com.uk

Thank you very much for your request for a reservation at the King's Hotel.
We are pleased to confirm the following accommodation:

Confirmation number: _____

Guest name: _____ No. of persons: _____

Address: _____

_____

_____ Telephone: _____

Arrival date: _____ ETA/Flight: _____

Accommodation: _____

Rate: _____ (inclusive of service charge and VAT)

Remarks: _____

Date: _____ Front Office Manager: _____

We look forward to welcoming you and assure you that everything possible will be done to make your stay an enjoyable one.

**Important:** *Please retain this letter and present it to the receptionist upon registration. Reservations are held only until 6 p.m. unless otherwise notified or the booking has been guaranteed.*

---

**Figure 6.7** (a) A reservation confirmation

6.7b), usually produced on specially designed paper using a word processor

- a pre-printed confirmation slip or form, usually printed by a computer on to specially designed paper

**KING'S HOTEL**

| | |
|---|---|
| *Address:* | *South Coast Road,* |
| | *Dover, Kent.* |
| *Telephone:* | *(0527) 723 6788* |
| *Fax :* | *(0527) 745 6345* |
| *E-mail:* | *kingsotel@hotemail.com.uk* |

Mr. P. Smith,
110 Plimsole Road,
London NE2 4WB,
United Kingdom.


Dear Mr Smith,

**RE: ROOM RESERVATION**

Thank you for your letter of 29 August. We have, as requested, reserved for you:

One double room with double bed, shower, sea view.
Rate: £90 per night, inclusive of service charge and VAT.
Date: 21-29 October, inclusive.

Unfortunately, we are not certain whether you require the room for nine nights or whether you plan to leave on the 29th. We would, therefore, appreciate it if you could confirm by return mail:

1) the actual number of nights required;
2) your estimated arrival time;
3) as we note that you are arriving by air whether you would require being met at the airport.

We thank you again for your valued custom and look forward to serving you in October.

Yours sincerely,
The King's Hotel




Gloria Todd (Miss)
Reservation Department

**Figure 6.7** (b) Personalized letter

## Activity 5

Complete the reservation confirmation form below, using the information on the reservation form in Activity 4 (p. 98).

---

👑

**KING'S HOTEL**

*Address:    South Coast Road,*
*            Dover, Kent.*
*Telephone: (0527) 723 6788*
*Fax :       (0527) 745 6345*
*E-mail:     kingsotel@hotemail.com.uk*

Thank you very much for your request for a reservation at the King's Hotel.
We are pleased to confirm the following accommodation:

Confirmation number: _____

Guest name: _____    No. of persons: _____

Address: _____

_____

_____    Telephone: _____

Arrival date: _____    ETA/Flight: _____

Accommodation: _____

Rate: _____    (inclusive of service charge and VAT)

Remarks: _____

Date: _____    Front Office Manager: _____

We look forward to welcoming you and assure you that everything possible will be done to make your stay an enjoyable one.

**Important:** *Please retain this letter and present it to the receptionist upon registration. Reservations are held only until 6 p.m. unless otherwise notified or the booking has been guaranteed.*

**Activity 5,**
Reservation
confirmation form

## AMENDMENT OR CANCELLATION OF A RESERVATION

A reservation amendment or cancellation form (Figure 6.8) is used to record any subsequent changes in the reservation details of an original booking. It is often attached to the original reservation form and correspondence for easy reference. As with the reservation forms, the design of the amendment or cancellation form may differ among hotels, but the basic information contained in the forms is quite similar.

| | |
|---|---|
| **KING'S HOTEL** | Address:    *South Coast Road, Dover, Kent.*<br>*Telephone: (0527) 723 6788*<br>*Fax :     (0527) 745 6345*<br>*E-mail:   kingsotel@hotemail.com.uk* |

☐ **Amendment**

☐ **Cancellation**

Cancellation no: _____

Guest name: _____

Arrival date: _____     Departure date: _____

Accommodation required: _____     Rate: _____

Remarks: _____

Date: _____     Completed by: _____

**Figure 6.8** Amendment/cancellation form

## SUMMARY OF THE RESERVATION PROCESS

In Chapter 5, we explained the different sources of reservations and the major reservation activities. In this chapter, we have concentrated on the systems and documents used at each stage of the reservation process.

The relationship between the reservation activities and the systems and documents used in the process is shown in Figure 6.9.

## CHOICE OF RESERVATION SYSTEMS

Virtually every hotel has its own system for recording and monitoring reservations; however, the principal functions performed by reservation systems are summarized below:

- collation of reservation details, regardless of the source (the reservation form)

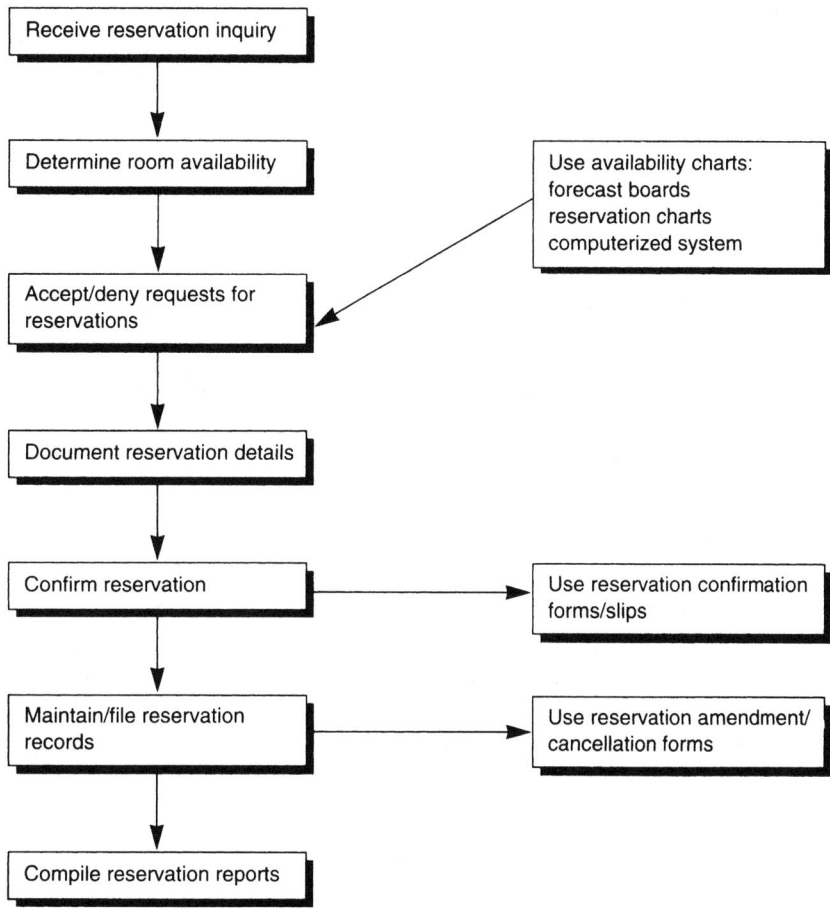

**Figure 6.9** Reservation procedures

- provision of immediate information about room availability (the reservation chart or forecast board)

- provision of a detailed record of each particular booking (the computer or booking diary)

- provision of a method recording any changes to the original bookings (the cancellation/amendment form or log book)

- provision of detailed lists of guests and their requirements on their day of arrival (the reservation report on expected arrivals and departures)

- provision of details of future arrivals and departures for other departments (the forecast list)

- provision of a method of filing guest correspondence (the chronological/alphabetical filing system)

In small hotels, the reservation system may comprise simple manual charts and forms such as conventional charts and reservation forms. But as hotels increase in size, such simple manual systems may become inefficient and frustrating to operate, and alternative systems have to be considered. These systems may include density charts, forecast boards or computerized systems.

The type of reservation system that a hotel will choose depends upon various factors, such as:

- the lead time of bookings, which determines the quantity of data to be stored

- the average length of guests' stay, which determines the turnover of rooms (for example, transient hotels usually have to store more details, as they have a larger number of bookings)

- the size of the hotel, as well as the actual number and variety of rooms available

While it is important for a hotel to choose an appropriate and efficient system for reservations, for any system to function effectively the reservations clerks must be well trained and skilled in operating the system. The incorrect recording of reservation details causes a lot of confusion and it invariably harms the reputation of the hotel.

---

**Activity 6** (a) What factors have to be considered when designing a reservation system for a hotel?

(b) Why is it important for a reservations clerk to be well trained in the procedures of accepting and recording reservations?

---

## SUMMARY

This chapter has covered the variety of methods by which a room booking may be taken and accurately recorded. It has also looked at the styles of speech and communication which are appropriate when taking a telephone booking.

The benefits of forecast boards were explained, as well as the merits and disadvantages of the conventional charting system. If the conventional chart is suitable for small hotels, the density chart is well suited to large properties. The reasons for this suitability were covered when the operating procedure of this system was given.

The main document of the reservation system is the reservation form. The details which should be recorded, and the reasons for taking them, were explained. In order to maintain an accurate room availability record, cancellations or amendments to room requirements need to be recorded. This chapter gave an example of the style and use of a cancellation/amendment form.

Each hotel has its own way of handling room reservations; as long as it is efficient and effective, it works. However, it must be remembered that reservations clerks go on holiday or leave their place of work. Therefore the system should be such that another member of staff can move into the reservations department and can operate the systems with the minimum number of problems.

As mentioned in Chapter 5, the reservations department is being recognized as one of the principal players in achieving and maintaining a profitable hotel.

# Review and discussion questions

The following tasks are designed to help encourage you to think about what you have studied in the chapter.

**1** (a) Explain the differences between a density chart and a conventional chart.

(b) Which of the two types of reservation charts is more appropriate for a small resort hotel? Why?

**2** Study the density chart overleaf which shows the reservation conditions of the King's Hotel for the period 19–21 February, and then do the exercises that follow. (Note: the density chart is being used as an availability chart.)

(a) List the number and types of rooms available on:

- 19 February

- 20 February

- 21 February

(b) Read the conversation below, then complete the King's Hotel reservation form that follows on p. 109. (Note: you might like to try this activity with a partner; take it in turns to be the reservations clerk and customer.)

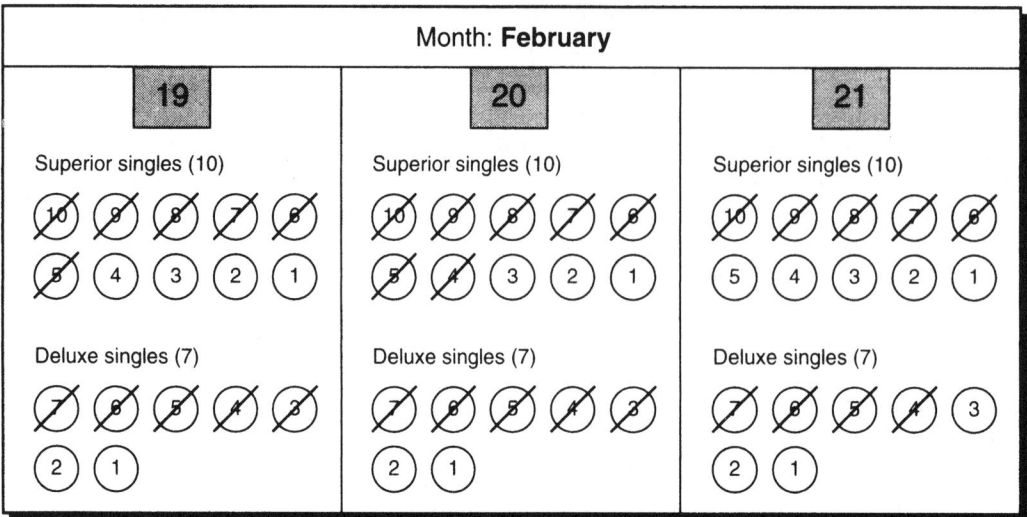

| | Reservations clerk: | Good morning. Reservations, Gloria speaking. |
|---|---|---|
| | Customer: | Good morning. Wheelok Holdings Ltd here. I'd like to reserve four single rooms from the 19th of February. |
| | Reservations clerk: | Arriving the 19th of February. For how many nights, please? |
| | Customer: | Two nights. |
| | Reservations clerk: | So that will be departing on Saturday, the 21st of February? |
| | Customer: | Oh ... no ... er, can you make that three nights please? |
| | Reservations clerk: | Checking out on Sunday the 22nd? |
| | Customer: | Yes, please. |
| | Reservations clerk: | Please hold the line one moment. I see your company has an arrangement with this hotel for deluxe rooms. At the moment we only have two deluxe singles at £90 per night. Shall I reserve two superior singles for the other guests? Your rate for these will be £85 per night. |
| | Customer: | Yes, that will be fine. |
| | Reservations clerk: | May I have the guests' names please? |

| | |
|---|---|
| *Customer:* | Please give the two deluxe rooms to Mrs L. Smit and Mrs P. Harper. |
| *Reservations clerk:* | Can you spell the names for me, please? |
| *Customer:* | That's Mrs L. for Linda Smit, that's S.M.I.T., and Mrs P. for Patricia Harper, that's H.A.R.P.E.R. |
| *Reservations clerk:* | Thank you, and the other guests' names? |
| *Customer:* | Mr D. for Daniel Swan, that's S.W.A.N., and Mr R. for Ronald Porritt, P.O.R.R.I.T.T. |
| *Reservations clerk:* | Thank you. I will note on the reservation that the two gentlemen should be upgraded to deluxe rooms should they be available when they check in. May I have your name please, madam? |
| *Customer:* | My name is Mrs Alison Long. |
| *Reservations clerk:* | What is your telephone number, please? |
| *Customer:* | 5625611, extension 262. |
| *Reservations clerk:* | That's 5625611. Do you have the guests' estimated time of arrival? |
| *Customer:* | Yes, they are arriving by air on flight BA 491, arriving at 10.15 a.m. |
| *Reservations clerk:* | BA 491, 10.15 a.m. Our check-in time is generally after 2.00 p.m., so we will try our best to accommodate the guests should they check in before that time. |
| *Customer:* | Yes, I understand. |
| *Reservations clerk:* | Will the company settle the full account? |
| *Customer:* | Oh ... er .. no ... Please split the account, and send the accommodation bill to this company. The guests will settle their own expenses on check-out. |
| *Reservations clerk:* | Can you confirm those payment details in writing please? |
| *Customer:* | Yes, what is your fax number please? |
| *Reservations clerk:* | It is ... 7456345. |
| *Customer:* | Thank you. |

*Reservations clerk*: Let me just go over these details, Mrs Long. Four single rooms, check-in date Thursday the 19th of February, check-out date Sunday the 22nd of February. Two deluxe singles at a rate of £90, each per night, in the names of Mrs L. Smit and Mrs P. Harper and two superior singles at a rate of £85 each per night in the names of Mr D. Swan and Mr R. Porritt. Your company is Wheelok Holdings Ltd, of 126 Crediton Road, Liddicote and your contact number is 5625611. The guests will arrive on flight BA 491 at 10.15 a.m. and you will confirm the billing arrangements in writing.

*Customer*: Yes, that is correct.

*Reservations clerk*: Thank you, Mrs Long.

*Customer*: Thanks for your help. Goodbye.

*Reservations clerk*: Goodbye Mrs Long, and I hope we can be of help again soon.

(c) Re-check the details on the reservation form (opposite). Correct them if you have made any mistakes. Now indicate on the density chart that the rooms have been booked. How many superior and deluxe single rooms are now available on 19 and 20 February?

(d) What should the reservations clerk do next after completing the reservations form?

3 With the aid of a diagram, illustrate the procedures that need to be followed when receiving a telephone reservation booking from the stage of initial inquiry to the stage of filing of the reservation documents.

4 You have been appointed as reservations manager of a large new transient hotel and you are asked to design a reservation system for the hotel. Which system should you choose? Why?

**KING'S HOTEL**

## Reservation Form

Dr/Mr/Mrs/Miss/Ms ..............................................................................................

Arr. date: ................................................ Dep. date: ................................................

ETA: ....................................................... No. of nights: ..........................................

Room type: ............................................. No. of rooms: ...........................................

No. of persons: ....................................... Rate quoted: ............................................

Home address: ........................................ Contact name: ........................................

.................................................................. Company name: ......................................

Phone no.: ............................................... Address: ..................................................

.................................................................. ...............................................................

.................................................................. Phone/fax no.: ........................................

Method of payment: ................................ Gtd booking: ...........................................

.................................................................. Cr card no.: ............................................

Remarks: ................................................. Conf: Yes/No ..........................................

Taken by: .................................................

Date: ........................................................

---

# Case Study: *The Case of the Mixed Up American*

It was 19.15 on the evening of May 6th when Evelyn Reinhold arrived at the reception desk of the Gladstone Hotel. She was tired and travel-weary after the long journey from her home in Phoenix, Arizona. She approached Tracy, the receptionist on duty.

'Good evening Madam, how may I help you?' said Tracy.

'My name is Evelyn Reinhold, I have a reservation for a single, no-smoking room with bath for five nights.'

Tracy immediately looked at the arrivals list. 'Can you spell your name please?'

'R.E.I.N.H.O.L.D.' said Ms Reinhold.

'No, you don't have a booking here,' said Tracy.

In her weariness Ms Reinhold was now getting upset over this mix up, and spoke to the receptionist with some irritation.

'What do you mean I don't have a booking, of course I do. I faxed all the details through to you myself, two weeks ago. AND your reservations department confirmed back to me by fax.'

Tracy re-checked the arrivals list, then glanced at the room status screen, noting that there were plenty of rooms available for tonight.

'Well I haven't got you on my list. Will you show me your confirmation fax, so that I can check,' replied Tracy, now showing signs of annoyance.

Evelyn Reinhold rummaged through her briefcase, produced air tickets, passport, and other business documents, but no fax. 'I'm sorry but I must have left it behind.'

'They all say that,' answered Tracy.

'Well I am not "they", I am "me" and I want the room which I requested,' snapped Evelyn Reinhold. 'Do you have rooms available?'

'Of course, we are a hotel.'

'Don't get clever with me young lady, just check me into a room NOW, and make it the no-smoking room I requested.'

'You don't have to shout, I am not deaf ... Fill in the registration card, and don't forget the part for foreigners,' responded Tracy, who was now becoming extremely cross. 'And by the way, you have to pay for your accommodation in advance, as you are a walk-in.'

Looking dumbstruck at the last statement, Evelyn Reinhold snapped back at Tracy, 'No way. I received a confirmation of my reservation from you. I guaranteed my booking with my American Express card. If you cannot find my booking that is your problem. Now once again will you please just give me a room.'

Tracy, more than a little taken aback by the anger shown by the newly arrived customer, processed the registration and allocated the first room that came up on the screen. However, not to be outdone by Ms Reinhold, when she gave her the key she said, 'Here's your key, it's room 427, that's on the fourth floor, which is just above the third floor, and the front office manager will want to talk to you about not giving us a deposit. It's the hotel rule, you know.'

Evelyn Reinhold went, unescorted, to room 427, and opened the door only to find that the room had not been made up. The room looked a mess, and smelt strongly of stale tobacco. This was the final straw; she went to the telephone, called the operator and demanded to speak with the front office manager.

As the front office manager you are called to room 427 to meet with Ms Reinhold. She shows you the room and explains exactly what has happened at the desk.

Meanwhile Tracy has phoned her friend Sharon, the reservations clerk, to ask her about the Reinhold booking. Sharon does remember the booking but tells Tracy that it was for June and not May. Tracy checks the June bookings, and sure enough finds Ms Reinhold's fax booking. Attached to this fax is the reply Sharon sent to America.

Upon your return to the front desk, Tracy explains that she has spoken with Sharon and hands you the correspondence. You take this to your office to try and find out how the mix up has occurred, but tell Tracy that you will want to see her later, in your office.

## Questions

1. What is the problem?

2. What are the causes?

3. What are you going to do about it?

4. What are you going to say to Tracy?

Reservation by guest

---

**THE MANAGEMENT CONSULTANCY CORPORATION OF PHOENIX**
Mojave Street, Phoenix, Az 10927
Telephone (879) 641 0212. Fax (879) 642 7613
President J.J. Mackworth/Vice President E.L. Reinhold

FAX TO: Gladstone Hotel, Main Street, Sydney

Fax No: 61 742 8888

DATE: 4/15

MESSAGE:

Please reserve 1 (one) single non-smoking room for 5 nights from 5/6. Please guarantee – Amex card number: 3562 054566 0009.

Thanks

E. Reinhold

---

**Confirmation by hotel**

# Gladstone Hotel
Main Street
Sydney
Telephone 61 742–3456. Fax 61 742 8888

FAX TO: E. Reinhold
Management Consultancy Corporation of Phoenix
Mojave Street Phoenix
Arizona U.S.A. Fax (879) 642 7613

DATE: 16/4

**MESSAGE**
We are pleased to confirm your reservation of a single non-smoking room for 5 nights from 5/6.

Please do not hesitate to contact me if I can be of any further assistance.

Sincerely yours

*Sharon Coates*
Reservations Clerk

# 7
# *Check-in of new arrivals*

## Introduction

The arrival at a hotel is a critical period for both the guests and for the hotel. It is at this time that the strongest impressions are made upon the guest. The reception department (sometimes called the front desk) is the department which deals with new arrivals.

This chapter introduces you to the work of the reception department. It starts with a brief description of the main reception duties and then discusses the work of this department in greater detail (which includes checking in new arrivals). The last section focuses on developing your skills of checking in guests.

## THE MAIN DUTIES OF THE RECEPTION DEPARTMENT

As already mentioned, the reception department is sometimes called the front desk. Throughout this chapter we shall stick to the term reception department' to avoid confusion. The reception department is often the first hotel department that a guest encounters when arriving at a hotel. The main duties of the department are:

- welcoming and checking in of new arrivals
- selling the facilities of a hotel
- maintaining records of resident guests
- providing guest information for other sections of the front office and other departments of a hotel

In this chapter, we shall look specifically at the first duty of the reception department, i.e. the welcoming of the guest and the checking in of new arrivals.

## WELCOMING THE GUEST

Guests have often travelled a long way and may be impatient and tired when they arrive at a hotel. They will, therefore, want quick, efficient check-in services provided by pleasant and courteous receptionists.

To a hotel, arrival is the occasion when a guest and hotel staff meet face-to-face for the first time. A well-functioning reception process gives the guest a good impression of the hotel. This helps to establish the hotel's image and reputation, as well as to encourage the guest to return in the future.

In order to give guests a lasting first impression, the reception staff need to be efficient and have good social skills. They should be knowledgeable about the accommodation product of their hotel and skilled in the check-in procedures, and the handling of guests' queries. Additionally, they should have pleasant manners, be cordial, empathetic, and always be ready to help. A neat and tidy appearance and the ability to communicate with guests is also essential.

## A CHECK-LIST FOR WELCOMING GUESTS

The following check-list may give you some idea of the appropriate social skills necessary when dealing with guests:

1. Maintain good eye contact; eye contact is very important because it shows attention and respect. However, do be careful not to turn your eye contact into a stare. It is also worth noting that positive eye contact is not regarded as courteous by the peoples of many Asian countries, especially Japan.

2. Smile when talking to the guest; it shows a warm and positive manner.

3. Stand up straight and avoid leaning or slouching. The way you stand is important; standing straight shows respect and attention. Leaning on the front desk, on the other hand, suggests that the receptionist is tired, bored and cannot be bothered.

4. Maintain a clean, neat and tidy personal appearance at all times. By paying attention to your dress and personal hygiene, you show that you have a pride in yourself and your hotel.

5. Speak clearly, using a pleasant tone. In this way, the guest will easily understand what you say and be impressed by your courtesy.

## Activity 1

(a) Use three words or phrases to describe how each of the following guests might feel at the time of arrival:
- a guest who has flown in from Australia, after a 24-hour flight with a 9-hour time difference

- a guest who was late arriving because of a long traffic jam on the motorway

- an American tour guest who has visited seven countries in ten days, and who wants to make a collect call home

(b) You are a receptionist who is checking in the following guests. In each case, write down three words or phrases to describe how you should behave in dealing with them:

- an elderly tourist who cannot find his travel voucher

- a young couple who have never been to Britain before

- a family, comprising parents and two young children, who have just had an 18-hour flight from Africa

– a businessman who has just arrived in Britain after a delayed flight from Rome, and is late for an important business appointment.

## BASIC CHECK-IN ACTIVITIES

The process of checking in new arrivals can be divided into five basic stages which are shown in Figure 7.1. However, you should note that

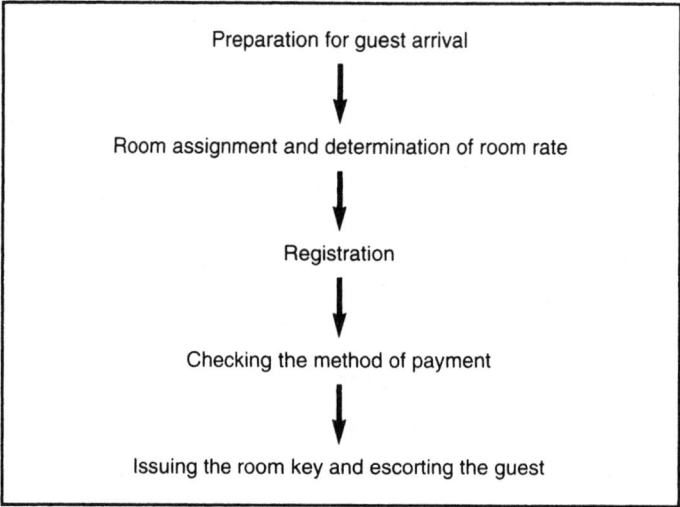

Preparation for guest arrival

↓

Room assignment and determination of room rate

↓

Registration

↓

Checking the method of payment

↓

Issuing the room key and escorting the guest

**Figure 7.1** Stages of check-in

the order of these stages may vary from hotel to hotel. Also, the reservation status of the guest may pre-empt some of the stages. For example, a VIP guest would normally have their room pre-allocated, and might well register in the room or suite.

In general, newly arrived guests at a hotel are classified into three main categories, as seen in Table 7.1.

Each category of guest will be handled differently at check-in, according to the differences in reservation status. However, it must be remembered that, under the law of contract, which applies to hotel room reservations, a hotel is expected to have a room available for a guest who has legally booked it. Similarly, it is expected that the guest will arrive (see Chapter 5). In legal terms it should not really be necessary to guarantee a room reservation.

The variation in the process of checking the method of payment of guest accounts is of particular importance. This will be explained in later sections.

**Table 7.1** Categories of guests

| Type of guest | Description |
| --- | --- |
| Guaranteed reservations | Guests with guaranteed reservations are expected and have reservations which have been guaranteed and, therefore, confirmed. In the event of their non-arrival, the room charge will still be paid. Most often, these reservations are guaranteed by the guest giving their credit card number. However, a prepayment or advance deposit, or a company booking which is confirmed in writing, should also guarantee the reservation. Rooms for guaranteed reservations must be held until the check-out time of the day following the date of expected arrival. |
| Non-guaranteed reservations | Guests with non-guaranteed reservations are usually those who reservation details are unconfirmed. If the guest does not show up on the expected day of arrival, the hotel will not receive any payment. Rooms for non-guaranteed reservations are usually held until a stated release time. If the guest does not show up before the release time, the rooms may be re-sold to another guest. |
| Walk-ins | Guests who arrive without having made a reservation are known as walk-ins. Such guests arrive at a hotel on the off-chance that a room will be available. It is usual for a substantial deposit or credit card imprint to be taken before checking the guest into the hotel. |

## PREPARATION FOR GUEST ARRIVAL

Before actually registering a guest or assigning a room, receptionists need to have at hand certain information which is essential in their work. Such information should include:

- room status and availability
- expected arrivals and departures
- arrivals with special requests
- VIPs and frequent-stay guests

Much of this information is determined the night before that day's arrivals. However, in hotels with computerized systems this information is updated with every room transaction. It is also permanently at hand and can be easily accessed through the keyboard.

It is also very important that reception and housekeeping have a close relationship. At times of high occupancy it is vital that housekeeping can return vacated rooms to the front desk quickly, but without loss of standards.

### The room status report

Before guests arrive, reception staff will need details on the status of the guest-rooms. This information is usually indicated by a room status report' (Figure 7.2) which shows whether a room is occupied, vacant and dirty, ready for occupancy or out of order.

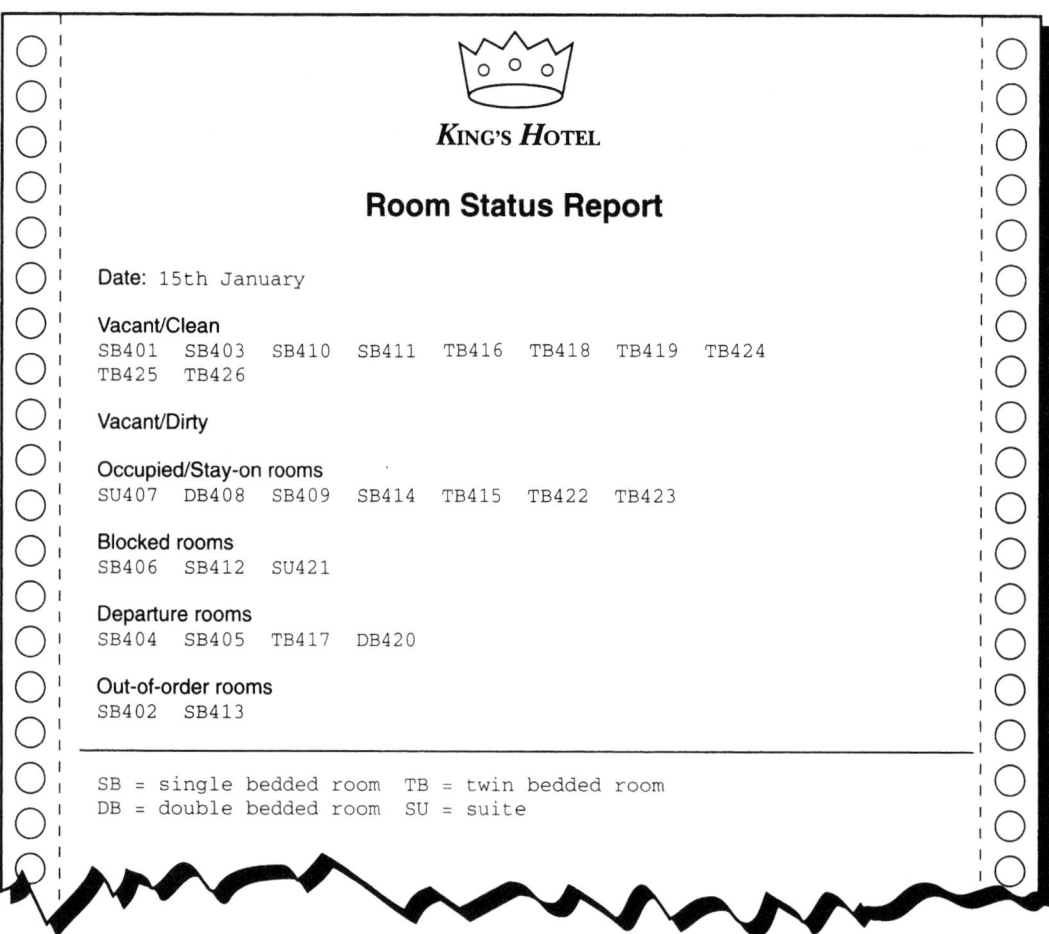

KING'S HOTEL

**Room Status Report**

**Date:** 15th January

Vacant/Clean
SB401   SB403   SB410   SB411   TB416   TB418   TB419   TB424
TB425   TB426

Vacant/Dirty

Occupied/Stay-on rooms
SU407   DB408   SB409   SB414   TB415   TB422   TB423

Blocked rooms
SB406   SB412   SU421

Departure rooms
SB404   SB405   TB417   DB420

Out-of-order rooms
SB402   SB413

SB = single bedded room   TB = twin bedded room
DB = double bedded room   SU = suite

**Figure 7.2** Room status report

From the example in Figure 7.2, you will see that the status of the rooms can be classified as follows:

- Vacant/clean. The rooms have been vacated and serviced, and are ready to be assigned to a guest.

- Vacant/dirty. The rooms have recently been vacated and await cleaning. Normally, it will take at least 30 minutes for housekeeping to prepare these rooms. These rooms may be pre-allocated to a guest who is due to arrive later in the day. Such rooms are sometimes called on-charge or checked-out rooms.

- Occupied/stay-on rooms. These are rooms still occupied by guests, who will stay on for one or more nights.

- Departure rooms. These rooms are occupied by guests who are due to depart later in the day. These rooms can be assigned to guests due to arrive later in the day.

- Out-of-order rooms. These rooms are not in use, usually because there is something which is faulty in the room, or the room is being re-decorated.

- Blocked rooms. These are rooms reserved for specific reasons (e.g. for VIPs or tours or because of their location).

From a room status report, reception staff will be able to identify which rooms are clean and ready for guests, which rooms will become available later in the day, or which rooms are unavailable on that date. Such information is essential to the reception department when assigning rooms, to ensure that a guest is not inconvenienced by being sent to an occupied, dirty or faulty room.

**Activity 2**   Answer the following questions with reference to the room status report in Figure 7.2.

(a) Which room should you assign to newly-weds Mr and Mrs Gordon, VIP guests, who were expected to arrive later on that day? Why?

(b) Which room should you give to Mr P. Svensen, a walk-in guest? Why?

### The expected arrivals list

The expected arrivals list provides basic information on guests who are expected to arrive on a particular date. Regardless of whether this information is given by computer or manually, the details should be the same (Figure 7.3). By checking the expected arrivals against the room status report, the reception supervisor will be able to determine:

**KING'S HOTEL**

## Expected Arrivals List

**Date:** 15 January

| Name | Requirements | Rate | Departure date | Remarks |
|------|--------------|------|----------------|---------|
| Archer, Robert Mr/s | D | 85 | 16/1 | Own a/c |
| Au, K.K. Mr | S | 75 | 17/1 | Company a/c |
| Baid, Vijay Mr/s | D | 85 | 16/1 | |
| Brown, W. Mr/s | T | 75 | 21/1 | Flowers in room |
| Longton, Dr/s | D | 85 | 21/1 | Part of medical conference |

**Figure 7.3** An expected arrivals list

- whether there are sufficient rooms to accommodate all the guests expected to arrive

- the number of rooms that will be available for accommodating any walk-in guests

If it is found that there are insufficient rooms to accommodate all expected arrivals on that date (i.e. when there is overbooking), the reception supervisor may have to seek additional accommodation in nearby hotels. This process of having to book an expected arrival into another hotel because you are full is sometimes called *walking the guest*. In most cases, the original hotel will pay for the transportation to and from the other hotel as well as any excess room charges. Overbooking is discussed in more detail later in this chapter.

### The guest history record

Most professional hotels keep guest history records which contain details on all previous guests. With the advent of computerization, this information is now easily made available to all hotels that use computers (Figure 7.4). If a guest history record is available, the names of

**KING'S HOTEL**

## Guest History Record

| | | |
|---|---|---|
| Guest name: | Epstein, James Mr | First visit: 9/3/98 |
| Group/Company: | ACME Import/Export Inc. | Total visits to date: 24 |
| Address: | 15/31 Sheraton Ave, Chicago, Ill USA | Total nights to date: 72 |
| | | Total revenue to date: £9648 |
| Credit: | Cr card (Amex) | Average spend to date: £134 |
| Passport no: | MH8997625 | |
| Total rate: | 85 | Comment: CIP |

| Arr. | Dep. | Days | Room | Rate | Payment | Revenue | Specials |
|------|------|------|------|------|---------|---------|----------|
| 4/9/99 | 7/9/99 | 3 | 416 | 85 | Amex | 416 | Fruit basket |
| 13/7/99 | 16/7/99 | 3 | 408 | 85 | Amex | 490 | |
| 2/3/99 | 4/3/99 | 2 | 408 | 85 | Amex | 287 | Bed board |

**Figure 7.4** A guest history record

all the guests on the expected arrivals list should be checked against the guest history record to see if any of the guests have previously stayed in the hotel. A check should also be made to ascertain what appropriate action should be taken to ensure that they will enjoy their stay. For example, if a guest has previously complained of a noisy room, the reception supervisor may assign a room on a floor away from the noise. If a frequent-stay guest had been previously upgraded to a better room, but on this occasion the hotel is unable to upgrade the guest, then extra amenities, like a fruit basket, may be placed in the room. A VIP or a frequent-stay guest should be greeted on arrival by the front office manager or guest relations officer. In some cases the guest may be met by the general manager.

---

**Activity 3**    Look at Figure 7.4, which shows the guest history record of Mr Epstein, an American guest, and then answer the following questions.

(a) How did Mr Epstein settle his bill in his previous stays?

(b) Why do you think the hotel has classified Mr Epstein as a commercially important person (CIP)?

(c) What special services has Mr Epstein received on his previous visits?

(d) Which room will you assign to Mr Epstein if he is expected to arrive at 4.00p.m. on 15 January? Why? (You need to refer to the room status report in Figure 7.2.)

---

### Expected arrivals with special requests

Some guests may request extra amenities or services when they make their reservations. The relevant departments must, therefore, be informed of these requests so that they can be prepared and are ready for the guests' arrival. For example, if an expected guest has requested a cot for a baby, the reception supervisor will assign a suitable room number for the reservation, and inform the housekeeper of the request for a cot. The housekeeper will then place the cot and any other items, such as a baby basket containing talcum powder, in the room before the guest arrives.

### List of important guests

Most hotels pay special attention to important guests. Important guests may include:

- VIPs (very important persons), e.g. frequent-stay guests, celebrities, guests in expensive rooms, guests with security risks, executives from the hotel's head office, and so on.

- CIPs (commercially important persons). May be guests and executives of large corporate account-holders, important journalists and media staff, travel agents and tour company staff, and guests whose companies could bring a lot of business to the hotel in the future.

- SPATTs (special attention guests) are guests who may need extra care and attention, such as handicapped guests, elderly or ill guests, and long-stay guests.

These important guests tend to be given special services or amenities during their stay. Such services may include the assignment of the guest's room before they arrive; the complimentary use of the hotel transport; registration in their room; and being greeted and escorted by special staff when they arrive.

In order to alert staff of the arrival of important guests, a list of important guests is produced and sent to other sections of the front office and to all other operating departments. An example is shown in Figure 7.5.

### KING'S HOTEL

## Expected VIP/SPATT Arrivals

**Date:** 15 January

Key: S = single   T = twin   (s/o) = single occupancy

| Guest name | Guest info | Rate | Room | Period | Remarks |
|---|---|---|---|---|---|
| Mr W. Peters | 1st visit 4/98 corp. rate | 75 | D (s/o) | 15/1–21/1 | Adjacent to Mr Duncan |
| Mr A Duncan | 1st visit 4/98 corp. | 75 | D (s/o) | 15/1–21/1 | Adjacent to Mr Peters |
| Mr G. Ferretti | Editor, Food & Wine Magazine | Comp. | T | 15/1–18/1 | Fruit basket and champagne on arrival. GM to meet. |
| Mr/s T. Scott | 1st visit 2/98 | 85 | D | 15/1–17/1 | Complained noisy air-conditioning. Fruit basket. FOM to meet. |

**Figure 7.5** A VIP/SPATT list

**Activity 4**  Answer the following questions with reference to the VIP/SPATT list in Figure 7.5.

(a) What are the possible reasons for the hotel to include Mr Ferretti on the VIP list?

(b) What special arrangements have been made for his room?

(c) Explain why the front office manager will personally greet Mr and Mrs Scott.

### Other preparations for guest arrivals

In addition to collecting information for check-in, receptionists may carry out other preparatory work before guests arrive at a hotel. For example, they may prepare registration documents and check whether the keys are available for vacant rooms, and check whether a newly arriving guest has any mail waiting.

The preparation of registration documents before guest arrivals can greatly reduce the time and work at check-in, thus speeding up the process during the busy hours. Some computer systems can pre-print the registration cards for the expected arrivals. This means that some of the personal details of the expected guests are printed on the registration card, e.g. name, address, dates of arrival and departure, and method of payment. When the guests arrive, all they then have to do is to check these details and sign the registration card.

## REGISTRATION

The purpose of registration is to record a guest's arrival and confirm their personal details, as well as to satisfy legal requirements.

### The Immigration (Hotel Records) Order 1972

This Order states that hotel proprietors are legally required to keep a written record of certain information about their guests for at least 12 months. According to the Order, the following details must be recorded for all guests over the age of 16:

- full name
- nationality
- date of arrival

It is not legally necessary for the visitor to sign the registration document. Nor is it necessary for them to give the information in person; it can be done through a third party and either orally or in writing. However, most hotels expect much more information and certainly a signature, as you will see in the section on the registration form.

The guest may be an alien; this is the legal term for someone who does not belong to any one of the following categories:

- British passport holders
- Commonwealth citizens
- citizens of the Republic of Ireland (Eire)
- members of NATO armed forces serving in the UK
- foreign nationals serving with the UK's armed forces
- foreign diplomats, envoys and their staff (this is under the Diplomatic Privileges Act 1964)
- citizens of a European Community country

For aliens, the following extra details must also be recorded:

- passport number, and place of issue
- next destination (if known)
- date of departure

When a guest arrives at a hotel, he or she is normally required to complete a registration form similar to the one illustrated in Figure 7.6. As mentioned previously in this chapter, there may be differences in the reservation status of newly arrived guests, and they will, therefore, be dealt with differently at the time of registration.

### Guests with reservations

For a guest with a reservation, the process of registration and room allocation occurs immediately on arrival. The receptionist will ask the guest to complete and sign a registration form and will check these details against the details held at reception. Should there be any discrepancies, these need to clarified at this point.

### Walk-in guests

If the guest is a walk-in, then the receptionist must first check the room availability before registering the guest. If a room is available, it will be offered, and the guest must be informed of all room charges. Upon acceptance, the guest will be asked to complete a registration form.

### The registration form

A registration form or card is used to record the personal particulars of the guest on arrival. The actual design or layout of the forms may vary among hotels, but they usually ask for similar guest information.

Figure 7.6 is an example of the details recorded on the registration form and how they should be entered. You should refer to Figure 7.6 while reading the sections which follow.

1. *Arrival date.* The arrival date is obtained from the reservation record and may be written or printed in the space provided.

2. *Departure date.* The departure date will be transferred, in the same manner as the arrival date, from the reservation record, and written or printed in the space. This detail must be confirmed by the receptionist at check-in.

3. *Arrival time.* The actual arrival time section will be completed by reception at the time of check-in.

4. *Number of rooms.* Information on the number of rooms is transferred from the reservation file and confirmed with the guest.

5. *Room type.* Information on the room type is transferred from the reservation file, and must be confirmed by the receptionist at check-in. It is possible for the guest to be upgraded, or be assigned another type of accommodation with their agreement at check-in.

6. *Daily rate.* If a guest has made a reservation prior to arrival, the daily room rate information will be transferred from the reservation file. For a walk-in guest, this has to be determined at the time of room assignment and recorded.

When the reservations clerk enters the room rate they must check if the guest may enjoy a special rate (e.g. a regular guest may be entitled to a reduced rate).

7. *Number of guests.* Information on the number of guests is transferred from the reservation file. It should be noted that the number of guests may not be the same as the number of beds in the accommodation. For example, one guest may be staying in a twin room on a single occupancy rate, or three guests may be staying in a suite or in a twin room with an extra bed.

### KING'S HOTEL

## Registration Form

Arrival date: .........1.........   Daily rate: .........6.........   Room no: .........9.........

Departure date: .........2.........   No. of guests: .........7.........

Arrival time: .........3.........

No. of rooms: .........4.........   Advanced deposit: .........8.........   Package Plan: .........10.........

Room type: .........5.........

Name: Dr/Mr/Mrs/Miss/Ms Surname:              First name:

.........11.........

Address:
Residential: .........12.........

Business: ...........................................

Passport no.: .........13.........              Date and place of issue: ...........................................

Nationality: .........14.........              Payment by: .........16.........
                                              • Cash
                                              • Company
                                              • Credit card
                                              • Coupon
                                              • Travel agent

Company name: .........15.........

Departing to: .........17.........

Guest signature: .........18.........

Reception clerk signature: .........19.........

Check-out time is 12 noon.
The standard rate of VAT will be added to your bill. Personal cheques are not accepted without the appropriate cheque card. Our liability for valuables is governed by the Hotel Proprietors Act 1956.
Guests are advised to read the notice at the reception desk.
Please use the safe deposit box at the cashier for your valuables.

**Figure 7.6** A registration form

*8. Advance deposit.* If an advance deposit has been paid, the amount of the deposit will be recorded. The details of the deposit will be transferred from the reservation file onto the registration form. The receptionist may then confirm the receipt of the deposit with the guest on arrival. The amount of deposit received will then be transferred from the advance deposit account to the guest folio.

*9. Room number.* Before printing out the registration form, the receptionist will assign a room to the guest. The room number will then be recorded on the registration form.

*10. Package plan.* The type of package or tariff to be paid by the guest will be printed in this space. The guest may be staying on 'room-only' terms, or 'bed and breakfast', or as part of a 'tour' package which includes some meals, or as a conference' delegate where meals, room, function room facilities and entertainments are all included in the plan.

*11. Name.* The guest's surname, first name and title are transferred from the reservation record. It is very important for the receptionist to check that the guest's name is spelt correctly, as otherwise the guest's bill, telephone messages and any other documentation will all have the name wrongly spelt. This may cause errors in operations and give the guest a bad impression.

*12. Address.* If the guest is to have their bill settled by a company, it is most likely that the company address will be transferred from the reservation record. Also, if the reservation was made by a travel agent, the agent's address will have been previously recorded.

If the guest is to settle their own account, then the residential address should be recorded.

It is useful to have the guest's residential address as well as business address. The residential address is needed to enable the hotel to forward any mail or contact the guest after departure; the company address may be used for marketing purposes.

*13. Passport number and date and place of issue.* If the guest is an alien, they must provide their passport number at check-in. The receptionist may have to request to see the guest's passport, and check the details.

*14. Nationality.* By law, the nationality of a guest must be recorded. If the guest has stayed before, this detail may be automatically transferred from the guest history record.

*15. Company name.* If the guest is to have the bill settled by their company, the name of the company should be checked against the approved company list prepared by the sales office or credit controller. If the booking was made by a travel agent, the agent's name may be transferred from the travel agent's file.

*16. Payment by.* The method of payment should be transferred from the reservation file. This information is very important to the hotel and care must be taken in confirming this with the guest. The procedures for checking the methods of payment for different categories of guests will be further elaborated later in this chapter.

*17. Departing to.* If this detail has been recorded at the time of reservation, then it will be transferred from the reservation file. If the information is not available in the reservation record, the receptionist should ask the guest where they plan to travel to next. This information is of interest to hotels because, should the guest be travelling to a city where the hotel group has another hotel, then the receptionist can suggest an onward booking.

*18. Signature.* It is important to ensure that the guest reads the details and signs the registration card. By signing the card, the guest acknowledges the terms and conditions of the hotel operation.

The signature is a vital record for the hotel's use because it can be used as a certification of guest's charges.

*19. Receptionist signature.* It is important that the reception clerk signs the registration form. Should any queries arise in the future regarding the guest, or any of the guest's details, then the hotel immediately knows whom to ask for further information, or clarification.

**Policy statements.** Many hotels print the policy statements of the hotel at the bottom of the registration card. This is an opportunity to ensure that the guest is aware of such policies.

---

**Activity 5**

(a) Study the registration form in Figure 7.6 again carefully. List two items of personal detail on the form which a guest is requested to complete but which are not legally required.

(b) If the details are not required by law, why do hotels collect such information? Illustrate your answer with the two examples you have given in (a).

---

### The blacklist

Some hotels have a blacklist, which is a list of the names of people who are not welcome at the hotel, e.g. rowdy persons, people who have not settled their previous accounts, and undesirables. The list can be compiled using information from:

- police reports

- the reports from other local hotels

- the corporate office

- the assistant manager's log book

- accounts department or credit manager

This list must be tightly controlled by the front office manager, and problems arising from the use of the list should be referred to this manager.

### Pre-arrival registration

One of the busiest times for the reception department is during the check-in hours. To ensure that newly arrived guests are greeted and given their rooms as smoothly and efficiently as possible, speedy registration procedures are required. One way is to pre-print all of the guest's details on a registration card prior to their arrival, as previously mentioned. All the guest then has to do is check that the details are correct, sign the card and receive their room key.

Pre-registration can also be the solution to checking in large numbers of guests simultaneously, e.g. groups, tours or conference delegates.

## ROOM ASSIGNMENT AND ROOM RATE

The process of assigning rooms and room rates differs with the different categories of guests.

### Expected arrivals

The room rate for expected arrivals (i.e. guests with reservations) is agreed by the guest when the reservation is made, and rooms are not normally assigned until the guest arrives at the hotel. However, this does not apply if the guest wants a specific room, or has made a special request, e.g. for a bed board or cot, or if the guest is a VIP or CIP. In such cases rooms are pre-allocated.

## Walk-in guests

Walk-in guests can only be assigned rooms and room rates after it has been confirmed that there is accommodation available. It is normal for the cost of at least one night's accommodation to be asked for in advance of the guest's stay.

## The Tourism (Sleeping Accommodation Price Display) Order 1977

This order provides for the display of the maximum and minimum current prices charged per night for accommodation. This information is displayed in the reception area where it can be easily read by all persons requesting accommodation. Examples of accommodation prices which must be displayed are:

- the price of a bedroom for one person, e.g. £100 per night or £100–£175 when there is a range of prices
- the price of a bedroom for two persons
- the price of a bed in any other type of room

But:

- If the prices include VAT, this must be stated, e.g. £100 per night, including VAT.
- If there is a service charge, it must be included in the price, e.g. £120 per night, including VAT and service charge.
- If the guest has to pay for meals as part of the charge for accommodation, this must be stated, e.g. £100 per night, including breakfast, VAT and service charge.

## Room assignment

When assigning a room to a specific guest, the receptionist has to ensure, as far as possible, that the needs and preferences of the guest are satisfied. In doing so, the receptionist needs to know:

- the status of all the rooms in the hotel
- the position and features of each room in the hotel
- the needs, preference and/or special requests of the guest

Information on room status will be obtained from the room status board or report, while the guest's needs and preferences can be obtained from the expected arrivals, and the special requests/VIP lists. The position and facilities of each room are usually indicated by a floor plan (Figure 7.7).

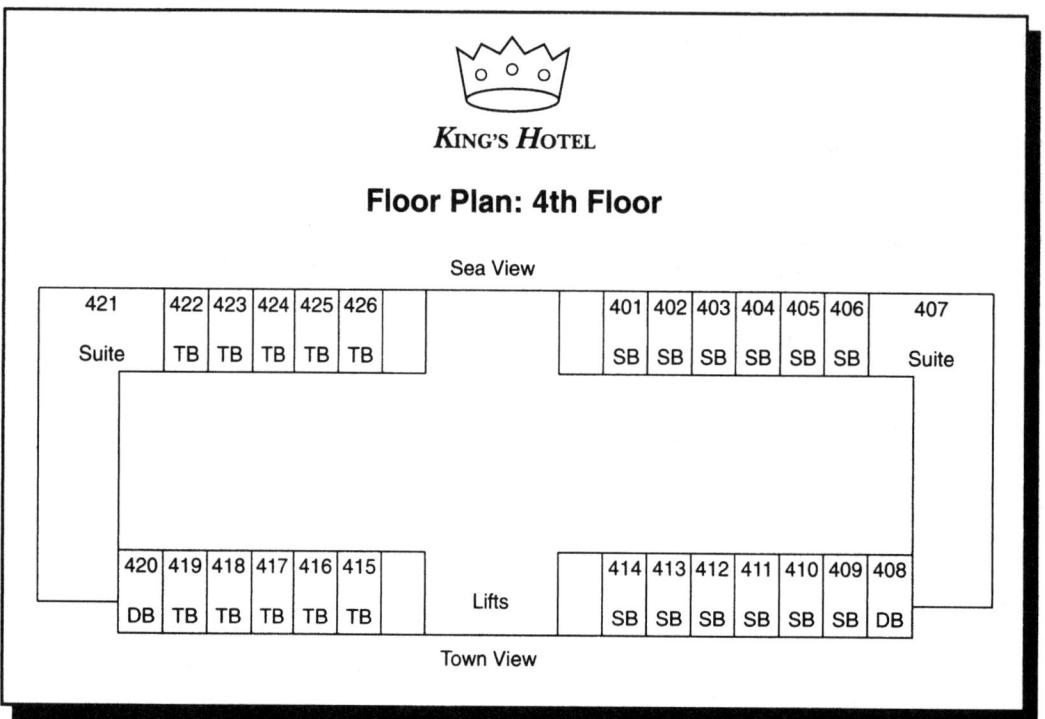

**Figure 7.7** A floor plan

## Room assignment by computer

In modern hotels, room assignment is often done by computer. When the receptionist enters the required room type and the requested period of stay into the computer, it will automatically display several suitable alternatives on the screen. It is then up to the receptionist to choose the most suitable room by using their knowledge of the facilities of the rooms (e.g. their view, floor and features), and comparing it with the details on the reservation (room type or special requests). The receptionist may also refer to the guest history record for the personal preferences of that guest.

Each time a receptionist checks a guest into a vacant room, the computer will change its record of the room status from vacant to occupied. This ensures that the room availability is continually updated.

## Early check-ins

On occasion, a guest may arrive earlier than expected and there may be no vacant or clean rooms available. In such circumstances there are a variety of options that the receptionist can take.

1. Check to see if there is an alternative type of room that is vacant/clean and offer that to the guest, e.g. a twin instead of a double.

2. If an alternative is not available, apologize to the guest and explain that their room has not yet been vacated and/or cleaned.

3. Register the guest, but do not assign a room until a suitable vacant/clean room is available.

4. Have a guest's luggage put into store until a room can be assigned. Then have it taken up to the room.

5. The guest should be given a time when they can return to collect the room key. Alternatively, a note should be made of the guest's whereabouts, so that they may be contacted as soon as the room is ready.

6. Contact housekeeping to rush the room (i.e. telephone the housekeeper to give a particular room priority on their cleaning schedule).

It is important to make sure that all staff members on the reception desk are made aware that there is a guest waiting for a room. This is especially true when one reception shift hands over to another.

Reception staff must also realize that guests may get very impatient if they cannot go straight to their rooms. The receptionist should be very empathetic, and make every effort to ensure that the guests feel comfortable while waiting. For example, the receptionist may inform the guests of the location of the bar and coffee shop, beach, promenade or children's play area, so that the guest can fill in time whilst they are waiting.

---

**Activity 6** Using the floor plan in Figure 7.7 and the room status report in Figure 7.2, assign rooms for the following bookings, and give reasons for your choice:

- two singles for non-guaranteed guests (early check-in)

- three singles for guaranteed guests (late arrivals)
- two twin rooms for a family (parents and two teenage children)
- one twin room for a handicapped person in a wheelchair

---

## CHECKING THE METHOD OF PAYMENT

When a guest makes a reservation, their intended method of payment is recorded. However, it is important to confirm the method of payment at the time of the guest's arrival, especially so for any walk-in guests. The main reason for doing this is to ensure that the hotel can know in advance if the guest needs to make special arrangements for settling their bill, e.g. wanting to pay by cheque, or to use uncommon foreign currency. This precaution helps to prevent embarrassment to the guest at check-out, as well as preventing walk-outs. (A walk-out occurs when a guest leaves without checking out and paying their bill.) The general rules for checking the method of payment are outlined below.

### *General rules for checking the method of payment*

1. If the guest is a walk-in or has a non-guaranteed reservation, take a pre-payment or a credit card imprint.

2. If the guest has a guaranteed reservation and is settling their own account, ask to take a credit card imprint, and phone for authorization for an amount which is estimated to cover the whole stay.

3. If the guest wants to pay by cash or foreign currency, inform them of the room rate and record the method of payment on the registration card. Confirm with the guest that the rates for the foreign currency are as displayed.

4. For settlements by cheque, ensure that the cheque guarantee card will cover the whole amount. Remember that it contravenes the cheque card agreement to use multiple cheques for settlement of one bill.

5. When a guest has a company or travel agent who is settling the account, the receptionist *must* ensure that accurate billing details are recorded, e.g. what is paid by the company or agent and what expenses are the guest's own responsibility.

### Advance deposits

Some guests may have sent an advance deposit to guarantee their reservation. The receptionist should confirm that the deposit has been received whilst the guest is checking in. A credit is then immediately posted (shown on) to the guest's bill.

### Paying by credit card

If a guest is to settle all or part of the account by credit card, it is common procedure to request an imprint of the card at check-in. This allows the hotel time to check whether or not the card is valid. If a guest wants to settle their account using a credit card which the hotel does not accept, then they must be immediately informed so that an alternative method of settlement can be arranged.

## ISSUING THE KEY AND ESCORTING THE GUEST

After registration and room assignment, a guest is issued a key to the room. It is common practice to give a key card, together with the key, to the guest. The key card is a personal record of the guest's room number and room rate, and a statement of the hotel's policies. It also serves as proof of the guest's identity to hotel staff. This may be necessary when the guest wants to collect the room key from reception or sign for a drink or meal.

**Welcome to**

**KING'S HOTEL**

Guest name: _____

Arrival date: _____  Departure date: _____

Room number: _____  Room rate: _____

Check-out time is 12 noon
**IMPORTANT You may be required to show this card
each time you collect your key and when you sign
charges to your room account.**

**Figure 7.8** A key card

The practice of escorting guests to their rooms depends on the standard of service offered by a hotel. In most budget hotels and motels, guests are not normally escorted to their rooms. Instead, they are given directions and may have to carry their own bags. On the other hand, full-service hotels usually offer a bell service. The bellboys frequently escort guests to their rooms, and at the same time handle their baggage.

In top-class hotels, where there are a large number of staff at the reception, the receptionist who checks in a guest may escort them to the room, and the bellboys will deliver the luggage shortly afterwards. The purpose of this attentive service is to show the guest that the hotel considers them important. The escorting staff will spend time explaining the facilities and services of the room, answering questions, and trying to make the guest feel welcome.

Some hotels employ guest relations officers (GROs) who greet VIPs and frequent-stay guests and personally escort them to their rooms immediately on arrival. In these situations the room will have been assigned and the key card and key prepared before the guest arrives. As soon as the guest walks through the hotel entrance they are escorted to the room, where the GRO carries out the registration procedure. In this way, an important guest does not have to wait in the busy front office area for check-in. This is a particularly important service for those guests who wish full anonymity or who, for security reasons, do not want to linger in a public place.

## THE CHECK-IN PROCESS: A SUMMARY

So far, we have described the various activities during the process of checking in new arrivals. These can be summarized by the chart in Figure 7.9.

## OVERBOOKING

It has been previously mentioned that 'overbooking' is the accepting of more reservations than there are rooms available, and is a standard practice in most hotels. This is done to compensate for the percentage of no-shows, cancellations and late departures which regularly occur. Customers who cancel their bookings at the last minute, or simply do not show up on the expected day of arrival, cost the hotel a large amount of money, because a room is being held for them, and the hotel does not receive the revenue because they do not arrive. Therefore, to achieve a full house and revenue it is necessary for hotels to adopt an overbooking policy.

To be able to implement an accurate overbooking procedure the

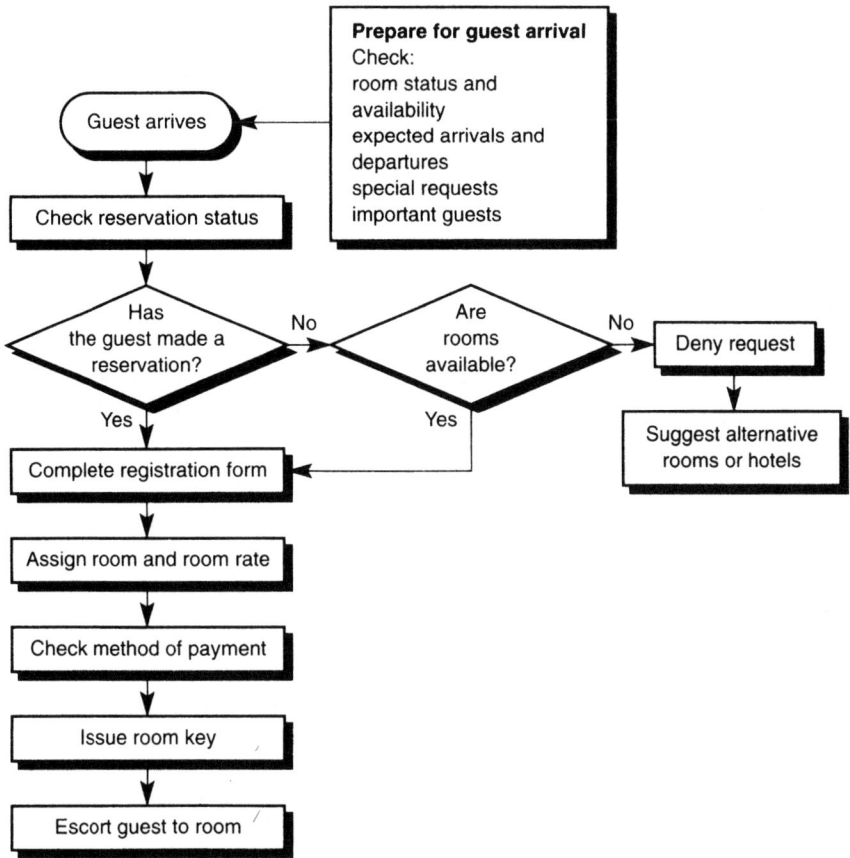

**Figure 7.9** The check-in process.

front office manager and reservations clerk need to have all the relevant historical data on the percentage of no-shows, guaranteed and non-guaranteed bookings, cancellations and early departures. With this information, management should be able to predict the overbooking percentage rates based on those figures. Additional information which is also important in achieving accurate overbooking figures is the possible number of walk-ins, the present reservations status, and the special events and functions which are happening in the hotel or surrounding area. The greater the information available for the front office manager, the more accurately the overbooking can be forecast. Many hotel companies now use computer systems in which to record all the relevant data, making it much easier to forecast the hotel's overbooking.

Overbooking is typical of transient or city centre hotels, which have a higher incidence of no-shows, cancellations and early departures. In order to maintain an accurate and up-to-date room availability record, good communication is required between reservations and the front desk, as well as the sales department. For example, if a guest wishesto extend their stay this should be communicated to the reservations department, so that the availability chart can be updated. Overbooking is also one of the basic strategies employed in yield/revenue management. (See Chapter 15.)

Occasionally, front office management may predict the wrong levels of overbooking. Consequently, the hotel finds that it is responsible for 'walking a guest'. 'Walking a guest' means turning away a guest who holds a reservation, owing to the lack of available rooms. Because the hotel is in breach of contract by not having a room available for the guest, every attempt should be made to mitigate the financial compensation that an irate customer might claim through legal action.

This may be done by locating the guest at another hotel of the same or a better standard, paying for transportation costs to the other hotel, and paying for any meals which may be included in the original hotel package and any increased room charge at the alternative hotel.

Despite all of these minimum measures, the hotel guest can still sue for breach of contract, and the inconvenience which it has caused.

If the receptionist finds that overbooking has occurred, a procedure to be followed prior to the guest's arrival could be:

1. Anticipate early in the day by how many rooms the hotel will be overbooked.

2. Check the arrivals list against room status, checking for non-guaranteed, guaranteed, release time and possible no-shows. This indicates the number of people who possibly may not arrive, as well as anticipating how many guests will have to be 'walked'.

3. Check the bed occupancy list against room status; this will indicate how many stay-ons, stay-overs and late departures there may be for that particular day.

4. Check with the housekeeper if any '000' rooms can be made available.

5. Check for company bookings, to ensure that they are guaranteed arrivals.

6. Is it possible for two regular business people to share? (Possibly offer discount or complimentary gift.)

7. Reserve the necessary rooms in another hotel in the immediate area.

8. If possible, book out only one night stays.

9. Check who to 'walk' – tourist or business person?

10. Arrange transportation for guests to the new hotel.

11. Inform the telephonist of the guest's alternative hotel.

12. Ensure that reception personnel and front office management are kept informed of all overbooking developments, especially at the changeover of shifts.

13. Notify the general manager of the overbooking situation, in case of any future repercussions,

14. Ensure that the duty manager is fully aware of the situation.

---

**Activity 7**  (a) If you find yourself overbooked, why would you try to relocate one-night stays first?

  (b) How would you discover who to walk if you are overbooked? What reception records would you use?

---

## DEVELOPING YOUR CHECK-IN SKILLS

In the previous sections of this chapter, we explained the duties of the receptionist in welcoming guests and checking in new arrivals. As you will have noted, a good receptionist should have, in addition to a full understanding of the reception duties, good social skills, and be well trained in the operational procedures of the reception department.

In this section, we shall try to help you develop such skills by giving you some examples of interactions between the guest and the receptionist during check-in. Through these activities, we hope that you can:

- develop the appropriate vocabulary and phrases

- adopt an appropriate manner and style of speech

- better understand the operational procedures involved in checking in guests

The following is a conversation between a front desk clerk and a guest with a non-guaranteed reservation. Read through the conversation then note the points that follow.

*Front desk clerk*:      Good evening, Sir. May I help you?

| | |
|---|---|
| *Guest*: | Good evening. I have a reservation. My name is Brothers. |
| *Front desk clerk*: | Thank you Mr Brothers. May I have your initial please? |
| *Guest*: | Yes, J. for John. |
| *Front desk clerk*: | Thank you. Yes, I have one superior single reserved for one night. Is that correct? |
| *Guest*: | Yes, that's right. |
| *Front desk clerk*: | Please will you complete this registration card with your name and address, and then sign at the bottom of the card. Would you like a pen, Mr Brothers? |
| *Guest*: | Yes, please. |
| *Front desk clerk*: | We received this telephone message for you earlier today. |
| *Guest*: | Thank you. |
| *Front desk clerk*: | What time do you plan to check out tomorrow, Mr Brothers? |
| *Guest*: | Well, I can be out of my room at 9a.m., but I'd like to leave my bags here until about 4p.m. because my flight doesn't depart until 7p.m. |
| *Front desk clerk*: | Yes, that will be fine, Mr Brothers. The porter will store your bags for you. Where is your next destination? |
| *Guest*: | Paris, France. |
| *Front desk clerk*: | How do you wish to settle your account, Mr Brothers? |
| *Guest*: | By Visa. |
| *Front desk clerk*: | May I have your card for an imprint please? |
| *Guest*: | Yes, here you are. |
| *Front desk clerk*: | Thank you. Here is your card, Mr Brothers, and here are your key and your key card. The key card should be shown each time you collect your key. Your room is a superior single and is located on the eighth floor. Your room rate is £120 per night including 10 per cent service charge and VAT, and your check-out date is the 14th November. |
| *Guest*: | Thank you very much. I'd like to place some items in a safe deposit box. Can I do it here? |
| *Front desk clerk*: | Certainly, Mr Brothers, would you like to deposit the items now? |
| *Guest*: | No, I need to unpack first. |

| *Front desk clerk*: | When you are ready to deposit your items, please see the cashier. Now, let me call a bellboy to escort you to your room. Have a pleasant stay at the King's, Mr Brothers. |
| *Guest*: | Thank you. |

---

### Key points
1. All guests should be treated with equal respect, courtesy, and attention, regardless of their status. Always extend a warm welcome, and a cheerful greeting.
2. The front desk clerk asked the guest for his name and initial and then checked against the arrivals list for that day.
3. A telephone message was taken before the guest arrived. The message was sent to the reception department, and was noted on the arrivals list so that when the guest checked in the message could be immediately given to the guest.
4. The front desk clerk can ask the guest to complete the registration form or, as an additional service, the front desk clerk can complete the registration card for the guest. The guest is then asked to sign the registration card.
5. No mention was made of this reservation being guaranteed, so the front desk clerk must ask how the account will be settled. Settlement may be secured by taking a credit card imprint or by the guest paying cash in advance. Mr Brothers wants to settle by credit card.
6. Mr Brothers also requested information on safe deposits. The front desk clerk offered to help him and did not immediately refer him to the cashier. Reception department staff should try to give immediate personal service when handling enquiries; this gives the guest a greater sense of belonging and importance.
7. The registration card, correspondence and credit card imprint may be given to a cashier. The cashier will check the credit card number against the special bulletin of void cards supplied by Visa, and open an account in the guest's name. However, this part of the check-in procedure is very often performed by reception.

---

## Activity 8

(a)(i) A message is received for an expected guest who has not checked in. How will the front office staff ensure they remember to give the guest their message as soon as possible?

(ii) Give two reasons why the front desk clerk should record a guest's home address on the registration card.

(iii) State why different members of the hotel staff request to see a guest's key card.

(b) Read the conversation below, which is between a front desk clerk and a guest who does not have a reservation, and then answer the questions that follow.

| | |
|---|---|
| *Front desk clerk*: | Good afternoon, sir. May I help you? |
| *Guest*: | Yes, I'd like a room for tonight, please. |
| *Front desk clerk*: | Certainly. Do you have a reservation, sir? |
| *Guest*: | No, I don't. |
| *Front desk clerk*: | May I have your name please? |
| *Guest*: | Davis, Mr Brian Davis. |
| *Front desk clerk*: | Is the room just for yourself, Mr Davis? |
| *Guest*: | Yes, I'm travelling on my own. |
| *Front desk clerk*: | For how many nights do you require a room? |
| *Guest*: | One night, although I may need to stay longer. |
| *Front desk clerk*: | Will you wait one moment please, Mr Davis, while I check? |
| *Guest*: | Sure. |
| *Front desk clerk*: | Mr Davis, we have a deluxe twin room on the 10th floor. |
| *Guest*: | How much will it be? |
| *Front desk clerk*: | At single occupancy that will be £150 per night, including service charge and VAT. |
| *Guest*: | OK. I'll take it. |
| *Front desk clerk*: | Here is your registration card. Would you please complete your full name and address and your passport details, and sign at the bottom of the card. May I know your approximate departure time? |
| *Guest*: | I'm not sure at the moment. I might need the room for another night. Can I let you know in the morning? |
| *Front desk clerk*: | Yes, that will be fine; check-out time is before 12 noon, so if you could inform us before then, it would be appreciated. |
| *Guest*: | OK. Here is the registration card. |

| Front desk clerk: | Thank you Mr Davis. And how do you wish to settle your account? |
| Guest: | Will you accept US dollars? |
| Front desk clerk: | Certainly, Mr Davis. As you do not have a prior reservation it is necessary for me to ask for the first night's room rate in advance, plus a sum for incidental expenses. Could you please let me have 200 US dollars as a pre-payment? |
| Guest: | Certainly, no problem. |

> **Key points**
> 1. The receptionist greets the guest, and asks for the guest's name to help make him feel welcome. The room type and length of stay is ascertained and then room availability is checked.
> 2. The front desk clerk must inform the guest of the room rate. When the guest accepts the room at that rate a contract has been made between the hotel and the guest.
> 3. As this is a walk-in, the guest is asked to prepay his accommodation and make a deposit towards his incidental expenses.

(i) Why does the front desk clerk use the term 'single occupancy' when referring to Mr Davis's room rate?

(ii) Why are walk-ins usually required to make a prepayment before check-in is completed?

---

## SUMMARY

Of all the tasks undertaken by the reception department, one of the most important is the checking in of the newly arrived guest, because it is at this time that the guest forms their strongest impressions as to the friendliness and efficiency of the hotel.

In this chapter we have looked at the basic activities undertaken by the reception desk from the time prior to the guest's arrival through to the assignment of the room, and the issuing of the room key.

Prior to the arrival the receptionist needs to be aware of the room status of the hotel. They must balance the rooms available against the expected arrivals for the day, remembering that some regular guests have specific personal likes and dislikes. This information is obtained from the hotel's guest history records. In most hotels rooms are assigned at check-in; however, there are certain categories of guest who need to be pre-allocated guests, for example, VIPs, CIP and SPATTs.

The registration process, apart from being a legal requirement, also gives the hotel the opportunity of collecting valuable information on the guest. The design of the registration form was shown, and the reasons for taking the information explained. Procedures for dealing with newly arrived guests with reservations were shown, as were the steps to be taken when checking in aliens, walk-ins and people who appear on the hotel's blacklist.

Once the registration process has been completed, the receptionist assigns the guest a room. Sometimes, if the guest arrives early, a room may not be ready and so the methods of dealing with this situation were covered.

To ensure that the guest and hotel suffer no problems or embarrassment when the guest checks out, the method of payment should be clarified at the time of checking in. Some of the problems which could arise were explained and the solutions were given.

In a number of better-class hotels, newly arrived guests are escorted to their rooms by reception department ('front desk') staff. The objective of this service was given, as were the tasks expected to be performed by the escort.

The length of this chapter is an indication of the importance that checking in has in the work of the reception department.

# Review and discussion questions

1 Explain the term 'walk-in'.

2 With the aid of a diagram, illustrate the check-in process.

3 Explain what the front desk clerk should do when a guest wishes to check in early.

4 Explain what is meant by 'blacklist'.

5 You are the reception manager of a hotel. You are expecting a VIP guest who is about to arrive later in the afternoon. Explain what you should do before and upon their arrival at check-in.

6 Explain the necessity of overbooking and its legal implications.

7 Explain the reasons why a guest history card can be useful to a hotel.

8 How can 'walking a guest' be harmful to both the guest and the hotel?

# Case Study: *The Blacklisted Guest*

One evening, Mr Bluster and his lady friend arrived at the reception desk of the King's Hotel. John, the receptionist, was on duty.

'Good evening, Sir, can I help you?' inquired John.

'My name is Tom Bluster, I have a reservation for this evening of a double deluxe room,' replied Mr Bluster. John immediately checked the arrivals list and finding the details gave Mr Bluster a registration card to complete.

'Welcome to the King's Hotel, Mr Bluster, may I have your credit card please?' John politely said.

Mr Bluster gave his credit card to John. However, before John asked for Mr Bluster's signature, he remembered that the guest name was similar to a name on the blacklist. He immediately checked the computer and found that the guest in front of him was the same person – someone who had, on a previous stay, deliberately damaged some furniture in a guest room and who had attacked a receptionist in a sister hotel.

Now aware of this, John informed Mr Bluster that the hotel was fully booked and asked if he could book a room in another hotel. Mr Bluster became furious and started to shout at John.

'You have got my registration details and credit card and NOW you tell me there is no room available?' Mr Bluster shouted. 'I don't wanna talk to you, get me the manager ... now!'

John immediately paged Mary the assistant manager on duty, and on her arrival took her to one side and explained the situation. Now aware of what was happening Mary calmly explained to Mr Bluster that the hotel was indeed fully booked and a room was being booked elsewhere, and to cause less inconvenience the hotel car was at his disposal.

'We don't want another hotel, or your bloody car,' shouted Mr Bluster. 'We have booked a room here, now where is it?'

Just at that moment Mr Williams, the front office manager, approached the desk to find out what was happening.

## Questions

1. **Explain what went wrong.**

2. **Did John handle the situation correctly? Give your reasons.**

3. **As front office manager, how would you deal with Mr Bluster?**

# 8

# *Other duties of the reception department*

## Introduction

In Chapter 7 we introduced the work of the reception department and looked at the welcoming of guests and checking in of new arrivals. In this chapter, we shall examine the other duties of the reception department.

The chapter is divided into three main sections. The first section examines the general responsibilities of the reception department for the maintenance of resident guest records. The second part describes how the information concerning resident guests is communicated to other sections or departments of the hotel. The last section deals with the duties of the reception department in selling the hotel facilities, and explains the knowledge and skills that reception staff should possess when promoting sales.

## MAINTAINING RESIDENT GUEST RECORDS

We explained in Chapter 5 that the reservations department is responsible for the compilation of the reservation reports which show the reservation details and expected guest arrivals and departures. However, such records cannot accurately show guest movements; they are only expected movements. Discrepancies may exist between the reservation reports and the actual guest movements because of the possibility of:

- no-shows, or late cancellations of bookings

- walk-ins

- early departures

- changes to the guests' residential status (e.g. an extension of stay, change of room or room rate, or a change of billing arrangement).

Because hotels have to keep accurate records of guests in residence, it is the responsibility of the reception department to communicate the information to other front office sections and departments in the hotel, regardless of whether this information is of a newly arrived guest or simply a change of residential status.

### Amendments to resident guest records

A resident guest's records may need to be amended during their stay, such as when there are changes in:

- room type or number

- departure rate

- room rates

- number of guests (e.g. when a businessman may be joined by his wife)

When the records have been amended, other sections and departments have to be notified immediately.

Examples of how a resident's records may be amended are given below.

## Situation 1

Two guests, Mr and Mrs Law, are staying in a deluxe twin room on room-only terms. They intend to stay in the hotel for three days. However, Mrs Law has to leave earlier than planned.

**Action.** The reception department has to amend the departure date and number of guests on the registration form; the in-house list has to be changed; and the cashier must be notified so that Mr Law is charged at a single occupancy rate after the departure of his wife.

## Situation 2

Mr Law wants to change to a single room on bed and breakfast terms after his wife's departure.

**Action.** The reception department has to assign a new room and issue a new key. As a result, the room number should be changed on both the registration form and the in-house list. Other sections or departments also have to be notified of the change, e.g. the cashier (Mr Law's account is transferred to the new room number and the room rate is altered), the housekeeper (Mr Law may require assistance with packing), the porters (Mr Law's baggage will need to be moved to the new room), the telephone section (calls must be connected correctly), and mail and information desk (a new key will be issued and mail and messages must be sent to the new room).

The importance of maintaining resident guest records cannot be overstressed. An accurate record of resident guests must be kept by the hotel in order to:

- comply with legal requirements, i.e. the Immigration Order 1972, which requires that certain personal details of guests must be kept by hotels

- provide up-to-date information on resident guests to all front office sections or other hotel departments

Up-to-date resident information is essential because it:

- provides an accurate and speedy service for guests during their stay (i.e. in handling mail, messages or telephone calls)

- ensures that guest bills are accurately and continuously updated

- allows other departments to plan their operations based on the actual guest movements (e.g. the food and beverage department can more accurately estimate the number of breakfasts required by knowing the number of guests staying in the hotel the night before)

## *Maintenance of registration records*

You will recall that when a guest checks into a hotel, their personal particulars and the details are recorded on the registration form. These registration details are kept by the reception department until the guest departs. After the guest has checked out, a summary of these details may be transferred onto the guest history records, whilst the original registration cards are kept by the hotel for at least one year. This is a legal requirement.

---

**Activity 1**    (a)  What problems may arise if a hotel does not keep an accurate record of the resident guests? Illustrate your answer with examples.

(b)  You are the reception manager of a hotel. What instructions would you give to your staff to ensure that the resident guest records are accurate and up to date?

---

## COMMUNICATION WITH OTHER FRONT OFFICE SECTIONS AND DEPARTMENTS

In the last section, we explained that the reception department plays an important role in maintaining the records of all resident guests. In order to provide high-quality services for the guests, other sections and departments of the hotel must be able to gain access to such records quickly. In most hotels information concerning the resident guest is obtained from their registration form and is circulated to the other relevant office sections and departments in the form of front office reports.

### *Front office reports prepared by the reception department*

The most common reports prepared by the reception department are the in-house list, walk-in and extra arrivals, guest amendments, departure list and checked-out list; these are described below. Remember, these are only examples; it is difficult to give a comprehensive list of all reception reports because different hotels have different policies about the types of front office report they want compiled.

- The in-house list. This is a list which shows all the guests currently residing in the hotel. The guest names are usually arranged in alphabetical order. The report should have the date and time printed at the top, so that staff can tell when it was compiled. This list has to be amended regularly to provide the most up-to-date information on resident guests.

- Current walk-ins and extra arrivals. This is a list showing all unexpected arrivals (walk-ins) and extra arrivals (guests who have telephoned earlier today to make their bookings) on that date. Apart from the guests' names and room numbers, it should show the level of credit the guest is permitted. This is particularly so for walk-ins.

- Guest amendments. This list shows any changes to a resident guest's details on that date (e.g. room number, room rate, number of guests, or duration of stay).

- The departure list. This list shows current expected departures. However, not all guests on the list may necessarily check out; some may decide to stay longer, and other names may not appear on the list because they have checked out earlier than expected.

- The checked-out list. This is a list of guests who have actually settled their accounts and left the hotel. Consequently, any telephone calls and messages for these guests must be handled very carefully. It is also possible that some of the guests have settled their accounts and vacated their rooms, but their baggage has been deposited with the porter's lodge. In this situation messages may be taken and given to the guests by the porters when they collect their bags.

- The guest history record. This is a record of the personal details of the guests who have previously stayed in the hotel. It is compiled and maintained by reception, but is not distributed throughout the hotel.

In general, the type of front office report depends on:

- The size of the hotel. Small hotels will have fewer arrivals or departures on a single date. Because of this, they often combine various lists or reports into a single list (e.g. arrivals, departures and stay-ons).

- The level of service of the hotel. Top-class hotels tend to provide more personalized services and thus need to know more about the specific requests or details of individual guests. Budget hotels, on the other hand, may not need such detailed information (e.g. a three-star hotel may not need a VIP or CIP list).

- The registration system used. A computerized system is capable of producing a wide variety of lists and reports in a short period of time. However, it is more difficult and time-consuming for hotels relying mainly on manual systems to produce similar reports.

The reports generated at the front desk are produced at different times during the guest's stay. Some are created after check-in and some during the guest's stay (e.g. the in-house list and the extra arrivals list), while some can only be completed after the guest has left (e.g. check-out list). As well as the variance in times, the format of the reports also varies from hotel to hotel. For example, the in-house list may be called the residents list, while the list of extra arrivals or departure list may be arranged according to room number in one hotel whereas in another it may be arranged alphabetically according to the guest's surname.

It is also possible that in some hotels a number of reports are combined to give a larger report. For example, hotels may compile a rooms report which could include information from the: in-house list (the stay-on rooms); departure list (current departure rooms); and arrivals list (current pre-assigned rooms). You can see that by this combining of reports, more comprehensive information is available to other departments on a single report. Combined reports are also more convenient to use, because departments do not have to check through different reports for information. For instance, from the rooms report the housekeeper can immediately identify which rooms need servicing and the type of servicing required on a particular day. Similarly, the reception supervisor will be able to know which rooms are available for unexpected guests.

---

**Activity 2**   For each of the following front office reports, state which front office sections and other hotel departments might need the information. Explain why.

- the in-house list

- the departure list

---

### Forms of communication

Very often, information on resident guests is communicated to other front office sections or hotel departments in the form of a written report. In many hotels, a computer system may be used to link all sections and departments together. This means that the information gathered by one section or department can be readily accessed by others. In this way, information can be communicated more quickly and effectively. This helps to improve the efficiency of guest services, and to provide the hotel management with up-to-the-minute information for decision-making purposes. Remember, however, that even in large modern hotels other forms of communication are often required, as follows:

Telephone:

- The receptionist may telephone the housekeeper and ask for an extra bed to be placed in a room at once for a walk-in guest.

- The cashier may phone the credit card company for an authorization code.

Person to person:

- The receptionist may directly inform the porter or bellboy of the room number of a newly checked-in guest so that the guest's luggage will be immediately delivered to the room.

- The porters/concierge may ask the reception for the room number of a particular guest so that an urgent message can be delivered to the guest.

From these examples you will see that an informal method of communication, such as person to person or the use of the telephone, is appropriate when action is needed or when an unusual problem has occurred which requires a speedy explanation or discussion. Very often, informal communication is followed up by a written notification, with a copy being kept, or the information may be stored in the computer.

---

**Activity 3**   Does the use of a computer system guarantee that resident guest records will be accurate and up to date? Why? Why not?

---

## FLOW OF GUEST INFORMATION BETWEEN SECTIONS OF THE FRONT OFFICE AND OTHER DEPARTMENTS

All hotel departments and sections are interrelated in their operations. Very often, the work of one section or department depends on that of another. Because of this, there must be a constant flow of information between them.

The front office is the centre of guest transactions in a hotel and the reception desk usually acts as the centre for the collection and distribution of guest information. We shall now examine, in greater detail, the information flow between the reception department and other sections and departments of a hotel.

### The reservations department

When you studied the work of the reservations department in Chapters 5 and 6, you should have noticed that the reservations department is a user as well as a provider of guest information. When reservations are received, the reservations department will use information on the guest which can be gleaned from the history records. Likewise, it will use the list of credit-approved companies which is provided by the sales or accounts departments. At the same time, it provides information on room availability and reservation details in the form of reservation reports for other departments to use (e.g. the expected arrivals list, the list of special requests, and the VIP/SPATT list), and the rooms forecast reports.

### The reception department

By now you should also be familiar with the process of checking in of new arrivals (Chapter 7). Remember that, when checking in guests, the reception department needs information on expected arrivals and anticipated departures, so that they can check mail and ensure key control, special requests, VIPs and so on, from the reservations department, as well as room status information from housekeeping.As you saw earlier in this chapter, the reception department plays an important role in maintaining the resident guests' records. It provides other sections and departments with reports showing the guest movements (e.g. the in-house list, list of extra arrivals, amendments to the status of resident guests, and guest history records).

### Other front office sections

Most of the other front office sections are users of information, as shown by Table 8.1.

**Table 8.1** Front office users of guest information

| Front office section required | Type of information | Purpose of information |
|---|---|---|
| Concierge/porters | Expected arrivals list<br>Departures list<br>Groups/tours list<br>VIP list<br>In-house list<br>Extra arrivals list | Baggage handling<br>Groups/tours<br>VIPs<br><br>Take messages |
| Front office cashier | Expected arrivals list<br>VIP list<br>Tour list<br><br>Guest history records<br>List of credit approved companies | Billing details<br>Payment details<br>Checking corporate accounts |
| Telephone | In-house list<br><br>Expected arrivals list<br><br>Checked-out list | Correctly connecting guest calls<br>Correctly charging guest calls |

Note: the charges for guest telephone calls may be monitored and charged to a guest's account directly by computer. If the guest cannot get through, the operator may be asked to place the call. In these situations, the charge for the call may be transferred to the cashier, either by a written voucher or via a computer terminal in the telephone room.

### The housekeeping department

The housekeeping department needs information on departures and stay-on rooms in order to organize room-cleaning schedules. It also needs details on special requests so that extra amenities and services can be arranged for specific rooms, as well as any VIP or CIP arrivals.

Housekeeping provides information on room status changes (e.g. the room status is changed from vacant/dirty to vacant/clean once a room has been serviced). This department is also responsible for the preparation of the housekeeper's report, which shows the number of guests occupying each room and the current status of that room. An example of a housekeeper's report is illustrated in Figure 8.1.

If the hotel is computerized then the housekeeping department will enter its report into a hotel's computer system. The computer will then compare the housekeeping room status with the room status infor-

*King's Hotel*

## Housekeeper's Report: Room Status Listing

**Date:** 26th March

| Room no. | Name | No. of Guests | Date in | Date out | Status |
|----------|------|---------------|---------|----------|--------|
| 101 | 0 | 0 | 0 | 0 | Vacant/clean |
| 102 | Lee | 2 | 26/3 | 7/4 | Stay-over |
| 103 | May | 2 | 26/3 | 3/4 | Stay-over |
| 104 | 0 | 0 | 0 | 0 | Vacant/clean |
| 105 | Leek | 2 | 22/3 | 26/3 | Check-out |

**Figure 8.1** The housekeeper's report

mation at the front desk. Should discrepancies be indicated, this shows that there is a potential error in resident guest records. This would be dealt with immediately by the housekeeper and the assistant front office manager or senior receptionist.

If the hotel operates on a manual system, then the receptionist physically checks the housekeeper's report against the front desk room rack. Again, any discrepancies are immediately investigated.

### The sales department

The sales department will need to have information on the room availability (provided by the reservations office) so that it may make reservations for groups, tours and corporate bookings. It also needs the guest history records of frequent and corporate guests so as to create a more personal approach to future or past customers. (It is interesting to note that in a number of hotels, reservations is now located in the sales department rather than the front office.)

### The accounts department

Information concerning the amount of advance deposits received by the reservations department and payments received by the front office cashier must be recorded and passed on to the accounts department. This department is responsible for the monitoring of guest accounts, monitoring credit limits, and seeking prompt settlement of ledger accounts. The department is also responsible for compiling the list of credit-approved companies, which is needed by the reservations and the front office departments.

## Management

The senior hotel management needs information on occupancy and revenue statistics. Most computer systems are programmed to produce management information in the form of a wide range of daily and monthly reports. By having this accurate, up-to-date information, management can make decisions based on facts rather than intuition. If a computer system is not used, then the same reports and statistics have to be prepared manually.

---

**Activity 4**  (a)  Which of the following reports will the receptionist need when assigning a room to a walk-in guest?

Checked-out list

Room status list

Extra arrivals list

Guest history record

(b)  Which of the following reports will the porters need if a visitor wants to contact a resident guest?

Arrivals list

Departures list

In-house list

Housekeeper's report

(c)  Which sections or departments will need the extra arrivals list for their daily operations?

Telephone, front office cashier, and reception

Reservations, cashiers, and porters

Telephone, front office cashier, and porters

Reception, reservations, and telephone

---

## SELLING THE HOTEL FACILITIES

We explained in Chapter 2 that unless a guest has stayed in the hotel before, that guest usually does not have any knowledge about the accommodation product. It is likely that many of the guests are not aware of the various services and facilities available when they arrive at the hotel. Thus, another important duty of the reception staff is to explain to guests the various types of accommodation and the other hotel facilities, and to encourage them to purchase them during their stay. This up-selling significantly increases the revenue to the hotel, especially from the sales of non-guest-room services.

In general, reception staff may help to promote sales by:

- encouraging guests to use the full range of the hotel services (e.g. business centres, coffee shops, bars, and so on)

- suggesting an upgrade in accommodation

### Salesmanship of reception staff

Good salesmanship is needed by reception staff when selling hotel facilities. The following are some guidelines for good salesmanship techniques:

1. Product knowledge: receptionist clerks must be able to describe and suggest the services and facilities of the hotel. You therefore need to have a thorough knowledge of your hotel and its products, including room types, rates, and all of the facilities or services available.

2. Willingness to sell: be willing to give guests your full attention and to offer assistance and knowledgeable advice whenever it is needed.

3. Communication skills: be able to communicate well. You must be able to listen, observe, and establish the needs of a guest. Additionally, you must be able to ask appropriate questions and discuss with guests the type of services that best suit their needs.

4. Selling techniques: possess good selling techniques so that guests are persuaded to purchase the hotel products without feeling that they are being pressurized.

### Some useful techniques in selling hotel facilities

Reception staff may promote sales of hotel services by employing certain useful selling techniques. These may include the following strategies.

### Offering alternatives

Guests are not always aware of the range of services available in a hotel. Reception staff can promote the sales of the services by suggesting the most appropriate service to the guest, or offering alternatives for the guest to choose from. Two strategies that can be used when offering alternatives of accommodation to customers are the top-down and bottom-up approaches.

The top-down technique requires the receptionist to start from the most expensive option, and then offer progressively cheaper ones if the guest does not intend to take the more expensive offer. This method is most appropriate with guests whose prime concern is comfort and service, rather than cost. The most expensive and costly option is described first, as this is likely to appeal most to this type of guest.

The bottom-up technique, on the other hand, requires the receptionist to start with the cheapest option, and then persuade the guest to take progressively more expensive packages. This method is most appropriate with guests whose prime consideration is the cost of the service. If the most expensive option is offered first, the guest would be put off right away. By starting with the cheapest option and then suggesting that for a small amount more the guest could have much better accommodation, the receptionist may be able to persuade the guest to accept services of the medium or higher price ranges.

When choosing a selling strategy, reception staff have to anticipate what will motivate the guest to use a service. For example, will the guest be attracted by offering a special promotional price, or will the guest be more interested in the exclusivity of expensive service?

In general, it can be said that:

- Well-dressed, affluent guests are less likely to be on a tight budget and may be more concerned with the quality of service than costs.

- Guests whose full accounts are settled by their companies tend to spend more than guests paying for themselves.

- Guests who want to impress business clients or colleagues tend to spend more on high-quality services.

- Guests who desire comfort are more likely to treat themselves to expensive services.

Reception staff, therefore, have to observe and listen to guests carefully. They may have to know more about a guest, such as the purpose of the guest's visit or the account details, in order to establish a guest's needs and to be able to recommend the most appropriate service.

### Suggestive selling

This is an important sales technique for front office staff. It involves a member of staff describing the services and offering to book them for a guest. The technique can be illustrated more clearly by the examples below. It is important to remember that when employing suggestive selling, care must be taken to avoid applying too much pressure on guests.

### Situation 1

A couple travelling with their baby.

**Action.** The receptionist may recommend the full range of the hotel services by offering to hire a baby-sitter for a family on that evening, reserving a table in the hotel's à la carte restaurant, or describing the laundry facilities and baby meals available from room service.

### Situation 2

An exhausted businesswoman.

**Action.** The receptionist may suggest that the guest upgrade to a room with a whirlpool bath. The guest may find the bath a well-deserved relaxation after a hard day's work, although it costs a little more. In addition, the receptionist may also inform the guest that meals and cocktails can be provided in the guest-room, and explain how the guest can ask for room service.

### Situation 3

An FIT businessman with a reservation for a standard room on rack rate terms.

**Action.** The receptionist may explain the benefits of the special business package (which may, for instance, include breakfast charge, use of the business centre facilities, and use of hotel transportation) and suggest that the guest change to the new tariff.

---

**Activity 5**  Imagine that you are a receptionist in a hotel.

    (a) Explain why good salesmanship is important when carrying out your duties.

    (b) What selling techniques would you employ when

offering accommodation for the following walk-in guests? Explain why.

- a mature man on an all-expenses-paid business trip

- a middle-aged couple who are on holiday

- a young man with a rucksack

(c) What kind of services would you suggest to the following guests in order to increase sales?

- an independent traveller coming to your city on business purposes

- a group of teenage pleasure travellers

- a newly-wed couple on their honeymoon.

## SUMMARY

In this chapter we have investigated the reasons why accurate records of all guest movements are needed. Apart from the fact that there is a legal requirement in certain circumstances, the other departments of the hotel often require guest information. Added to this, we learnt how front office records assist in making the guest feel more welcome and 'at home' in the hotel.

Because the hotel industry is all about dealing with people, we saw how it can often be necessary to alter the information relating to a guest's stay. This required amending the guest status information, and distributing these amendments to other departments.

It was shown how it is essential that the front office has excellent communications with other sections within the rooms division as well as other departments. Examples of the information which needed to be communicated were given as well as explanations as to who wants what and why.

One of the major duties of every good front desk clerk is to be a sales-person. The reasons for this and some useful techniques were explained.

Further aspects of communication and social skills will be discussed in Chapter 14.

## Review and discussion questions

1   A guest history record is a useful record for the front office. However, only some hotels keep such records.

(a) What types of hotels are more likely to keep this record? Why?

(b) What information can be found on the guest history record?

2 Explain what is meant by 'suggestive selling'.

3 Explain the differences between top-down and bottom-up selling techniques.

4 What is the purpose of the housekeeper's report?

5 Explain why communication between the housekeeping department and the front office is important. Give examples.

6 Why is it important to keep an accurate record of the resident guests?

# Role play situations

(a) An FIT businessman with a guaranteed reservation walks up to the front desk and asks to check in. What procedure would you follow?

(b) Mr Chin Man Wong arrives at the desk asking to check in. You are unable to find his reservation details. What would you do, assuming you have rooms?

(c) A guest arrives late in the evening with a confirmed booking and asks to check in. You discover that the hotel is full and no rooms are available. What would you do if you were the receptionist on duty?

(d) Mr Jones (Room 101) comes down to the front desk asking to change rooms. He complains that his present room is noisy. What procedure would you follow?

(e) Mrs Smith wishes to stay one extra night. What procedure would you follow?

(f) Mr Walker, staying in Room 107, asks for his account to be settled by his company, IBN Ltd. What procedure would you follow?

# Case Study: Room Discrepancy

*King's Hotel – Housekeeper's Room Report*
*Monday 17th June*

| 1st floor | | 2nd floor | | 3rd floor | | 4th floor | |
|---|---|---|---|---|---|---|---|
| 101 | O (2) | 201 | O (2) | 301 | O (2) | 401 | OOO |
| 102 | O (1) | 202 | O (1) | 302 | OOS | 402 | OOO |
| 103 | O (1) | 203 | O (1) | 303 | O (1) | 403 | OOO |
| 104 | B | 204 | O (1) | 304 | O (1) | 404 | OOO |
| 105 | V | 205 | V | 305 | O (1) | 405 | OOO |
| 106 | V | 206 | V | 306 | O (1) | 406 | OOO |
| 107 | OOO | 207 | O (2) | 307 | L | 407 | OOO |
| 108 | O (2) | 208 | O (1) | 308 | X (2) | 408 | OOO |
| 109 | O (1) | 209 | O (1) | 309 | V | 409 | OOO |
| 110 | O (1) | 210 | V | 310 | L | 410 | OOO |
| 111 | O (2) | 211 | V | 311 | V | 411 | OOS |
| 112 | O (1) | 212 | V | 312 | O (1) | 412 | OOS |
| 113 | X (1) | 213 | V | 313 | O (2) | 413 | OOO |
| 114 | V | 214 | L | 314 | O (1) | 414 | OOO |
| 115 | V | 215 | OOO | 315 | V | 415 | OOO |
| 116 | V | 216 | X (1) | 316 | V | 416 | OOO |

*Key*

| | | | |
|---|---|---|---|
| O | Occupied, baggage in room | OOO | Out of order |
| L | Door locked inside | OOS | Out of service |
| X | Occupied, no baggage in room | ( ) | No. of occupants |
| B | Baggage, not slept in | V | Vacant |

The above housekeeper's report shows the room status and relates to 9.30a.m. on Monday 17th June. On checking the reception records the following differences are noted:

(a)  Room 302  occupied, 2 sleepers
(b)  Room 107  vacant
(c)  Room 301  occupied, 1 sleeper
(d)  Room 111  vacant
(e)  Room 309  occupied, 1 sleeper

**After double-checking with the housekeeper, state the action to be taken, in each case giving reasons why these differences may have occurred (taking into account what documentation you would refer to).**

# 9

# *Front office accounting*

## Introduction

The objective of a hotel is to provide facilities and services for guests in return for money, ultimately to make a profit. To ensure that all guest bills are properly settled, hotels need to have an accurate and constantly updated record of all guest financial transactions.

This chapter deals with the front office accounting system which records all of the guest's financial transactions. It begins by explaining the main functions of the front office accounting system and the different types of guest accounts held at the front office. The basic front office accounting cycle and the procedures necessary in creating and maintaining guest accounts are then described. Finally, the posting of charges and credits to guest accounts and the verification of postings is examined.

## FUNCTIONS OF THE FRONT OFFICE ACCOUNT SYSTEM

Each day, a hotel engages in a large number of transactions with guests. In addition to using bedrooms, and food and beverage operations, guests may use other services and facilities during their stay, such as the laundry, room service or the business centre. Therefore, charges obviously have to be made for the services used.

On most occasions, guests do not have to pay for the hotel service immediately after its use; instead, they may be provided with services on credit. That is, they use the service or facility and pay for it at the end of their stay. The charges must therefore be recorded on a guest account so that they are ready for settlement when that guest checks out.

A hotel may receive advance deposits or part payment of a bill from guests. In order to have an accurate and up-to-date record of all these financial transactions, a front office accounting system has to be set up by a hotel to deal with credit payments as well as debit charges.

The main function of the front office accounting system is to:

- maintain an accurate and current record of all guest transactions

- provide an effective internal control by monitoring credit given to guests, and prevent fraudulent staff practices

- provide management information on departmental revenue

A front office cashier may be employed whose specific duty is to perform various tasks, such as preparing and settling guest accounts, administering the safe deposit system, as well as offering foreign currency facilities to overseas guests.

The front office cashier is normally assisted by night audit staff, who conduct many of the checks or audits and who print the management reports (see Chapter 10). Staff from the credit control section of the accounts department may also perform some of the credit monitoring and fraud prevention aspects of bill preparation and settlement. However, in many hotels the role of cashier is combined with that of a reception clerk, which means that the duties of a receptionist and a cashier are performed by the same person.

The front office accounting system, which involves the above functions of bill preparation and control, must be able to integrate with the main accounting system operated by the hotel's accounts department. The function of the accounts department is to monitor the financial operation of all areas of the hotel, i.e. the running costs and earned revenue.

The information supplied by the food and beverage accounting system and the front office accounts system, together with financial and statistical information from other departments, is transferred to the accounts office. From this information the accounts office produces two main types of report:

- The operational reports, which are used by management for daily decision-making.

- The financial reports, which are concerned with profitability and revenue. The financial reports indicate the overall performance of the hotel and are used by senior and corporate management.

**Activity 1** List the problems which could arise if a hotel does not have an accurate and up-to-date record of its transactions with guests.

## TYPES OF ACCOUNTS MAINTAINED BY THE FRONT OFFICE CASHIER

A guest account is a record of all the financial transactions between the hotel and the guest. It is sometimes called a folio or a bill. Figure 9.1 shows an example of a hotel guest folio.

There are two main types of entry on an account: debit and credit. Most guest accounts have a debit balance, because the guest is in debt to the hotel for the services which they have had and had charged to their account. Thus each time a guest charges an amount, it is a debit entry. A credit entry refers to payments or subtractions from the balance of a guest bill.

A guest's account tells the story of their stay in the hotel. Look at the story as told by the account in Figure 9.1.

Mr and Mrs Gibson arrived on the night of 8 May; they had prepaid the accommodation charge, so their account shows a credit entry. The necessary room charge for that night was then posted to their bill. They had a drink in the bar, and then had a meal from room service. These charges are shown as debits on their account. At the end of the day, a balance of the debit and credit entries for that day was shown. This shows that with all the debits added together minus the credit of £150 for the prepayment, there is an outstanding amount to be paid of £74.00. In the morning, the Gibsons had breakfast from room service, which was charged to their account by the room service waiter. They then checked out and settled their outstanding balance by cash. A credit

## KING'S HOTEL

| | |
|---|---|
| Address: | South Coast Road, Dover, Kent. |
| Telephone: | (0527) 723 6788 |
| Fax : | (0527) 745 6345 |
| E-mail: | kingsotel@hotemail.com.uk |

| | |
|---|---|
| Name | Mr/s Gibson |
| Arrival date: | 8/5/99 |
| Departure date: | 9/5/99 |
| No. in party: | 2 |
| Room no. | 1032 |
| Rate | £150 |
| Folio no: | 283833 |

| Date | Item | Description | Debit | Credit |
|------|------|-------------|-------|--------|
| 8/5/93 | 1 | Cash | | 150 |
| 8/5/93 | 2 | Room | 150 | |
| 8/5/93 | 3 | King's Bar | 10 | |
| 8/5/93 | 4 | Room service – dinner | 64 | |
| 8/5/93 | | Balance | 74 | |
| 9/5/93 | 5 | Room service – breakfast | 15 | |
| Amount to be settled by guest | | | 89 | |
| | 6 | Cash | | 89 |
| | | Balance | 00 | |

**Figure 9.1** A guest account or folio

entry of £89.00 is shown, which leaves a nil balance, showing that all charges have been paid.

There are three main types of account maintained by the front office cashier, which record a hotel's transaction with three different types of customer.

### Resident guest accounts

Most of the accounts held by the front office cashier are the resident guest accounts, which show the financial transactions with guests who have registered and who are currently staying at the hotel.

As previously explained, some of the resident guests may have their accommodation charges settled by their company, while they settle incidentals themselves. In these situations, the resident guest has to have two folios:

- The master folio or account for the room charges, which will be sent to the company for settlement. A copy of this account is sent to city (sales) ledger.

- The folio for the incidentals, which the guest will settle personally.

## City accounts

City accounts are records of financial transactions between the hotel and non-resident guests. These could include accounts held by:

- Local business people who are not resident in the hotel but who use the hotel facilities and services for entertainment or business meetings.

- Guests who walk out of the hotel without settling the outstanding balance on their account. Walk-outs are no longer resident so their account is transferred to the city (sales) ledger, to either await eventual payment, or to be written off by the account as a 'bad debt'.

- Guests who have sent prepayments to guarantee their bookings, but have not arrived or checked in. This amount is normally recorded in the city (sales) ledger.

## Management accounts

Management accounts are expense accounts or allowances given by some hotels to the hotel manager. These accounts are used to entertain guests or potential clients. For example, if a guest has a complaint about the hotel, the assistant manager may invite them to have a drink with him or her in the hotel bar after the problem has been resolved. This may help to encourage the guest to relax and to think well of the hotel. The charge for the drinks is debited to the manager's expense (management) accounts.

Some resident accounts are transferred to city (sales) ledger, such as company accounts and non-bank credit cards (American Express and Diners Club). These accounts, along with city and management accounts, are transferred to the accounts department, which handles their settlement at a later date.

**Activity 2**   Complete the grid below by stating the number of folios, type of account (resident or city ledger) and place of settlement (front office cashier or accounts department) for each of the following guests.

| Type of guest | No. of folio | Resident account or city ledger | Place of settlement |
|---|---|---|---|
| An FIT arrived today for four nights and will pay by cash. | | | |
| Two conference delegates, who shared a twin room, checked out on a full corporate account. | | | |
| A couple with a travel voucher for room charge, and US dollars for incidentals. | | | |

## THE FRONT OFFICE ACCOUNTING CYCLE

The first important function of the front office accounting system is to maintain an accurate and up-to-date record of all the financial transactions between a hotel and a guest so that all outstanding accounts are settled without delay. In this process the basic activities involved are as shown in Figure 9.2. From this, it can be seen that the front office accounting process can be divided into three main phases:

- creation of accounts

- maintenance of accounts

- settlement of accounts

In this chapter, we are mainly concerned with the creation and maintenance of accounts, particularly those of resident guests. The final part of the settlement of guest accounts will be discussed in the next chapter.

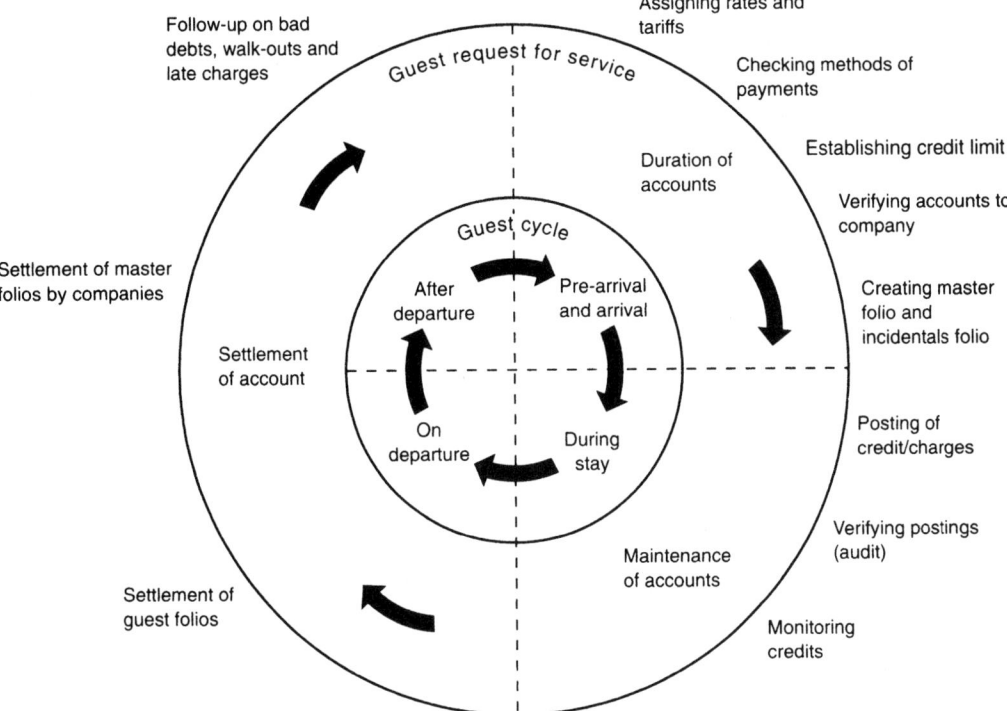

**Figure 9.2** The front office accounting cycle

## CREATION OF ACCOUNTS

A guest account, or folio, is usually created immediately after the guest checks in. As you saw in Chapter 7, part of the check-in procedure is to enter the guest details into the computer, which automatically opens an account, or to open a guest account manually. Credit limits or house limits are often set, which means that guests may not charge more than a pre-set amount to their accounts.

**Activity 3**   Explain why a hotel allows credit to some guests but not to others.

## MAINTENANCE OF ACCOUNTS

Once the guest account has been opened, all financial transactions between the hotel and the guest will be recorded on that account. The act of recording the transactions onto to the guest account is called posting.

### The posting process

In general, the posting of a charge or credit involves a five-stage process which is illustrated in Figure 9.3. This process is dramatically speeded up if the hotel is computerized.

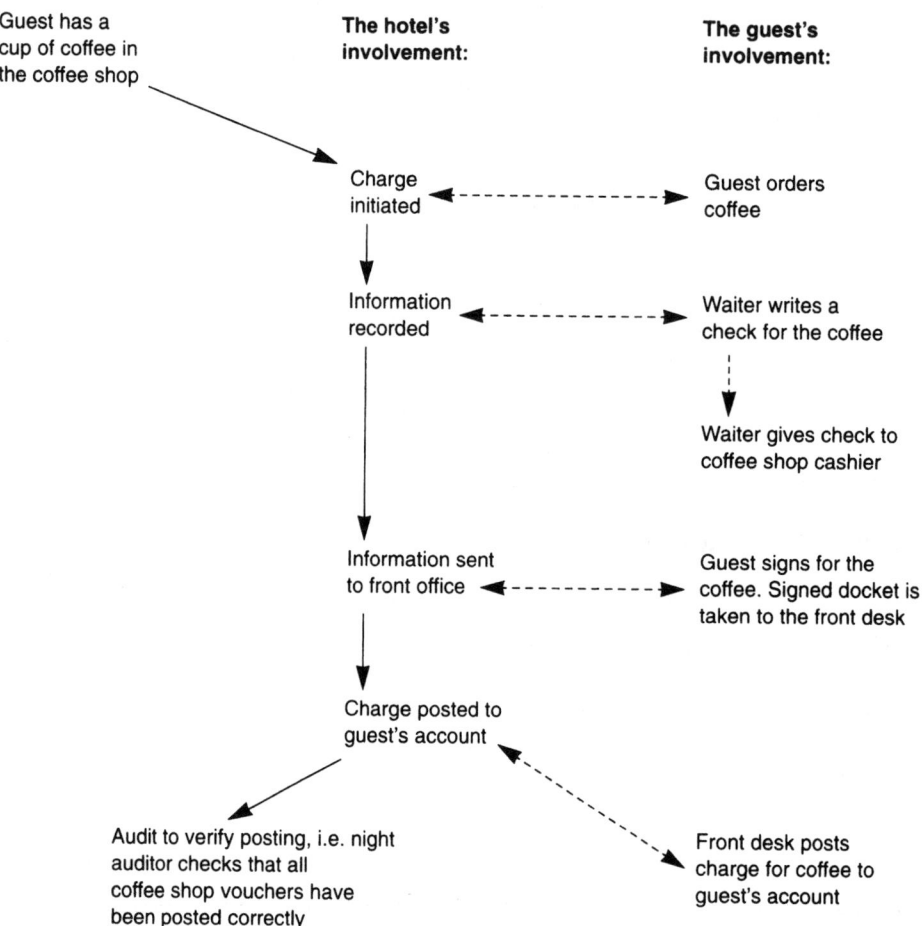

**Figure 9.3** The process of posting a charge to a guest's account

### Types of postings

There are two basic types of transactions that are posted to a guest account: debit entries and credit entries.

The most common debit items include:

- room charges
- restaurant/coffee shop/bar
- telephone
- laundry
- use of hotel facilities (e.g. health centre, business centre and transportation)

Credit entries:

- prepayments
- payments for part of the bill during stay
- payments for final settlement
- amendments to the bill

### VPO (visitors paid out) or Guest Disbursement

A guest may sometimes request services which the hotel does not provide. In these situations the hotel will often employ the services of an outside organization (e.g. a car-hire agency, secretarial bureau or sightseeing tour operator, florist). The porter will usually arrange and pay for these services and notify the cashier or reception of the charge to be added to the guest's bill. These charges are usually termed visitors paid outs (VPOs) and mean that the hotel has paid out sums of money on behalf of the guest for a service. These charges have to be entered into a guest's account as debit items for settlement. Common items for VPOs include theatre tickets, car-hire service, sightseeing tours and postage stamps.

### Special types of postings

In addition to the debit and credit entries mentioned, there are special types of postings which sometimes may be needed in order to adjust for certain irregularities that can arise during the posting process. These are as follows.

### Account corrections

Account corrections are required when there has been a posting error to a guest's account. Examples of necessary corrections are:

- The correct amount has been posted to the correct guest

account, but the wrong department identified. If a charge for a coffee shop meal has been incorrectly posted as a room service charge, the charge must be subtracted from the guest account (i.e. credited) as a room service charge and added to the guest account (i.e. debited) as a coffee shop charge.

- The incorrect amount has been posted to the right department and guest account. For example, £250 is posted instead of £150. A correction in the form of a credit entry of £100 has to be made to the guest's account as well as the department account.

- The correct amount has been posted to the right department, but to the wrong guest account. For example, an £8.00 telephone charge is posted to room 612 instead of room 611. This needs a correction of a credit entry to room 612 of £8.00. Room 611 is then debited with the charge.

### Account allowance

An account allowance is a type of credit posting which is given to a guest during their stay, or sometimes on their departure, and can be either for an over-charge, or as a form of compensation. For example, if a guest has been charged for a meal in the coffee shop, but complained that the service was very poor, the assistant manager may offer to reduce or deduct the charge as a compensation for the bad service. This amount will then be deducted from the guest's account as an account allowance.

### Account transfer

An account transfer is needed when a charge is removed from one account and transferred to another account. For example, if a couple with their two children are occupying two twin rooms, they may ask for the charges of the children's rooms to be transferred to their account, so that the two accounts can be settled together.

---

**Activity 4**   What type of posting entry will be made to a guest's account for each of the following transactions?

- A prepayment has been received from a guest.

- A hotel has paid for concert tickets on behalf of a guest.

- A guest wishes to settle the bill for his son's room.

- A guest has consumed drinks from the mini-bar.

---

## METHODS OF HANDLING GUEST ACCOUNTS

To ensure that guest accounts are accurate and current, all guests' credit or charge information must be promptly communicated to the front office cashier for posting.

There are two methods by which such information can be communicated and handled:

- manually (preparing bills by hand)
- by computer

In most hotels, computers are widely used because they are accurate and fast in the transfer of credit or charge information. In addition, computers can be programmed to analyse a hotel's revenue in great detail and produce reports for management in a very short period of time.


## HANDLING OF GUEST ACCOUNTS BY COMPUTER

If a hotel is using a computer system, a guest account will be created when the guest details are entered into the computer at check-in. The information will be stored in the memory of the computer.

Once a guest account is created, any subsequent debits or credits may be posted directly to that account. This can be done in a number of ways, as illustrated in Figure 9.4.

In the example of Figure 9.4, credits or charges are posted to the guest account, which is held on the main computer processor at the front office, in the following ways:

- Processor. Some charges are posted by the computer automatically: for example, the room charge (the room rate which is recorded in the computer at check-in) can be automatically added to a guest's account each night by the computer.

- Charges can also be transferred directly from computer terminals in other departments. For example, a waiter can enter a guest's breakfast charges by means of a small computer terminal in the coffee shop. The charge will then be transferred to the main processor at the front office and posted directly on to the guest's account.

- By a computer link from one computer system to the main system. In some hotels, smaller computer systems are set up to monitor special types of guest services and are linked to the

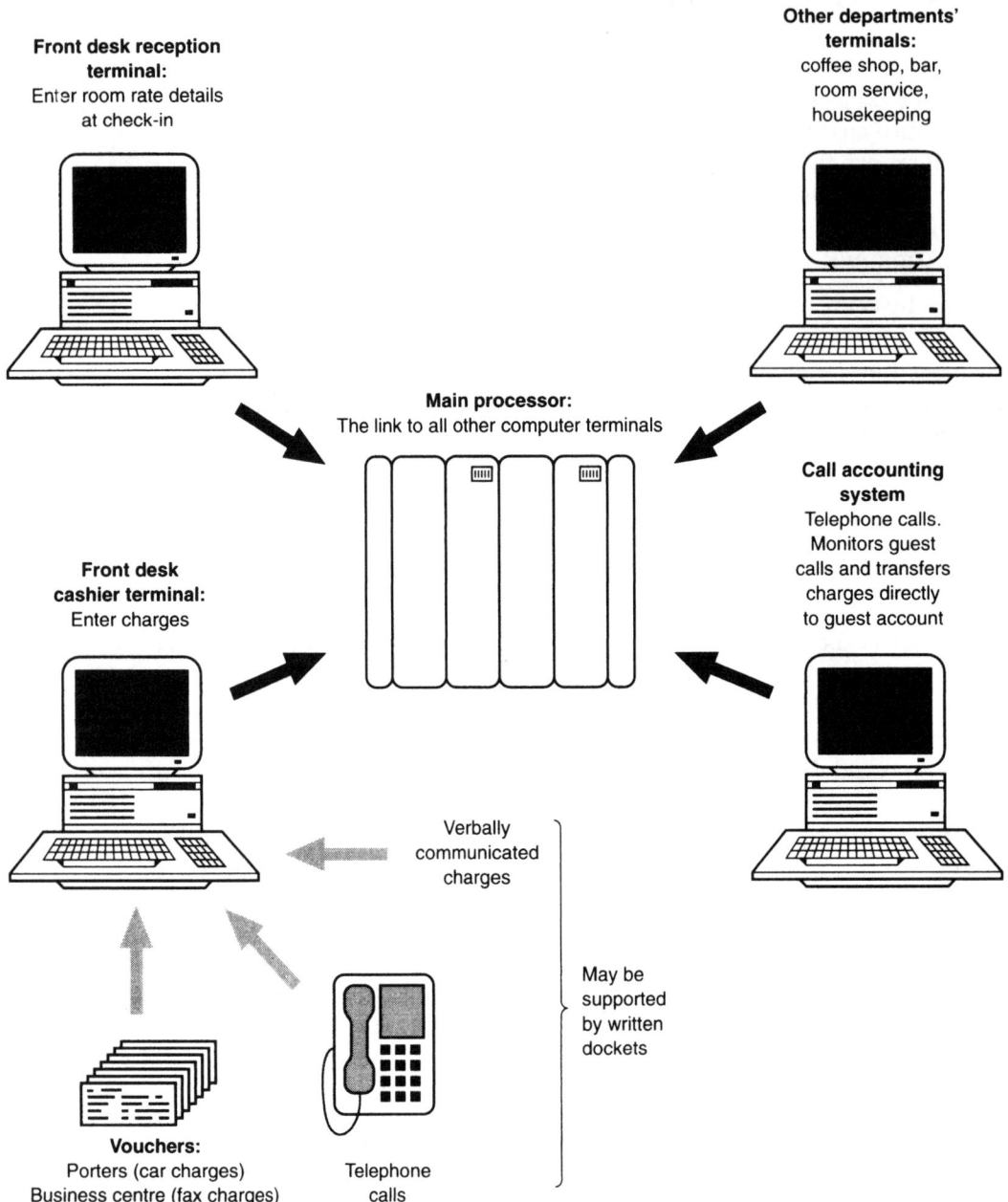

**Figure 9.4** A computer-based front office accounting system

main system at the front office. For example, some hotels have a call accounting system, where calls made from guest-rooms are monitored by a small computer. The charges for telephone calls are recorded by the small computer and transferred into the main computer at the front office for automatic posting.

- By vouchers or dockets. In the case where a department is not linked to the computer system at the front office, the front office cashier will be notified of any charges or credits by a voucher or docket (Figure 9.5). After receiving the information from other departments, the front office cashier will input the credit or charge onto the guest's account accordingly.

### KING'S HOTEL

## Fax Charges

| | | | |
|---|---|---|---|
| To: | Front Office Cashier | | |
| From: | Business Centre Supervisor | | |
| Guest name: | Mr W. Hunt | Room no.: | 262 |
| Date: | 16/12/99 | Time: | 12.40 p.m. |
| No. of pages: | 2 | Fax no.: | 83451245 |
| Charge: | £17.00 | | |

**Figure 9.5** A charge voucher/docket

**Activity 5**  Study Figure 9.4 again, and then answer the following questions.

(a) How will the charges for the following services be transferred from the department to the front office?

- A guest requesting extra flowers from the housekeeping department

- A guest making an international direct dial telephone call

- A guest requesting a car-hire service from the porter

- A guest purchasing some postcards from the hotel kiosk

(b) What benefits can a hotel enjoy by using a computerized front office accounting system?

---

## THE IMPORTANCE OF NIGHT AUDIT AND ITS ROLE IN THE HOTEL

The hotel industry operates 24 hours a day, 365 days a year. Therefore, all residents', non-residents' and management accounts should be reviewed and checked for accuracy on a daily basis. As previously mentioned, the front office accounting process can be divided into three phases: creation, maintenance and settlement of accounts. To ensure this has been done correctly a team of staff, normally called night auditors, is needed. Traditionally, night audit was performed during the night shifts because that was the period of low activity and would cause least disruption at the front desk. The function of night audit, whether it be with a manual or computerized system, is to:

- post any outstanding charges

- balance and verify all accounting transactions, including room charges and taxes

- detect and correct any accounting errors

- prepare cash receipts for deposit

- prepare and submit accounts for guests and non-guests who have reached or extended beyond their credit limit.

The night auditor should be aware of these credit limits, whether credit card limits or company account floor limits. If these limits are reached or exceeded, the night auditor will create what is called a high balance report, and either prepare the guest folio for settlement or create a report so that the information is passed to the front office manager for action. Also, the night auditor will prepare and distribute other relevant reports and statistical information for operational and management use, and finally, when using a computerized system, do a complete back-up of the day's business.

## Activity 6

(a) Explain why night audit is important in front office operations.

(b) Using a front office computerized system, list what reports could be prepared during the night audit function, and why.

### *Responsibilities of the night auditor*

The responsibilities of night auditors vary according to the size of the hotel. For example, in smaller establishments their roles and responsibilities increase in that they not only have the task of the night audit but also that of night manager, receptionist, security officer, telephonist, cashier, porter, etc., and all the other tasks that relate to those extra roles.

In larger hotels there are often two or more night auditors, one for food and beverage and one for rooms. On duty at night will be a porter, a telephonist, a security officer, a maintenance person, a duty manager, cleaners, a pastry chef, and very often night housekeeping crews.

### *Food and beverage night auditor*

The food and beverage night auditor is responsible for the food and beverage outlets, the balancing of each shift and the analysis and accurate totalling for each restaurant or department. In a non-point-of-sale (POS) system each register has to be 'Z'd' off. This is an expression that originated from the older days when all accounting machines were either mechanical or electromechanical. At the end of each day a 'Z' key was used to clear the machine of all figures of that day's activities, so that it left an empty machine for the next day's business. Despite the fact that computers no longer use 'Z' keys to clear the system, the expression to 'Z' off a machine is still used (much as we still talk about 'rack rates' when we no longer use racks to store the room rate). Credit cards, cash, signed guest charges and city ledger are all totalled separately, and all figures are entered on a spreadsheet on which the debits and credits are balanced. Food, beverage and miscellaneous charges must also be balanced against their various methods of payment.

## Activity 7

Explain what is meant by the term 'Z' and how it can apply to a computerized hotel accounting system.

### Rooms night auditor

It is normal for the rooms night auditor, whether in a large or small hotel, to have the roles of cashier, receptionist and reservations clerk for the 11p.m. to 7a.m. shift: checking in and out people who arrive or depart during those hours, as well as posting charges (where a POS is not used), recording reservations, dealing with foreign exchange and safety boxes, counting floats, posting room charges and reconciling guest charges.

### Verifying room status

As one of the objectives of night audit is to post and verify room and tax charges, it is important before doing so to check the status of each room. Checking the front office room status against the housekeeper's report will normally highlight any discrepancies. Figure 9.6 illustrates this. The front office room status shows that Room 102 is vacant, and the housekeeping report status shows it is occupied with one sleeper. It is important for housekeeping to check who is actually in the room and notify front office accordingly. The reason for the discrepancy could be that front office omitted to update their records for a new arrival, or there may have been a change of room. Similarly, Room 103's guest could have vacated the room and left without paying the account. It is important at this stage for the rooms night auditor to check for any discrepancies, especially as room revenue constitutes the main revenue for the hotel.

| Front Office Room Status | | Housekeeper's Report Status | |
|---|---|---|---|
| Room 101 | Occupied (2 sleepers) | Room 101 | Occupied (2 sleepers) |
| Room 102 | Vacant and clean | Room 102 | Occupied (1 sleeper) |
| Room 103 | Occupied (1 sleeper) | Room 103 | Vacant and clean |

**Figure 9.6**

### Arrivals, in-house and departures lists

Throughout the day, the arrivals, in-house and departures lists will change according to the guests actually arriving, staying on and departing. When using a computerized system the job is made easier. Until the guest actually checks into the hotel he/she will be shown as an expected arrival on the arrivals list. Once the guest registers into the hotel, the front office computer system will automatically update the arrivals list and room status. The same principle operates when a guest departs. Similarly, when a guest leaves early (understay) or decides to stay longer (overstay), the computer system will automatically amend the relevant lists. When using a manual system this is more difficult, and it is the responsibility of the night auditor to ensure that all these lists are checked carefully. They are important when posting or amending room charges, and when calculating the basic rooms sold from the arrivals and departures lists.

previous night's + today's rooms − today's rooms = tonight's rooms
rooms sold      arrivals      departures      sold

To calculate the number of rooms left to sell, simply deduct the number of rooms sold tonight from the total rooms available, but taking into account OOO and OOS rooms.

---

**Activity 8**    Either using a front office computerized system or a manual system, discuss how an arrivals, in-house and departures list can be used when checking the front office room status to verify that day's room charges.

---

### Examples of the duties of the night auditor

1   *Posting room charges.* A manual system would require these charges to be posted individually to each account – very tedious, time consuming and open to error. A fully computerized system will do this automatically upon request. It will post room charges including any taxes or service charges and any packages (Christmas, Easter, weekend specials, modified American plan, etc.). Although the computer posts the total charge to the guest's folio, it breaks down the expenditure to the relevant departments: for example, breakfast, lunch, dinner, bottle of wine, etc.

2   *Assembling guest charges and payments.* If a non-POS system is being used, all charges must be posted manually to the guest's account at the front desk. The auditor must reconcile these charges by comparing the charges posted to actual relevant paperwork. This can also be called 'marrying up', where the original voucher/document is checked and verified with a duplicate copy.

3   *Reconciling departmental financial activities.* All of the various cashiers' work (both restaurant and front desk) is audited and

totals are checked in order to confirm that all postings have the supporting paperwork and are correct. The cashiers must submit all supporting paperwork and summaries that confirm the total of all the various types of payment. Each department or outlet may well have more than one set of paperwork for the day, i.e. breakfast, lunch and dinner, and each has to be audited separately and then a grand total per outlet established. This is done so that the hotels can have accurate performance figures for different meal times as well as for the entire day. Once shift and outlet paperwork has been audited and balanced, the methods of payment, i.e. credit cards, cash, city ledger and signed dockets are separated and each outlet's payment group individually totalled. They are then combined with all the other outlets' methods of payment once they have been audited and a cumulative total reached. This will give a total manual figure for each method of payment, and this is then balanced against the machine or computer figure,

e.g. debits (food) − credit (settlement).

Any account corrections should also be audited, for example, an incorrect amount posted. Normally the front office or restaurant supervisor will countersign any corrections on the supporting documents which could affect the overall balance.

4  *Running the trial balance.* This is a first run of a set of debits to determine their accuracy against a set of credits:

previous balance + debits − credits = new outstanding balance.

We are basically determining what the product is that has been sold, and its cost, and how it has been paid for. In an ideal world this should balance every time. However, this depends on amounts being posted correctly, credit cards being charged the correct amount, and amounts being recorded correctly. The failure to successfully do any or all of these transactions is always due to human error. The trial balance (D-Report) is usually run several times during the night so that errors can be picked up and subsequently rectified. The auditor checking vouchers, transfers and paid-out slips against the various cashiers' summaries and transaction analyses picks up the errors. Once the trial balance has been completed the night auditor frequently prepares a cash deposit voucher as a part of the night audit function. For cash which has not been banked, the night auditor will compare the postings of cash payments and paid-outs with actual cash on hand and the front office cashier shift report. Any shortages or overages should be recorded.

5   *Reconciling accounts receivable.* The city ledger is an 'accounts receivable' ledger that is held at the front office. This is a register of accounts of guests not staying at the hotel who have received approval to sign for goods and services received in the hotel. In exactly the same way as with guest-room account charges, the city ledger charges must be verified and justified by the night auditor.

6   *Preparing the night audit report.* This is a report of all of the financial transactions of the day. This report is structured specifically for each individual establishment, and is based upon what information is required by that hotel. Some may require only actual figures, while others may also require budget figures and goal percentages. Daily review of the night audit report allows management the opportunity to be flexible in meeting financial goals and in assisting with yield management.

---

**Activity 9**   Explain what is involved in the actual operations of a night auditor working in a small hotel.

---

### The importance of the reports generated by the night audit

The night audit process generates many reports as a result of information recorded on activities, both financial and physical, in the hotel during the day. This information is essential in order to enable management to keep up-to-date on room availability, reservations, average room rates, guest credit levels, restaurant activity, and so on. The reports generated by the night audit process on the property management system or manual system are distributed to the relevant departments for their immediate information.

### PRODUCING MANAGEMENT REPORTS

Computers are capable of producing a great variety of management reports. Figure 9.7 gives a list of some of the kinds of management reports which are available from one computer system. More detailed information on management reports will be given in Chapter 11.

Some of the purposes for which management uses front office reports are as follows:

```
┌─────────────────────────────────────────────┐
│           Management Reports Menu 1          │
├─────────────────────────────────────────────┤
│  1. Management statistics report:            │
│         room occupancy and %                 │
│         no. of guests and %                  │
│         rooms revenue and %                  │
│         commissions paid                     │
│         yield %                              │
│         average room rate                    │
│                                              │
│  2. Room type usage report                   │
│                                              │
│  3. Marketing statistics graphs:             │
│         client types                         │
│         guest origin                         │
│         sources of business                  │
│         room rate mix                        │
│                                              │
│  4. Future revenue forecast                  │
│                                              │
│  5. Marketing analysis: revenue by segment   │
│                                              │
└─────────────────────────────────────────────┘
```

**Figure 9.7** The management reports menu of a computer system

- Guest origin report. This report analyses the number of guests by their country of origin (i.e. nationality). It can be used to compare the origins of the previous year's guests, to see whether the proportion of people of different nationalities using the hotel has changed. For the sales and marketing departments this is useful because they can organize services to suit different nationalities, and possibly arrange sales promotions in countries which are not using the hotel.

- Room rate uptake report. This report identifies which room rate is most popular, and which tariffs are rarely used. Once again, the marketing department can use the information to choose the most effective tariff structure to attract guests.

- Future revenue forecast report. This report shows the revenue which can be expected according to the number of reservations in the computer. It can highlight periods of low revenue to the front office and rooms division manager. Information from this report can be used to promote sales as well as encourage the letting of more rooms during the low period to tour and corporate companies.

The importance of the front office in the collecting of statistical information cannot be overstressed. A lot of important planning decisions rely on accurate information from the rooms division.

## SUMMARY

In this chapter we have looked at the main functions of the front office account system, i.e. the maintenance of accurate records of all guest accounts, the provision of effective internal controls, and management information.

To ensure that guests are billed correctly for the services and facilities used, good procedures must exist whereby these charges are speedily transferred to the cashier's desk. The easiest way of looking upon the details recorded on a guest bill is as a story. It is a story of the movements and transactions the guest had within the hotel.

Apart from a resident's bill, other accounts are held at the front desk. These are city accounts for non-residents who use the hotel, and management accounts, which are accounts primarily used for management entertainment.

The cycle of the front office account system is very much in chronological order. It begins when the guest arrives and is assigned a room, with the accompanying rate, and ends upon settlement of the final bill. In some instances the bill is simply signed by the guest and sent on to a company or travel agent for eventual payment.

Guest accounts are created when the guest uses a service or facility and, instead of paying cash, signing a docket in acknowledgement that they have used the hotel's services. This docket or charge will eventually be posted onto the guest's bill. This is known as a debit entry. Occasionally, corrections or alterations are made to a bill and amounts are removed from it; the removal of charges is called a credit entry. This is also the case when a guest part pays their bill.

A VPO or visitors paid out is another form of guest posting.

Many hotels use manual account systems, but, with the reduction in cost of electronic equipment, computerization is becoming more and more popular. The benefits are that the transfer of charges and information is almost instantaneous, and their accuracy is exceptional, provided that the operators are careful with their information input.

# Review and discussion questions

1   What is an audit? Why is it necessary?

2   You are the front office manager and have been asked to introduce a front office accounting system

into your hotel. Explain which system you would introduce and give your reasons why.

3   Explain the differences between debit and credit entries, giving relevant examples.

4   Explain what is meant by the term 'VPO'.

5   Explain how a computer system has been modernized in recent years to handle front office accounts.

# 10

# Check-out and settlement of accounts

## Introduction

In Chapter 9, we examined how guest accounts are prepared. In this chapter, we shall look at the settlement of accounts and check-out procedures.

We start by explaining the duties and procedures of the front office at the time of check-out. We then discuss the problems associated with late check-outs and late charges and the different types of accounts and settlement methods which are used. Finally, we examine the role of the front office staff in the updating of front office records after the departure of a guest, and in the creation of a good lasting impression to guests.

## A SUMMARY OF FRONT OFFICE DUTIES AT CHECK-OUT

One of the last contacts the guest has with the hotel is the check-out procedure. It is also most probably the last chance for a guest to interact face to face with hotel staff. It is, therefore, of great importance that guests' financial transactions with a hotel are properly settled before they leave. The quality of service that guests receive at check-out will also influence their final impressions of a hotel. A bad meal can be resurrected by a good dessert. The same is true of a guest's stay. If they had experienced some dissatisfaction with the hotel, the check-out clerks can improve their opinion of it by being friendly, courteous and efficient.

After departure, a guest's room will be available for resale to other guests. Consequently, room status information has to be updated immediately and the front office records must also be amended.

In summary, the process of check-out (usually performed by the front office cashier) involves the settlement of guests' accounts and the updating of front office records. The main duties of the front office at check-out include:

- settlement of guest accounts
- updating front office records after guest departures
- creating good, lasting impressions

## THE CHECK-OUT PROCEDURE

When checking out a departing guest, front office staff should follow certain basic procedures (Figure 10.1).

Here is a list of guidelines which you should follow when checking out guests:

1. Greet guest. Always greet guests with a smile and say, 'Good morning' or 'Good evening', and always try to use their names.

2. Confirm guest details (i.e. name and room number) against the guest's account.

3. Check departure date. If the guest is leaving earlier than expected, other departments will need to be informed.

4. Check whether late check-out charges should be applied. If the guest is leaving after the 12 noon check-out time, and is not a

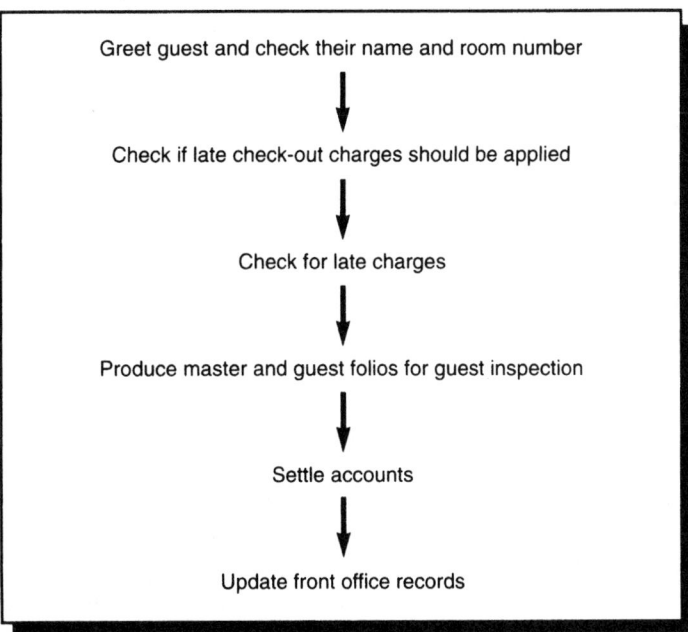

**Figure 10.1** Basic check-out procedures

frequent guest, add the relevant late check-out charge to the account.

5. Check for late charges. Examine current entries on a guest's account, and in particular check out any mini-bar, breakfast or telephone charges.

6. Give the guest the master and/or guest folios for checking. When the guest checked in, the receptionist will have determined whether one or two folios are to be produced. All queries must be handled without fuss and in a pleasant, helpful manner, in order to give a good impression of the hotel.

7. Guest settlement of accounts.

8. Provide front office services upon guest departure such as receiving the guest's key and checking if they have used a safe deposit box which now needs to be emptied.

9. Offer the assistance of the bell staff to collect the luggage.

10. See if the guest would like to make a future reservation, or an onward reservation in another hotel within the chain.

11. Update front office records. The most important records to update are the room status list and the residents list. It is

important to do this, in order that other departments can accurately know the room and guest status.

## LATE CHECK-OUTS

When a request for check-out is received from a guest, the front office staff should first determine whether a late check-out charge is to be added to the guest account. Most hotels have a stated check-out time at which departing guests must vacate their rooms. In general, check-out time is between 10.00a.m. and noon. The information regarding this should be written on the key card, as well as stated in the information folder in the hotel guest-room. If guests do not vacate their rooms by the check-out time, a late check-out charge may be imposed. To avoid misunderstandings between guests and the hotel, guests are often asked about their expected departure time at check-in, and they should be informed of the extra charge which could be levied for late check-outs.

Check-out time can sometimes be a problem for tour groups. Pleasure travellers want to enjoy every moment of their holiday, so if their coach does not leave the hotel until 4p.m., for example, they dislike being asked to vacate their rooms at 12 noon. In these situations hotels usually arrange to have the guests' luggage stored with the concierge, and reserve one or more hospitality or complimentary rooms at no extra charge. These arrangements allow the group rooms to be vacated for subsequent guests, while the hospitality rooms are still available for the comfort of the tour group.

---

**Activity 1**

(a) What are the benefits to the hotel in asking guests their expected departure time when they check in?

(b) A walk-in guest requests a late check-out of 4.00p.m. on the date of departure. Explain how their request should be handled.

(c) If the guest in (b) is a frequent guest, would their request be dealt with differently? Why? Why not?

---

## LATE CHARGES

A late charge is a charge for a service or facility which is sent to the cashier too late to be added to a guest's account for settlement. For example, a laundry charge may arrive at the front office cashier after the guest has already settled the bill and possibly left the hotel. In such situations, it may be difficult for a hotel to collect payment from its guests.

In order to reduce the losses due to the late arrival of charges, the cashier should confirm whether there are outstanding charges before producing the guest's accounts. The cashier may, for example, ask the guests whether they have used the mini-bar or other services that morning, and check the bill to see whether charges for breakfast that morning or other charges have been included. However, this is relying upon the honesty of the guest, and does not reflect a particularly organized or professional hotel.

This investigation of late charges is not easy and, apart from inconveniencing the guests while checks are made, it creates extra work for the busy cashier. Many hotels accept that a certain level of loss will be experienced due to late charges, and consequently charge high prices for items such as mini-bars to compensate. To avoid an unnecessary delay and inefficient service at check-out, a well-designed and well-functioning accounting system is needed. This will ensure that:

- guest charges from various departments are sent to the front office as soon as possible if not immediately.

- all charges are posted to the guest account once they are received.

It is for these reasons that computerized accounting systems are advantageous; they greatly speed up the transfer of charge information between departments and the front desk.

---

**Activity 2**　(a)　Why do hotels need to prevent late charges?

(b)　Explain what the following hotel personnel could do to help reduce late charges:

- the front office cashier

- the room attendants from the housekeeping departments

---

## METHODS OF ACCOUNT SETTLEMENT

As you will have noted, the settlement of guest accounts is a comprehensive process; we will now look at the methods used.

### Own accounts and company accounts

Accounts to be settled at check-out can be divided into two main types: own accounts and company accounts. They differ mainly in terms of who is paying the bill. Own accounts are those accounts which will be settled by the guest.

The guest may pay the bill on their departure with currency (local or foreign), personal cheques, traveller's cheques, bank credit cards or charge cards.

Company accounts, on the other hand, are those accounts which are not settled directly by the guest, but are settled by a company or a travel agent. These accounts are transferred to the accounts department after the guest has checked and signed the bill as being correct.

The accounts department then sends the bill and invoice to the company or travel agent for payment.

### Types of settlement

There are two main types of account settlement: cash and credit.

### Cash settlements

A cash settlement is any form of settlement which can be paid into the bank on the same day as it is received. Under this classification, cash settlements can include settlements:

- in local currency

- in foreign currency

- in traveller's cheques

- by personal cheques

- by bank credit cards – these are cards which are issued by banks, and are considered as being equivalent to cash settlements because their imprints can be taken to the bank each day, and the charge amount will be paid into a hotel's account on the same day. The best-known examples are Visa and MasterCard.

### Credit settlements

Credit settlements are settlements for which a hotel does not receive immediate payment on the day of departure. These include:

- settlements by charge card

- settlements of corporate accounts

- travel agent vouchers

Charge cards are credit cards which are issued by private credit card organizations, e.g. American Express and Diners Club. When a guest settles their account with a charge card, the hotel does not receive payment on the same day. Instead, at the end of each shift the cashier will transfer all of the bills settled by charge card to the accounts department for them to follow up.

At the end of the week or month, the accounts department will send out statements of the total amount charged to the private credit card organizations, together with copies of all the imprints. On receiving the statement and imprints, the credit card company will pay the amount to the hotel less its commission.

In the cases of corporate accounts and travel agent vouchers, the bills will also be transferred to the accounts department. The accounts department will then mail the account and invoice to the company or agent, and later receive a cheque in settlement. Once again the travel agency will send its settlement less their commission. Figure 10.2 summarizes the types of accounts and the settlement methods.

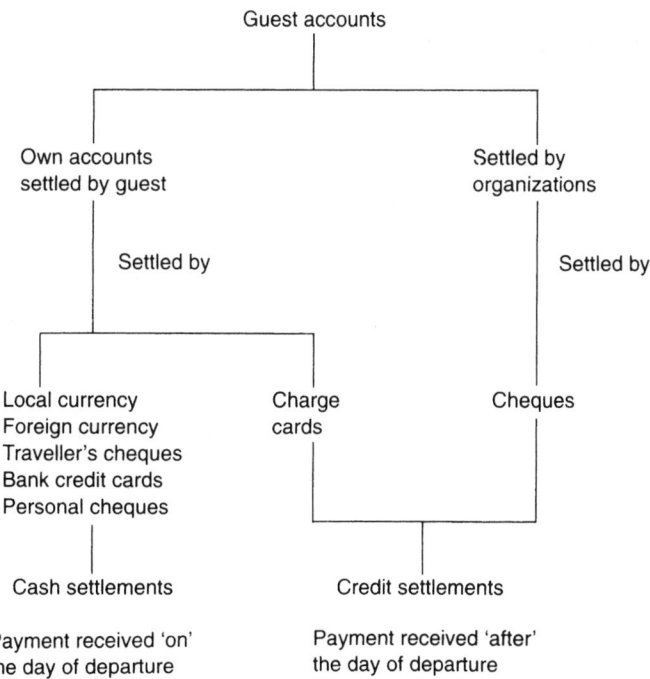

**Figure 10.2** The types of accounts and the settlement methods

## Activity 3

For each of the following cases, state the types of account and whether the settlements are in cash or credit.

- A business person whose full account will be paid by IBM Ltd.

- An FIT who agrees to settle his account by American Express card

- A couple whose accommodation is to be settled by Oriental Tours Co. Ltd., but who will settle their incidentals by Visa card

### Procedures for accepting settlements

The guest usually agrees the method of bill settlement upon arrival. The actual settlement process then consists of checking that the account is accurate and that the correct accounting procedures are followed.

### Corporate and travel agent's accounts

Very often a company or travel agent will settle only the guest-room and possibly the breakfast charges. Incidental charges such as telephone, laundry and drinks must be settled by guests themselves. In these cases, the guest account is divided into two, i.e. master accounts, settled by companies or travel agents, and incidental accounts, settled by the guests.

The different techniques for handling corporate and travel agent accounts are explained in Table 10.1.

## Activity 4

A guest whose full account is settled by her company is planning to leave the hotel today.

(a) What effects does it have on the hotel if she does not come to the front desk before she leaves?

(b) What has to be done by the hotel after the guest has checked out to ensure settlement?

### Guest or incidental accounts

Guest accounts are settled by the guests themselves, and they may choose to pay by credit card, cash, traveller's cheque or personal cheque. The procedures of accepting these forms of settlement are as follows.

**Table 10.1** Different techniques for handling corporate and travel agent accounts

| Type of account | Coroporate account | Travel agent's account |
| --- | --- | --- |
| Master | Settled by company. Shown to the guest for inspection, verification and signature at check-out. | A voucher is issued by the travel agent to the guests At check-in the voucher is collected from the guest by the receptionist The cashier ensures that the travel agent is on the approved travel agent list (compiled by the sales and accounts department) At check-out the cashier must ensure that the guest pays for all items not covered by voucher The master account is *not* given to the guest at check-out (because the room rate paid by guest to the travel agent might not be the same as that paid by the travel agent to the hotel) After check-out the master and attached voucher will be transferred to the accounts department. At the end of the week or month the vouchers and a statement of the total account will be sent to the travel agent. Guests will be given their incidentals account for settlement. |
| Incidental | Settled by guest, by cash, credit card, or personal cheque A receipt is given to the guest | Settlement is usually by cash, credit card or personal cheque. A receipt is given to the guest |

### *Accepting credit card or charge card settlements*

On arrival when a guest proposes to settle their account by credit card, the cashier must carry out various checks. The cashier should check that:

- the card is accepted by the hotel

- the name and signature on the card are the same as those on the registration card

- the card has not passed its expiry date

- the card number is not listed on the cancellation bulletin as stolen or invalid

An imprint of the card will then be taken by the receptionist. If the guest is a walk-in or has a non-guaranteed reservation, the receptionist will pass the card through the electronic PDQ credit card machine or manually phone the credit card company for authorization. The registration card and imprinted voucher are then handed to the cashier after check-in and stored in the bill tray.

Upon check-out, when the account is finally settled by credit card, the cashier enters the bill total and date on the credit card voucher. The guest then signs the completed, detailed imprinted voucher and hands it back to the cashier, who will check to ensure that the signature matches the signature on the credit card. During the signing of the voucher the receptionist should mask the signature on the card from the guest.

Should the bill be higher than the hotel's 'floor limit', then, regardless of the guest's reservation status, authorization must be obtained. A floor limit is the limit given to an establishment by the credit card company up to which a guest's bill may reach, before the hotel has to phone for permission to exceed that limit.

The last action of the cashier is to complete the guest's account. The top copy of the account, and the cardholder's copy of the credit card imprint, are given to the guest.

### Accepting cash settlements

The procedures for accepting cash settlements are summarized in Table 10.2. Bear in mind that there will be some variations in these procedures among hotels (see also Figure 10.3, p. 196).

---

**Activity 5**   A guest is checking out and the outstanding balance of the account is £895.00. The guest agreed at check-in that they would settle their account by Visa card.

(a) What checks should the cashier carry out before finalizing the settlement?

**Table 10.2** Procedures for accepting cash settlements

| Method of payment | Procedures |
| --- | --- |
| Local currency | The cashier accepts and counts cash in front of the guest<br>Any change and a receipt are given to the guest. |
| Personal cheques | Do not accept a cheque without a cheque card<br>Is the cheque card limit sufficient to cover the bill?<br>Has the cheque card expired?<br>Is the signature on the card the same as on the cheque?<br>Is the date correct?<br>Does the amount in words agree with the amount in figures?<br>Is the name of the hotel spelt correctly?<br>Cheques drawn on foreign banks and third party cheques should not be accepted. |
| Traveller's cheques | The cashier must ensure that the second signature on the cheque is written in front of them (the first signature was made when the guest collected the traveller's cheques from the bank/travel agent).<br>The cashier may also ask to see the guest's passport as a double check of identity, and record the number on the back of the cheques.<br>If the traveller's cheque is in a foreign currency, the cashier must calculate the foreign exchange rate conversion.<br>All change must be given in the local currency |
| Foreign currency | The cashier converts the bill charge into the foreign currency before account is settled.<br>A record of the currency (foreign exchange voucher) transaction is given to the guest; this is to show the guest the exchange rate and to prevent fraud.<br>The cashier may request the guest to sign for each currency transaction as proof of acceptance.<br>All change must be given in the local currency. |

(b) If the guest had chosen to settle the account by American Express card instead of Visa card, would the procedures of accepting the settlement be different? Why? Why not?

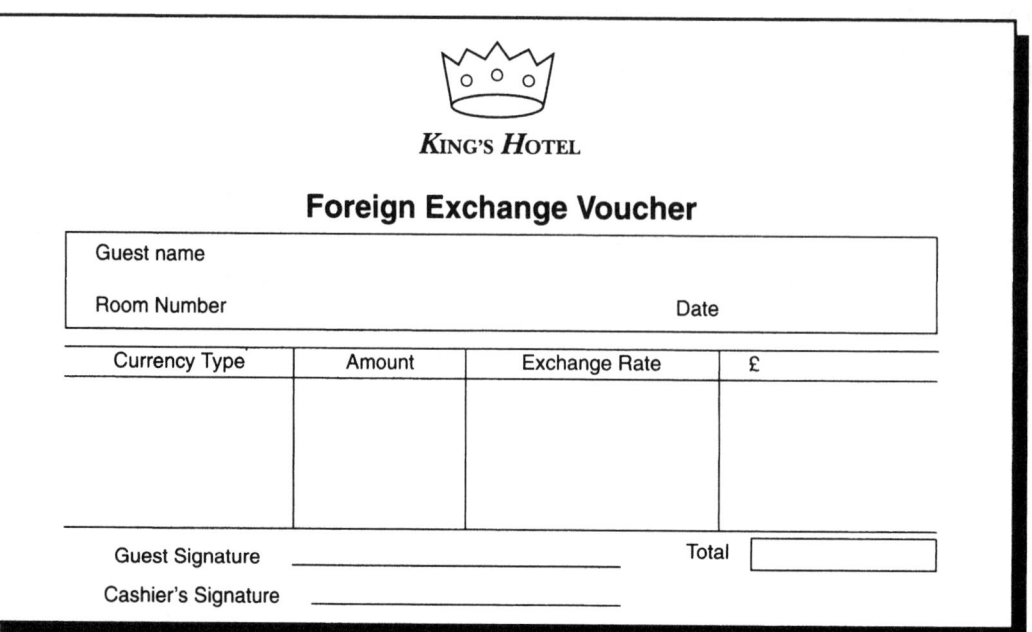

**Figure 10.3** A foreign exchange voucher

Figure 10.4 summarizes the procedures for handling different types of accounts and the settlement methods used.

## EXPRESS CHECK-OUT

In most hotels guests tend to check out at approximately the same time, and consequently the cashier's desk becomes very busy during that period. Hotels therefore offer an express check-out service (Figure 10.5) which allows guests to check out without having to queue at the cashier's desk. This also helps the cashier by reducing the pressure of work at busy times. In hotels with express check-out services, special forms are placed in guest-rooms as well as being available from the front office. By signing the express check-out form, the guest agrees to have the account finalized by the front office cashier after they have left the hotel.

On the morning of the date of departure, a copy of the guest's account, indicating the approximate total, may be sent to the guest's room. The guest may now leave the hotel at their convenience without having to call at the cashier's desk. After the guest has left, the cashier will finalize the account, including any late charges, and complete the imprinted credit card voucher.

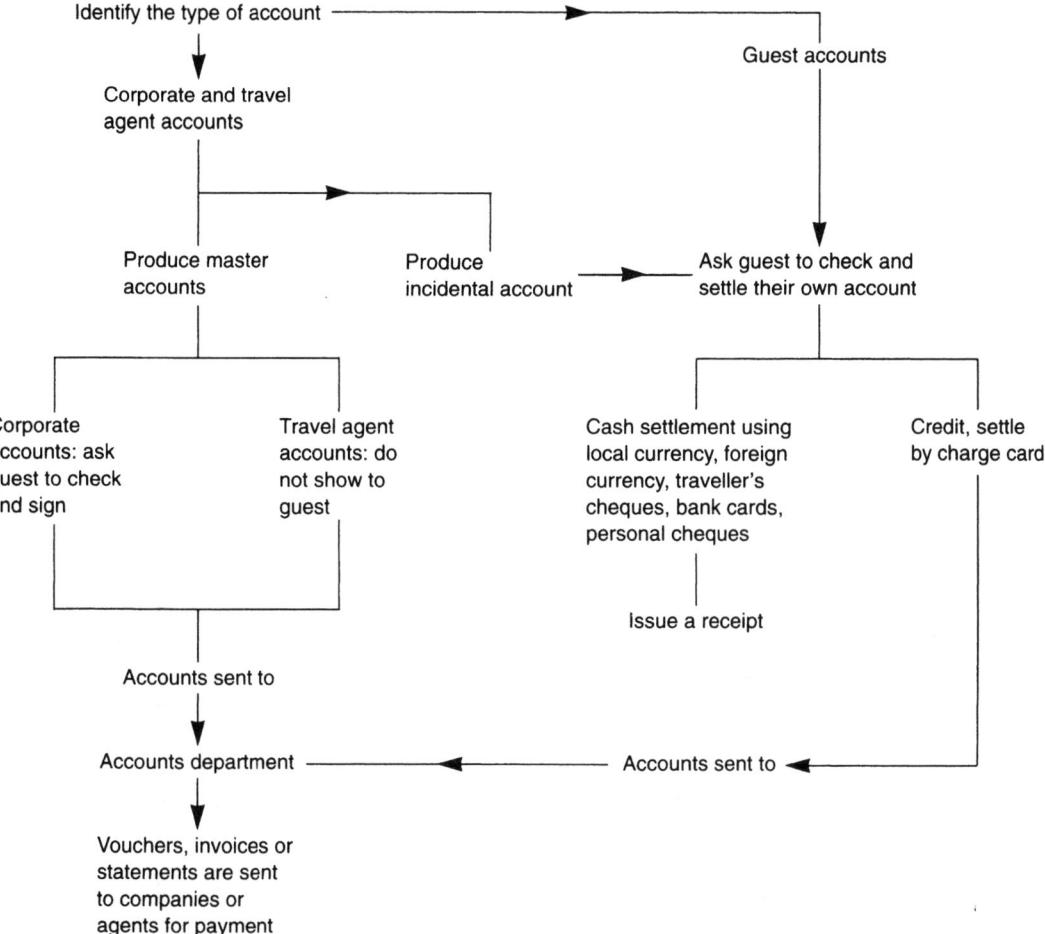

**Figure 10.4** Accepting settlements

The signature on the express check-out form will replace the signature on the credit card voucher as the guest's agreement to the payment. The imprint and the signed check-out form will be sent to the credit card company for settlement.

In some hotels a copy of the guest's final account is mailed to the home address of the guest so that they may check the balance on the monthly statement from the credit card company.

**Activity 6** Would you recommend the express check-out service to the following guests who intend to leave the next day? Why or why not?

- A businesswoman who needs to leave at 7.00a.m.

- A young couple who will check out at 4.30p.m.

- A businessman who has an important business appointment at 9 a.m. on his date of departure

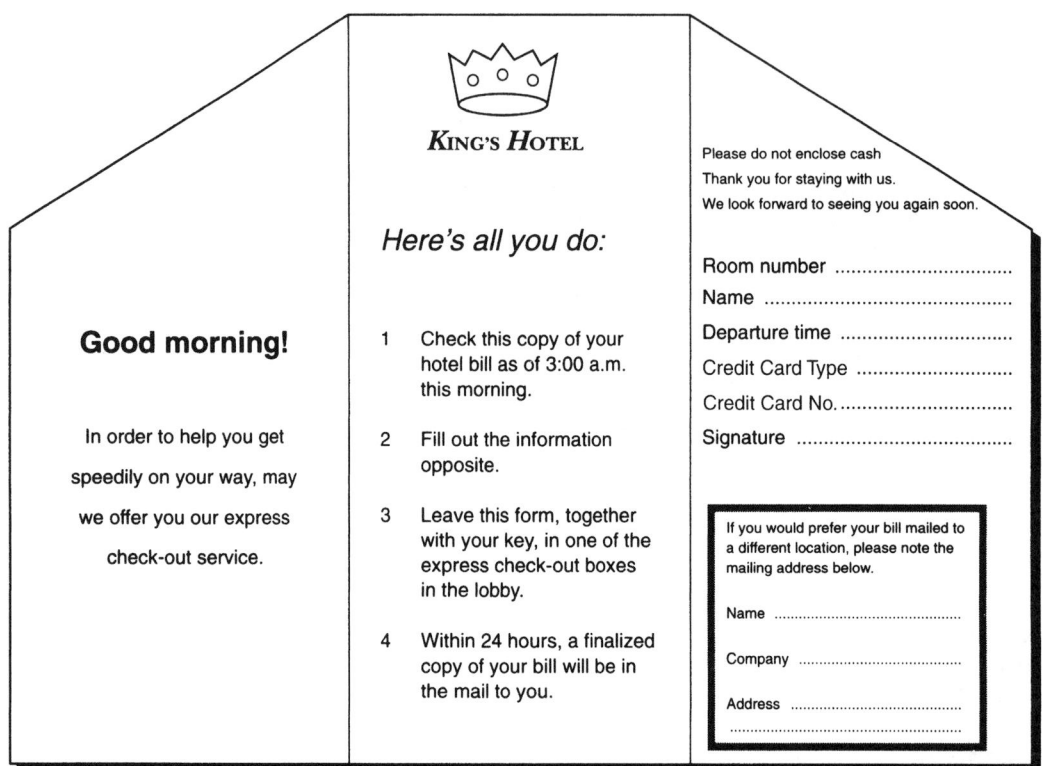

**KING'S HOTEL**

*Here's all you do:*

**Good morning!**

In order to help you get speedily on your way, may we offer you our express check-out service.

1   Check this copy of your hotel bill as of 3:00 a.m. this morning.

2   Fill out the information opposite.

3   Leave this form, together with your key, in one of the express check-out boxes in the lobby.

4   Within 24 hours, a finalized copy of your bill will be in the mail to you.

Please do not enclose cash
Thank you for staying with us.
We look forward to seeing you again soon.

Room number ...............................
Name ...............................
Departure time ...............................
Credit Card Type ...........................
Credit Card No. ...........................
Signature ...........................

If you would prefer your bill mailed to a different location, please note the mailing address below.

Name ...........................

Company ...........................

Address ...........................
...........................

**Figure 10.5** An express check-out form

## CREATING A GOOD LAST IMPRESSION

We have already discussed the need for creating the right first impression at check-in; it is equally important that at check-out a guest should be given a good last impression. Staff who are not warm, friendly or willing to help can make guests feel unwanted and uncared for, and as a consequence they may feel that they do not want to return to the hotel. The following guidelines may help you to create a good last impression at check-out.

1. The accounts must be accurately and neatly produced. Incorrect amounts mean delays to guests at the check-out desk, which cause the guest annoyance and make the front office desk appear inefficient.

2. The front office cashiers should be well trained in social skills and check-out procedures. They should be pleasant and helpful, and skilled and efficient in checking out guests. Their manner should not be so hurried that they make departing guests feel that the hotel is no longer interested in them, but should be speedily efficient.

3. Sometimes, guests may have queries or complaints concerning their accounts. These should be handled without fuss, always trying to ensure that the guest is satisfied. If a guest wishes to make a complaint, the cashier must listen patiently and with empathy. Should a guest complain and demand a reduction of the account, the cashier should again listen empathetically and do what they can to rectify the situation. However, on occasion it may become necessary to refer the matter to the front office manager.

## UPDATING FRONT OFFICE RECORDS

When a guest has checked out, the front office is responsible for updating all records as soon as possible.

### Room status and front office records

After a guest has checked out, their room will become vacant and available for letting to other guests. Consequently, the guest is no longer a resident of the hotel, and, therefore, the room status information and front office records (e.g. the resident guest list) must be changed immediately to keep them current.

In large hotels with computerized front office systems, the updating process is automatically done by the computer. After the guest has been recorded as having checked out, the system will automatically change the room status from occupied to vacant/dirty. The name of the guest will be removed from the residents list and transferred to the checked-out guests list and the guest's account will be transferred into a past guests file in the computer. However, it must be remembered that the registration card must be stored for the legally required 12 months.

### Guest history records

In some hotels a guest history record is kept. This is a record of the guest's room, and rate charged, their likes and dislikes if known, as well as the amount which they spent in the hotel. One member of the front office staff will be given the duty of the daily updating of the guest history record. The records may be kept on the computer, or on handwritten record cards.

When creating and updating the guest history record, a hotel will need to decide which guests should be added to the guest history records (i.e. all guests, or frequent guests only). In hotels with a computerized front office system, the computer will automatically open a new guest history record for guests who stayed in the hotel for the first time. The computer system will also automatically update existing guest history records on check-out by transferring the account details onto the existing guest history record.

Apart from creating and updating guest history records, an annual review of all guest history records is needed. Some records may have to be discarded (e.g. records of guests who have not returned for a long time, or whose company no longer has a corporate account at the hotel). In smaller hotels, guest history cards may not be kept, but this is very much up to the policy of each property.

---

**Activity 7**   Imagine that you are a front office cashier. One day, a guest who was checking out complained that her laundry had not been returned as quickly as she had been led to expect and asked for the charge to be removed from her bill. What actions should you take to deal with the incident? Why?

---

## SUMMARY

At the beginning of this book we discussed how important first impressions are to guests; the way they are greeted and made to feel at home sets the tone for the rest of their stay. The treatment a guest receives when he or she comes to check out is equally important. The guest can see the welcome and courteous attention they receive on settling their bill as final evidence of an enjoyable stay in the hotel. On the other hand, it may be the salve that was needed to repair the damage done if the guest had experienced mediocre service. Either way, the front desk cashier plays a vital role in customer relations.

Apart from ensuring that guests leave the hotel in a contented frame of mind, other duties at check-out include the preparation of the bill, confirmation of late or delayed charges and receiving settlement for the bill. The late check-out procedures were explained. To ensure that guest misunderstanding does not occur, it was suggested that reception inform the guest at check-in exactly what time they are expected to vacate their room.

Another problem for the cashier is how to handle late charges, i.e. those charges which arrive at the desk after the guest has gone. Usually it is not possible to claim this money, so a routine has to be established at check-out to find out what services the guest may have used just prior to their departure.

It was explained how guest methods of payment are split into two distinct sections: forms of payment where the hotel has the settlement on the day the guest departs, i.e. cash settlement; and credit settlement, when the hotel has to wait for reimbursement. Cash settlements include local currency, foreign currency, traveller's cheques, bank credit cards and personal cheques. Corporate accounts, travel agents' vouchers and travel and entertainment cards (American Express and Diners) are seen as forms of credit settlement. The necessary steps to be taken when receiving these types of payment were explained.

Finally, the express check-out system was covered. This system is used primarily to help relieve congestion when several guests are all waiting to check out at the same time.

# Review and discussion questions

1   Discuss the differences between cash and credit settlement.

2   Explain what the term 'incidental expenses' means and give relevant examples.

3   Discuss why late charges can concern the management of a hotel operation.

4   The worth of cash and credit settlements can affect the cash flow of a business'. Explain this statement.

5   Cash can be a security problem. Can this apply to all methods of payment?

6   You are the front office manager of a hotel. Recently, there have been a lot of complaints from guests that they had to wait for a very long time when checking out. On investigation, you find that the delays are due to: peak check-out at 8.30a.m.; time spent checking for late charges; and guest accounts not being ready for presentation when the guests check out. Suggest what you could do to help solve the problem.

7   Explain the advantages of an express check-out service.

# Case Study: 'There Must be Easier Ways to Earn a Living' – Mr O'Leary

It was nearly 11.00a.m. and at last you had managed to sit down in your office after an extremely fraught and upsetting 2 hours at the reception desk. It had seemed as though all of the problem guests had decided to depart at the same time, but in fact it had just been three separate incidents that had caused all of the problems.

Firstly Mr O'Leary had arrived to check out and pay his account. He had initially checked into the hotel for three nights on a special weekend package rate; however he then extended his stay for a further three nights to conclude some business in town. Upon printing out the bill for Mr O'Leary the receptionist noticed that he had been charged the extra three nights at the special weekend rate rather than the normal full rate. Accordingly she amended the bill and presented it to Mr O'Leary.

On seeing the rates that he had been charged he became most irate, and explained that he had approached the receptionist on Monday morning to extend his stay and was assured that he could have the special rate also extended. Therefore he was refusing to pay the extra pounds. At this point you had been called in to sort things out. On checking you found that it was one of the trainee receptionists who had spoken to Mr O'Leary. Although she felt sure she had not said that he could have the special rate, she could not be absolutely certain.

## Action as front office manager regarding Mr O'Leary

1. How would you handle Mr O'Leary?

2. Would you charge the extra pounds?

3. What systems or procedures would you put into place to ensure that such a mishap would not happen again?

4. What would you say to the trainee receptionist?

# 11

# *Credit control*

## Introduction

We pointed out earlier that in many hotels, guests are allowed to enjoy hotel services and facilities on credit. In other words, hotels will receive payment only on or after a guest's departure. In these cases, a hotel must take some measures to ensure that guests' accounts will be settled in full and at the agreed time. Otherwise, a lot of revenue will be lost, and there will be a problem with cash flow.

In Chapters 9 and 10, we looked at how guests' bills are prepared and settled. In this chapter, we shall concentrate on how a hotel can control its credit to guests in order to ensure a healthy cash flow.

We shall start by explaining the meaning of and the reasons for credit control in a hotel. We shall then describe the credit control measures that are taken by the various front office sections at the different stages of a guest's stay, and find out why they are needed. The last part of the chapter will discuss the legal rights of the hotel should a guest fail to settle their account.

## THE MEANING OF CREDIT CONTROL

Credit control refers to the various measures taken by a hotel to ensure that guests settle their accounts in full at an agreed time.

Controlling credit is the responsibility of the credit manager or clerk, who is a member of the accounts department. However, the process also necessitates that specific measures be taken by various departments of a hotel at different phases of the guest cycle. A credit manager cannot fulfil his or her role unless all hotel staff cooperate and perform their own credit control duties.

As you work through this chapter, you will find that many of the credit control measures have been mentioned in previous chapters.

## WHY CREDIT CONTROL IS NECESSARY

Hotels, like any other businesses, need to have a healthy cash flow in order to survive and succeed, and try to achieve this by exercising control over the credit given to guests. The cash flow of a hotel is the money which moves in and out of the business.

## OBJECTIVES OF CREDIT CONTROL MEASURES

The main objectives of credit control measures are:

- To prevent walk-out (skips). As you will remember from previous chapters, walk-outs are guests who leave a hotel without settling their accounts. They include guests who deliberately intend to leave the hotel without paying their accounts as well as those who do not realize that they have to check out with the cashier. This is because they know that their companies have agreed to settle their accounts.

- To reduce the problems caused by walk-out guests. As well as the lost revenue, they cause a great deal of inconvenience to a variety of people, such as the cashier, who will not have verification of bills, the housekeeper, who will not know the room status, the management, who may decide to instigate legal proceedings, and the police, who would have to alert other properties in their search for the guest.

- To prevent late settlement of accounts. Since most accounts are settled by the guests on departure, there are few problems of late settlement for these accounts. But corporate or travel agent accounts are sent to the companies or travel agents after the guests have departed. While hotels usually expect that a cheque for settlement should be received within 30 days, in some cases they may have to wait a long time before a cheque is actually received. In some instances the agent or company may go out of business before settling the invoice, in which case the hotel does not receive any payment.

Delay in payments can cause cash flow problems for a hotel. When companies or travel agents take time to settle their accounts, the threat of a bad debt should be considered. Bad debts are incurred when a debtor (a person who owes the hotel money) does not settle the account. Therefore, the account has to be written off, resulting in lost revenue to the hotel. It is, therefore, important that the accountant carefully checks the debtor's collection period, and any accounts which have not been paid within a certain time period must be followed up.

- To avoid guests' dissatisfaction. Guests feel embarrassed and annoyed if, on checking out, they discover that they cannot satisfactorily settle their accounts for reasons such as a credit card not being accepted by the hotel, possession of insufficient cash to pay the account, refusal by the hotel to accept certain foreign currency, or their account balance being over the hotel's floor limit, the credit card organization refusing to approve a higher limit.

Many of the possible causes for walk-outs, late payments and guests' dissatisfaction when settling their accounts are the responsibility of the front office cashier and accounts department. Common causes for these problems may include:

- unclear instructions to the guest at check-in (e.g. not informing the guest which credit card or foreign currency is or is not acceptable)

- lack of communication between departments (e.g. the credit manager not notifying the cashier when a guest's account is over the hotel's credit limit)

- Breakdown in front office procedures (e.g. the front desk or reservations clerk not checking the blacklist for previous walk-outs)

Various procedures are necessary to ensure that these problems are minimized, and can include the following:

- Give the guest clear instructions at check-in regarding account settlement.

- Notify the guest when their account has reached the hotel's credit limit.

- Provide a list of previous skips to all relevant departments.

- Ensure good coordination and communication between all departments on matters relating to guests' charges.

- Ensure that guests with company accounts have been notified that the account has to be verified and signed before check-out.

Non-settlement and delayed payment of accounts seriously hamper the cash flow of a hotel. However, most of these problems can be avoided or minimized if credit control policies are set up by a hotel, and if all the staff concerned take great care in following credit control procedures. In the following sections, we shall explain the credit control measures taken by the various sections and departments in different phases of the guest cycle.

**Activity 1**

(a) Why do hotels need to control the credit given to guests?

(b) Who may be responsible for carrying out the credit control duties?

(c) Why is the delayed settlement of an account considered a problem to a hotel?

## HOTEL CREDIT CONTROL POLICY

Hotels will normally allow guests to charge their hotel expenses to their room account. To ensure that final settlement is paid, hotels must be certain that the guests are able to pay their bills in full before they are given credit. The credit limit (sometimes called the house limit) refers to the maximum level to which a guest's bill can amount before some form of settlement is required. Credit limits may vary, and often depend on the guests' reservation status and the method of payment.

In general, hotels tend to allow credit to three types of guest (although this depends very much on a hotel's policy):

- those who have guaranteed bookings with the hotel

- those whose accounts will be settled by their companies

- those who will settle their accounts by credit or charge cards.

### Guests with guaranteed bookings

Most hotels give credit to guests who have guaranteed their bookings (either by a credit card or a deposit). These guests are allowed to enjoy the hotel facilities and services on credit, and to settle their accounts personally at check-out.

On the other hand, walk-in guests and guests with non-guaranteed bookings or late bookings are usually not given any credit if they settle their bills by cash or cheque. They are usually required to prepay their room rate, together with a deposit for incidental expenses, at check-in. If a walk-in guest pays an advance deposit or gives a credit card for imprint in order to cover accommodation and incidental expenses, then credit status may be allowed.

### Settlement by corporate accounts

When a company wishes to have credit facilities at a particular hotel, the hotel will have to check to ensure that the company is solvent, i.e. that it is capable of paying its accounts. The hotel will need a reference from the company's bank; if the reference is favourable, the company is approved to receive services on credit. The obtaining of a credit rating of a company can be conducted through organizations that specialize in this type of work. The company will then be listed on the list of credit-approved companies prepared by the accounts department. This list will be distributed to the reservations department, reception and sales office so that other sections or departments can know clearly which companies are entitled to credits at the hotel. However, you should note that a hotel often approves different credit limits for different companies. For example:

- A large local firm which regularly reserves a large number of rooms at the hotel and which has a good record of settling bills promptly will have a high credit rating. It may be allowed to have a large balance outstanding on individual accounts and the company's total account before payment is asked for.

- A new company, a small company, or a company which has been late in settling its account may be given a low credit rating. The company will be required to settle the bill once the account has reached a certain limit.

## Activity 2

(a) What benefits will a hotel obtain by giving credit to companies and travel agents?

(b) You are the credit manager of a hotel. What credit policy would you recommend for each of the following companies?

- A company with a good credit record which has substantially increased the number of bookings at the hotel

- A travel agent which has not paid its account for six months

- A new company which has applied for credit facilities at the hotel but whose bank reference shows that the financial condition of the company is insecure

## ACCOUNTS SETTLED BY CREDIT OR CHARGE CARD

In most hotels, credit is also given to guests who settle their accounts by credit or charge cards that are accepted by the hotel.

The types of charge or credit card which are accepted by hotels vary from hotel to hotel. Reasons for this may be the popularity or otherwise of the card, the fee the hotel pays on accepting a particular charge or credit card, and the time period taken by the charge or credit card company to settle the account.

To ensure that guests and hotel personnel are aware of which charge or credit cards can be used, signs are displayed at the front desk and relevant payment areas, showing which charge or credit cards are acceptable. This policy can be emphasized to hotel personnel during training sessions and their induction programmes, so as to ensure that guests are not embarrassed at check-out. It is important that they and all hotel personnel are fully aware of which cards are accepted.

Remember that different charge or credit cards may have different floor limits agreed by the card-issuing company.

## Activity 3

Explain the credit status of the following guests:

- An FIT with a guaranteed reservation, who will settle the account in cash

- A walk-in guest who intends to pay the bill with a gold Visa card

- A guest with a non-guaranteed reservation who will settle the account in cash

## CREDIT CONTROL MEASURES REQUIRED WHEN RECEIVING RESERVATIONS

In Chapters 5 and 6, we described the procedures for receiving reservations. In fact, many of the same procedures are needed for credit control purposes. Figure 11.1 summarizes the main credit control measures that have to be followed when receiving reservations.

**Activity 4**  A request for a booking has been received from a company. Explain:

(a)  what measures the reservations clerk should take for credit control purposes

(b)  why the measures are needed

## CREDIT CONTROL MEASURES AT CHECK-IN

We examined the check-in procedures in Chapter 7. Similarly, many of the procedures for credit control are set up to control the credits given to guests and ensure full settlement of accounts.

Table 11.1 summarizes the main credit control measures at check-in and the reasons for such measures.

**Activity 5**  What measures are needed at check-in to ensure that a guest on a corporate or travel agent account will settle their incidentals account?

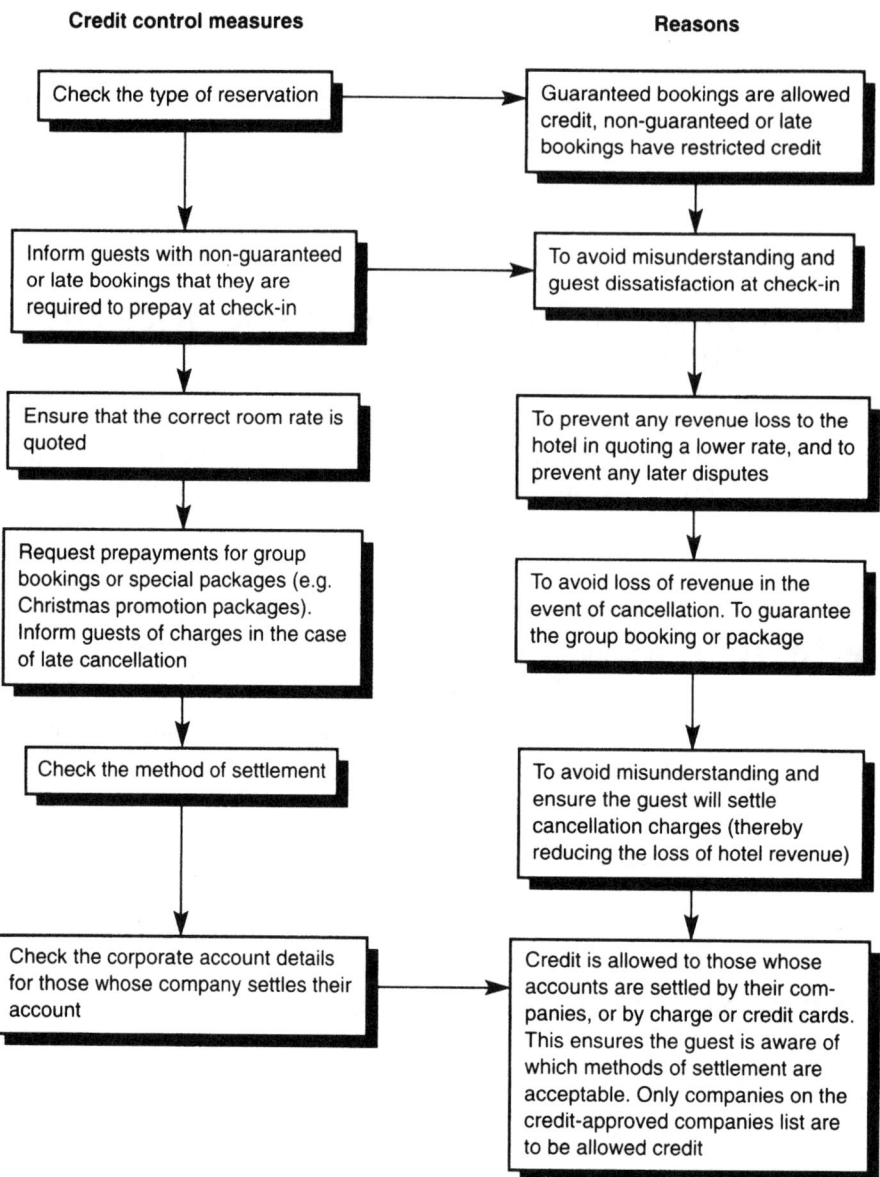

| Credit control measures | Reasons |
|---|---|

Check the type of reservation → Guaranteed bookings are allowed credit, non-guaranteed or late bookings have restricted credit

Inform guests with non-guaranteed or late bookings that they are required to prepay at check-in → To avoid misunderstanding and guest dissatisfaction at check-in

Ensure that the correct room rate is quoted → To prevent any revenue loss to the hotel in quoting a lower rate, and to prevent any later disputes

Request prepayments for group bookings or special packages (e.g. Christmas promotion packages). Inform guests of charges in the case of late cancellation → To avoid loss of revenue in the event of cancellation. To guarantee the group booking or package

Check the method of settlement → To avoid misunderstanding and ensure the guest will settle cancellation charges (thereby reducing the loss of hotel revenue)

Check the corporate account details for those whose company settles their account → Credit is allowed to those whose accounts are settled by their companies, or by charge or credit cards. This ensures the guest is aware of which methods of settlement are acceptable. Only companies on the credit-approved companies list are to be allowed credit

**Figure 11.1** Summary of main credit control measures when receiving reservations

## CREDIT CONTROL MEASURES DURING OCCUPANCY

Most transactions between a guest and a hotel take place during a guest's occupancy. Therefore, during this phase of a guest's stay the hotel needs to monitor the credit given to guests very closely. This is achieved by monitoring bills with high balances.

The cashier will monitor all the bill totals against the hotel's set

**Table 11.1** Summary of the main credit control measures at check-in

| Credit control measures | Reasons |
| --- | --- |
| Check reservations status: collect prepayments from walk-ins and non-guaranteed bookings | Credit is given to those with guaranteed bookings; walk-ins and guests with non-guaranteed or late bookings have restricted credit if they pay by cash or credit card, depending on the hotel's policy |
| Check types of accounts:<br>• Travel agent voucher. Ask for voucher and check what charges are covered. Check with the guest the method of settlement for incidentals | To ensure that the guest will pay for incidentals by an agreed method of settlement |
| • Tour groups. Check with the tour leader about the billing arrangements (e.g. master account to the travel agent and/or incidentals to the tour members | To ensure that the incidentals will be paid for |
| • Corporate accounts. Check whether the full account is to be settled by the company; if not, agree with the guest on the methods of settlement for incidentals | To ensure that the incidental account will be properly settled |
| Check methods of settlements:<br>• For cash settlement, record the room rate on the registration card and key card, and remind the guest of the room rates; inform the guest of the hotel's policy on house limits | Guests can estimate their account total and the amount of cash they need on check-out<br>Guest will not be annoyed when asked to settle part of the account should the bill be close to the house limit |
| • For charge or credit card settlement check that the card is accepted by the hotel | Ensure that guests will settle their accounts by methods which are acceptable to the hotel, to prevent the guest's dissatisfaction when a card is refused at check-out |
| Take an imprint of the card | To check the validity of the card; to seek authorization; to guide against walk-outs |

credit limit. Each day, a high-balance report will be produced which lists all the accounts whose totals are near to or in excess of the limit. An example of a high-balance report is shown in Figures 11.2 and 11.3.

**KING'S HOTEL**

## Guest Ledger High-balance Report

Date: ...........................................................................

Auditor: ..................................................... Reviewed by: .................................................

| Room no. | Guest name | Amount | Action taken |
|----------|------------|--------|--------------|
| 103 | Green, L. | 498.00 | Contacted. Paid £200.00. Address and credit verified. |
| 122 | Church, W. | 155.00 | Direct billing. |
| 247 | Smith, D. | 355.70 | Left three messages. No contact. Action necessary. |
| 295 | Tong, L. | 285.50 | Amex. approved. |

**Figure 11.2** An example of a high-balance report

The reception, night auditor or the credit manager is usually responsible for handling accounts with high balances. The guests will be asked to settle their account to date, and a new account will be started for the rest of their stay. The credit manager will send the bill, together with an accompanying letter, to the guest's room, asking the guest to settle the account with the reception. If the guest has any queries about their account or the credit policy, the reception or the assistant manager should explain them to the guest.

Sometimes, guests may fail to call at the reception desk as requested. In this case, the assistant manager has to contact the guest personally. They may telephone the guest in their room, or contact them when they next collect their keys from the front desk. In serious cases, where the guest cannot be reached and has made no attempt to see

*King's Hotel*

## Notification of High Balance

Room no: ................................................................ Date: ........................................................................

Dear: ...........................................................................

I would like to notify you that your expenses up until ..................................... are .....................................

This amount is in excess of the level of credit the hotel normally extends to its guests. We would, therefore,

be most grateful if you would contact our duty manager on ................................ or the front office manager

to establish how you wish to settle your account.

Yours sincerely,

...................................
Front Office Manager

**Figure 11.3** Notification of high balance

management or the front desk staff, their room will be double-locked. This means that the guest has to contact the assistant manager before they can be let into their room.

## CREDIT CONTROL MEASURES BY OTHER SALES DEPARTMENTS

Whenever a guest wants to charge a service from a sales outlet to their account, the staff in that outlet must check the credit status of the guest carefully. They must check that:

- the guest is a resident and/or has an account at the hotel
- the guest is allowed to charge services to their account

Remember:

- A walk-in may not be allowed to charge services to their account and consequently will have to settle the incidentals by cash or credit card at the sales outlet.

- If the guest is part of a tour, their package may allow a meal in the hotel but only up to a certain value (e.g. £10.00). Any excess on the bill must be settled at the sales outlet. Often the front desk will issue these guests with vouchers, which the guest will hand to the restaurant captain or head waiter upon entering the hotel restaurant.

## THE ADVANTAGES OF USING COMPUTERS

In Chapter 9, you learnt how computerization speeds up the transfer of guest information and is useful, for the same reason, in transferring charge information from different departments. Computers, therefore, help to ensure that guests' accounts are always accurate and up to date.

A computerized accounting system is also useful in controlling credit. Computers can automatically monitor bill totals and produce high-balance reports, thereby notifying the cashier when to seek higher approval on credit cards. The computer can also be programmed to prevent charges from being added from other departments when the guest is not allowed credit.

---

**Activity 6** A guest plans to stay at your hotel for four days and has left a Visa imprint at the reception at check-in.

(a) What credit control measures should the front office cashier take on receiving the imprint?

(b) If, on the second day of their stay, the guest's bill has accumulated to an amount of £780.00, what further actions are required? (Hotel credit limit is £500.00.)

(c) If, on the date of departure, the guest has breakfast at the hotel coffee shop and asks for the bill to be charged to their account, what measures should the coffee shop waitress take to ensure payment?

---

## CREDIT CONTROL MEASURES AT CHECK-OUT

In the previous sections, you learnt about the various credit control measures taken by hotel staff when accepting reservations, at check-in and during the guest's occupancy. You also saw why these measures are needed. In this section we shall ask you to identify measures needed at check-out and to explain their purposes.

---

**Activity 7**    Explain, using a flow-chart similar to Figure 11.1, the various credit control measures at check-out, and the reasons for such measures.

---

## CREDIT CONTROL MEASURES AFTER GUEST DEPARTURE

You are aware that corporate accounts or travel agents' accounts are not settled at check-out. Therefore, after a guest's departure these forms of account will be transferred to the city ledger held by the accounts department, which holds an individual account for each company. At the end of each month, the accounts department will send statements of these accounts to the companies for settlement. It is expected that payment will be made within 30 days.

However, some companies may be late in settling their accounts. In such cases, follow-up measures need to be taken by the accounts department to speed up the payment. An example of the procedure is as follows, however, the time frame may be reduced in many hotels.

1.  After having failed to receive payment within 30 days, telephone the company as a reminder.

2.  After 45 days, write officially to the company, requesting immediate payment.

3.  After 60 days send a strongly worded letter. Possibly threaten legal action.

4.  If nothing has been received after 90 days, proceed with legal action through the hotel's solicitor. At this point the hotel accountant may have to consider writing off the bill as a bad debt.

## PREVENTING WALK-OUTS (SKIPS)

Because a walk-out costs the hotel not only in lost revenue, but also in actual food and drink costs, much is done to prevent this type of occurrence. Front office staff should take great care when dealing with newly arrived guests. It may be possible for staff to identify potential walk-outs by paying closer attention to the behaviour of the guest, and to thus take measures to guard against them.

### On arrival

When guests arrive, the bell staff should check the number of bags, and assess their weight. People who intend to walk out sometimes have very little luggage, or carry empty suitcases which they will leave behind in the room when they walk out.

### During the stay

Extravagant purchasing patterns can be a feature of walk-outs, so the cashier should monitor the guest's account carefully. A person who intends to walk out is more likely to order expensive meals, and eat and drink from room service. The hotel credit limit can be reached quickly.

### On the day of departure

The hall porter may contact a departing guest to request the time to collect the luggage. By doing this, the porter will keep the bags in store until the guest has paid their account. Some hotels have a system of luggage passes. When the guest has checked out with the cashier they are issued a receipt or luggage pass. The guest will then show the receipt to the porter who, knowing that the account has been settled, will release the luggage.

### The right of lien

On some occasions a guest may be unable to pay the account, and in this case the hotel can exercise right of lien. The right of lien means that a hotel has the legal right to detain a guest's suitcase, and the belongings which they bring into the hotel, if they are unable to settle the account. However, the hotel is not allowed to keep the clothes which the guest is wearing.

If a guest cannot pay the account (e.g. if they have lost their traveller's cheques) then the hotel may keep some of the luggage as security until the account is settled. This means that the guest could leave the hotel to arrange finance and then return to pay the bill and have the luggage returned.

If the guest cannot pay the bill and the luggage has to be held, the hotel does have the right to sell that luggage to recover the debt. However, there are various conditions attached to the sale:

- The luggage or belongings must be held by the hotel for at least six weeks and then sold by public auction.

- The sale must be advertised in the press.

- After the sale any surplus of cash (after deducting the amount of the guest's account) has to be returned to the guest.

---

**Activity 8**   (a)  How can the hall porter help prevent walk-outs?

               (b)  What actions can a hotel take when a resident guest is unable or has failed to pay the bill?

---

## SUMMARY

For a hotel to be successful and profitable, it is necessary for it not only to be busy, but to receive all the revenue owed to it by resident guests. To do this requires a series of stringent credit control systems. This chapter has looked at the reasons why hotels have such systems, i.e. to prevent walk-outs (skips), late settlement of accounts and guest upset at check-out.

The credit rating of the various guests was looked at, and the difference in rating according to reservation status explained. Why do guaranteed have a better rating than walk-ins and non-guaranteed, unconfirmed guests? Apart from individual credit ratings, travel agents, tour groups and companies need a rating. How these organizations achieve their rating was explained.

The operational procedures for handling credit and charge cards were explained. This chapter has stressed the need to obtain authorization for any card which exceeds the hotel's floor limit.

The techniques and processes of credit control were examined as they applied during the guest cycle, i.e. at the time of making a reservation, at check-in and during occupancy. One of the most important tasks for a hotel in its efforts to maintain good credit control is the monitoring of high-balance accounts. The procedures for handling guests who have exceeded the hotel's credit limit were shown.

Credit control is also practised after the departure of the guest. Although usually conducted by the accounts department, the chasing of city ledger accounts which have not been paid can sometimes be done by the front desk staff.

Finally, the chapter examined the legal practice of right of lien, whereby a guest's luggage and belongings can be held and eventually sold, if a guest is unable to pay the bill.

It always seems easier to sell and fill a hotel than it does to control it. However, it is the control of a hotel that can make it an efficient and profitable establishment.

## Review and discussion questions

1 Explain the right of lien.

2 Why can a late settlement of an account be a burden to the operation of a hotel?

3 Explain your understanding of credit control.

## Case Study: 'There Must be Easier Ways to Earn a Living' – Mr Nonjoma

The final straw for the morning occurred when you had to meet a foreign guest, Mr Nonjoma, to ask about his bill.

Mr Nonjoma and his family had been checked in to the hotel for a week by a travel agent. He then asked and received an extra week's extension of stay. All of the accommodation expenses for the first week were covered by the travel agent but all extras were to be paid by Mr Nonjoma, as were all of the expenses associated with the extra week.

Earlier in the week it was noticed that Mr Nonjoma and his family had run up an excessive bill, so he was asked to give an imprint of his credit card or pay some of the bill. However, he was unable to produce either a card or money because he said that his wallet had been stolen or lost. But he told the hotel staff not to worry as he was the president of a large company in his own country and was in town to set up a branch here. Not being convinced, the duty manager of the day asked Mr Nonjoma for his passport for surety. Two days ago the Nonjomas were expected to check out but as yet no remuneration had been received and so Mr Nonjoma's passport was not returned until he paid his bill.

Today you had to approach Mr Nonjoma to ask about settlement. However, once again Mr Nonjoma had not been able to get any money. At this point you noticed that his bill had become excessive, mainly due to room service and international telephone calls.

## Your actions and responses regarding Mr Nonjoma

1. How would you handle Mr Nonjoma?

2. What would you do next and who would you inform and why?

3. How could such a situation have happened in the first place?

4. What needs to be done to ensure that such an incident does not happen again?

# 12

# Sundry guest services

## Introduction

In previous chapters we were concerned with the reservation processes and procedures for dealing with guests at check-in and check-out. These procedures are the main duties dealt with by the front office personnel, but there are other services and functions offered by a hotel which are also normally carried out by the front office staff.

As was mentioned in Chapter 4, the front office department in smaller hotels often provides several services to guests which, in larger hotels, are performed by a number of individual sections. These services can include:

- mail and information

- telephone

- guest requests met by the porters

- foreign currency exchange and safe deposit boxes

- security

This chapter is concerned with looking at each of these services in depth and will show how they integrate the guest with other areas of a hotel. In addition, this chapter will identify the front office personnel responsible for the above services, and will explain what each service should include.

Remember that the work of these independent units within large hotels can differ. This is mainly due to the policies and procedures laid down by each individual hotel, together with the volume of work carried out within each particular unit. For example, the handling of mail and providing information to guests can be the responsibility of the mail and information desk, or porter, or front desk.

## MAIL AND INFORMATION

Many large hotels used to have a separate mail and information desk, sometimes known as the inquiries desk, in their front lobby. But nowadays they have tended to follow smaller hotels, where the work of the mail and information desk may be conducted by front desk personnel or the porter/concierge.

The main duties and responsibilities of the mail and information clerks are shown in Figure 12.1.

### Handling mail

Handling mail and messages on behalf of a guest and the hotel is an important responsibility of the front desk personnel. For example, if a registered letter is received by a hotel but not delivered to the guest, the hotel may be held liable for any losses or inconvenience caused to that guest. Therefore, an efficient system of handling mail and messages is essential. As a protection against charges of negligence, against both the hotel and the person dealing with the mail, many hotels insist that all incoming mail is time and date stamped upon arrival.

All incoming mail is divided into three main categories:

- hotel mail, which is normally distributed to the relevant departments concerned

- staff mail, which is normally distributed through the personnel or staff office

- guest mail, which consists of resident (i.e. current guest) mail, past guest mail, and future guest mail

When handling mail, the following procedures should be followed.

### Current guest

Letters should be placed in the mail rack. Parcels that are too large for the rack should be stored and a note placed in the mail rack. In some hotels a mail light connected to the guest-room is switched on, notifying the guest that a letter or message is waiting for them in the mail rack.

### Past guests

In many hotels, guests prior to departing are required to complete a mail forwarding card (Figure 12.2) which contains a forwarding address. This helps the clerk to re-direct the mail. (Note: registration forms can also be used as a reference for re-directing mail.) At the time of checking

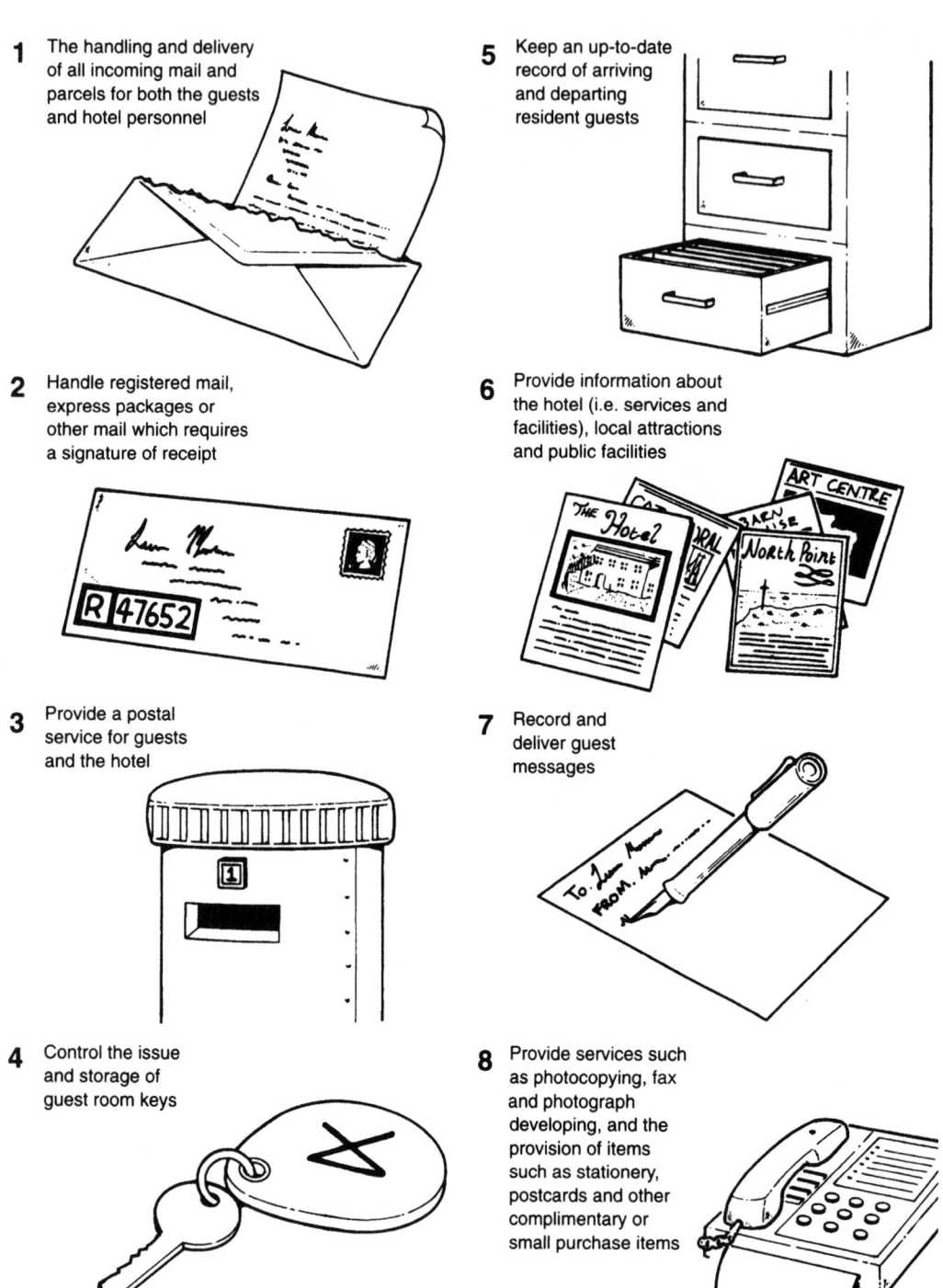

1 The handling and delivery of all incoming mail and parcels for both the guests and hotel personnel

2 Handle registered mail, express packages or other mail which requires a signature of receipt

3 Provide a postal service for guests and the hotel

4 Control the issue and storage of guest room keys

5 Keep an up-to-date record of arriving and departing resident guests

6 Provide information about the hotel (i.e. services and facilities), local attractions and public facilities

7 Record and deliver guest messages

8 Provide services such as photocopying, fax and photograph developing, and the provision of items such as stationery, postcards and other complimentary or small purchase items

**Figure 12.1** Main duties of the mail and information clerks

```
            ♔

       KING'S HOTEL

    Mail Forwarding Card

Please forward any mail arriving for

Dr/Mr/Mrs/Miss/Ms: ...........................................................

room number: ........................ during the next ........................ days,

to the following address:

............................................................................................

............................................................................................

Date:................................    Signature: ....................................
```

**Figure 12.2** Mail forwarding card

out the cashier could inquire whether the guest is expecting any mail which will need forwarding.

### Future guests

Details of the guest arrival date are obtained from the reservation file and this date is written on the guest mail. A note is then made on the computer or recorded on the guest reservation file, or in the booking diary, against the name of the addressee. The mail is then stored in a secure drawer in alphabetical order.

---

**Activity 1**  You are the head receptionist of the hotel. You have a new member of staff who has just started; design a training programme for them in the handling of mail.

---

### Registered mail

If items of value are sent through the mail, the sender usually registers the package. When a package is delivered to a hotel, a staff member must sign the postman's receipt of delivery. On receiving a registered envelope or package, a hotel accepts responsibility for the mail. The registered mail should be noted in a registered mail record book (Figure 12.3). Once the mail has been recorded, it is placed in a secure safe or locked drawer.

| Registered Number | Date Received | Address | Guest's Signature | Date Collected | Clerk's Signature |
|---|---|---|---|---|---|
|  |  |  |  |  |  |
|  |  |  |  |  |  |
|  |  |  |  |  |  |
|  |  |  |  |  |  |
|  |  |  |  |  |  |
|  |  |  |  |  |  |
|  |  |  |  |  |  |

**Figure 12.3** Extract from a registered mail record book

A guest will be informed that registered mail is awaiting collection by means of:

- a note placed in the mail rack
- a message sent to the guest's room
- a guest message light which is switched on in the guest's room
- a message displayed on the in-room television or computer

When guests come to collect their registered mail, they must give proof of identity and sign the registered mail record book.

**Activity 2** (a) How does the procedure for handling registered mail differ from that for ordinary mail?

(b) Why do hotels need to handle registered mail with special care? How could a guest prove their identity?

---

## Outgoing mail

The front desk clerk may have to collect all the mail which is being sent out from the departments, arrange for its delivery to the post office and often pay the postage charges. Therefore, a record needs to be kept of the quantity and costs of the mail being sent out. Any letters or parcels posted for guests must be weighed and a voucher of the charges sent to the cashier's desk.

## Messages

The recording of guest messages can be done manually or by computer. Guest messages are important, and if not promptly given to the guest concerned may cause problems or embarrassment, which would result in a strong complaint. The accurate handling of messages and their delivery is essential. Figure 12.4 summarizes the main procedures in dealing with messages.

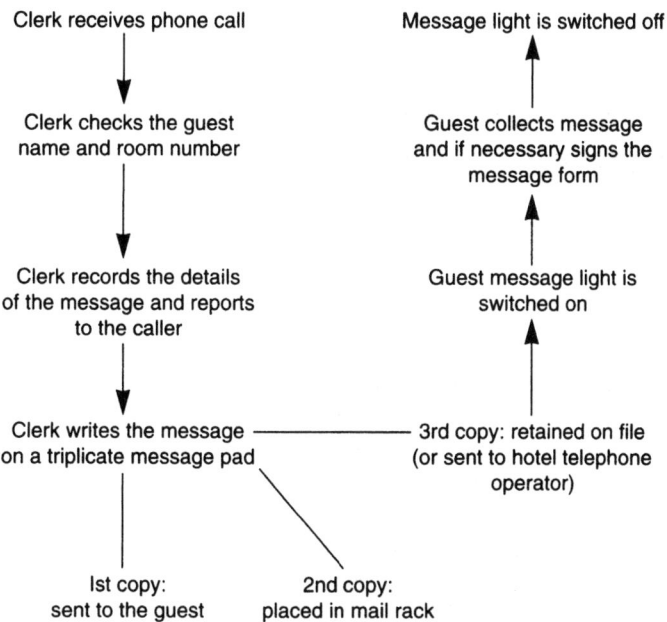

**Figure 12.4** Procedures to follow when handling a guest's message

If the hotel has a sophisticated computerized system, messages can be viewed by guests on the television screens in their rooms.

Alternatively, a triplicate message pad can be used, similar to the one illustrated in Figure 12.5.

**Message Record**

KING'S HOTEL

To: ................................................................ Room number: ................................................

**YOU WERE CALLED**

By: ........................................................................................................................................

Of: ........................................................................................................................................

☐ Please call back ☐ Will meet you at ☐ Will call again

**MESSAGE**

........................................................................................................................................

........................................................................................................................................

........................................................................................................................................

Taken by: ......................... Date: ............................... Clerk's signature:.........................

**Figure 12.5** Triplicate message from

Messages received for guests who are expected to arrive at a hotel on a particular day should be attached to their registration cards at the front desk. Guests who are expected to arrive in the future will have their messages filed in alphabetical order, and a note attached to their reservation file to remind reception that a message is being held for their arrival. The front desk clerk will take out the message and attach it to the guest's registration card on the day of their arrival. Messages for guests who have departed will be checked against the mail forwarding record and if necessary redirected.

Messages for non-residents will be kept at the front desk to await collection.

Periodically the front desk clerk must carry out a mail and message check to ensure that mail and messages have been collected by guests. Mail should not be kept for too long; different hotels may have varying policies concerning the time period for which mail should be kept. All uncollected mail should be returned to the post office.

---

**Activity 3**  You are a front desk clerk on duty. A message has been received for a guest who has already checked out. With the aid of a flow-chart, explain the procedure you should follow in dealing with this.

---

### Sundry information

Guests may ask for local information at any of the desks in the foyer. The following is a list of reference books and guides which should be available for general use.

Transportation:    Timetables for buses, trains and airlines.
Entertainment:    A list of specialist restaurants, bistros, clubs and night-life, as well as an up-to-date guide of what is on at cinemas, theatres and exhibitions.
General information:    Street maps, consulate telephone numbers, religious information, a list of doctors, dentists and opticians, information on telecommunications, local travel agents and tour operators, local and international hotel telephone and fax numbers, and yellow pages and business directories.
Local facilities:    List of hairdressers, chemists, banks, shopping centres, etc.

### TELEPHONE

Most hotels provide a 24-hour local and international telephone service. This service is mainly used to direct incoming calls to guests because most hotel telephone systems have direct dialling from the guest-rooms. Direct dialling can be for both local and international calls.

Telephone and fax recorded by the telephonist or front office clerks should be time stamped and held in a guest's mail rack until retrieved. If guests' telephones are equipped with message indicator lights, these are switched on to notify the guest that a message for them has been received.

Finally, the telephone services offered to a guest may include early morning wake-up calls to ensure the guest does not oversleep.

Alternatively, a guest may choose to use an automatic wake-up call system, a facility that many modern telephone systems now possess. Some hotel telephone systems may also provide 'do not disturb' or call-barring services, where the guest's calls are intercepted by the switch-board until the guest wishes to receive their own calls.

---

**Activity 4**  Investigate other telephone services and facilities which are now available for hotel guests.

---

## GUEST REQUESTS MET BY THE HALL PORTERS

The range of duties performed by the head hall porter and their staff will vary according to the size of a hotel and its standard of service. Sometimes the services provided by the mail and information desk are the responsibility of the porter. Other duties can include:

- baggage handling
- arranging transportation
- escorting guests to their rooms
- providing information and miscellaneous services (e.g. flight confirmation, and airline, theatre, and restaurant reservations and tour bookings)

### Handling baggage

At the end of each day's operation, the porter will receive two lists from the front desk; these are the arrival and departure lists for the following day. These two lists will include the following information:

- the estimated time of arrival or departure of the guests
- names of the guests
- size of the parties
- special requests (if any)
- flight/rail details, if any

With these details to hand, the porter can mobilize their staff to assist guests who are part of a group or tour, and to complete the incoming/ outgoing' record form (Figure 12.6).

KING'S HOTEL

**Incoming/Outgoing Group Record Form**

| | |
|---|---|
| Date: ........ | Name of group: ........ |
| Arr/dep flight no.: ........ | Hotel arr/dep time: ........ |
| Number of persons: ........ | Number of pieces of baggage: ........ |
| Supervised by: ........ | Handled by: ........ |
| Travel agent: ........ | Remarks: ........ |

**Figure 12.6** An example of an incoming/outgoing group record

Assistance is also given in the transporting of baggage from the lobby to the guest's room or vice versa, as well as the counting, tagging and storing of luggage if required (Figure 12.7).

When handling baggage for FITs and groups, the porter should carry out the following procedures.

***FIT.*** The bell staff (baggage attendant) removes the baggage from the taxis and will accompany a guest to the front desk. On completion of registration, a key card and key are issued to the guest. The bell staff will then escort the guest to their room, inspect the room and introduce the facilities available.

***Group.*** In order to release the pressure of group arrivals, the baggage tags have been completed in advance. This information is usually obtained from the tour list, in which guest-rooms have been pre-allocated. On arrival at the hotel, the bell staff tags the luggage, counts the number of bags, sorts the baggage into room numbers and floors and delivers it to the guest-rooms.

The procedure to follow in order to ensure the safety and security of guests' baggage are described below.

1. A service call record sheet (Figure 12.8) is completed every time bell staff collect or deliver baggage. This record enables the captain to keep track of the crew, by noting where their

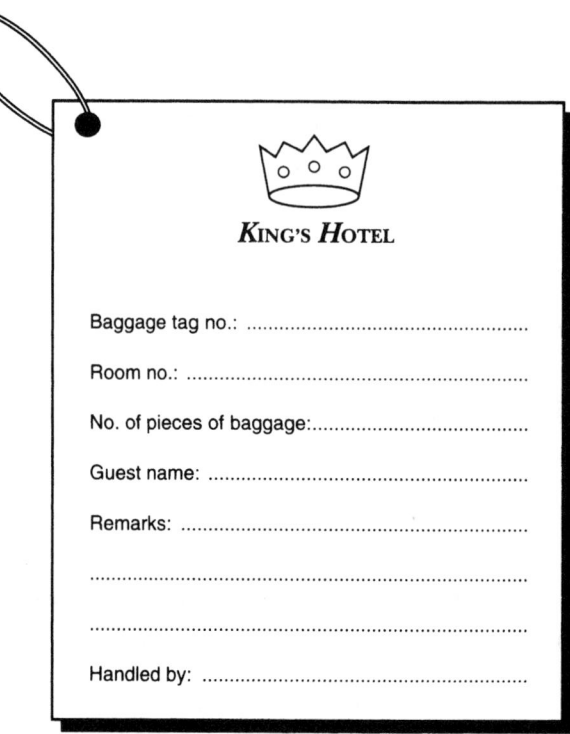

**Figure 12.7** An example of a baggage tag

staff are at various times; the record also offers protection from accusations in the event of theft or other problems

2. The number of bags handled must be recorded.

3. Nets should be used to bind group baggage together and thus avoid loss or theft.

4. Missing baggage must be reported immediately to the management.

---

**Activity 5**  You are the head porter of a hotel. A group of 50 visitors is due to depart tomorrow. Describe what you have to do to prepare for the handling of the luggage.

---

### Arranging transportation

It is usually the duty of the porter to arrange any guest transportation requests, especially if the hotel has its own service. The porter must keep an accurate record of the times a car or mini-bus is in use and who it is used by. If it is the policy of the hotel to charge for this service, then

## Service Call Record Sheet

KING'S HOTEL

Date: ............................. Shift: ............................. Shift leader: .............................

| Room no. | Porter | Time | No. of bags | Remarks |
|---|---|---|---|---|
| | | | | |
| | | | | |
| | | | | |
| | | | | |
| | | | | |
| | | | | |
| | | | | |
| | | | | |
| | | | | |
| | | | | |

**Figure 12.8** An example of a service call record sheet

it is the responsibility of the porter to arrange for the charge voucher to be sent to the cashier's desk.

### Escorting guests to their rooms

Once guests have completed their registration procedures, the bell staff are normally responsible for escorting guests to their rooms. In addition, the bell staff will:

- assist in the transportation of a guest's luggage to the room
- introduce the facilities of the room to the guest, and demonstrate their usage

### *Providing information and miscellaneous services*

The porter may also be responsible for acting as a booking agency for such things as:

- theatre tickets or concerts

- car hire

- local tours

- airline reservations (the department would also be expected to provide airline guides and timetables)

- travel services

- restaurant reservations

Remember, the above are only a few of the services which may be offered by the porter's lodge. Other responsibilities may include requests as diverse as having a pair of shoes repaired, or organizing a flower arrangement or arranging for a private aircraft. If any payments are made by the porters on behalf of the guest a visitors paid out voucher should be completed and sent to the cashier.

Finally, as the porter's desk is usually positioned near the entrance of the hotel, the porter staff can easily note and observe any suspicious persons or abnormal situations. Because of this, the porter maintains a close communication with the security department.

---

**Activity 6**   A VIP guest is due to arrive at the airport late in the afternoon. Explain the services that you, as head porter, would provide for this guest.

---

## FOREIGN CURRENCY EXCHANGE AND SAFE DEPOSIT BOXES

Many hotels, especially those with a high proportion of overseas visitors, will offer foreign exchange facilities. The hotel exchanges the foreign currency for local currency. However, the hotel cannot sell foreign currency. When receiving foreign currency in settlement of a bill, it must be remembered that change must be given in local currency.

Hotel management is also obliged to ensure the safety of guests' property. This obligation is stated under the Hotel Proprietor's Act 1956.

### Foreign currency exchange

There are no legal restrictions on the exchange rates offered by hotels, so the hotels are free to offer whatever price they wish. Normally the price offered is higher than the normal bank rate. For example, if the bank is quoting US $1.70 for £1.00, then the hotel may charge US $1.60 for £1.00. The difference is to allow for administrative costs, sudden changes in the exchange rate, and often a small profit. Exchange rates for major currencies are displayed in the cashier's office or reception area.

It is important that the front office cashier understands the different types of foreign currencies offered by the guests, and which particular rate of exchange to use. Normally foreign notes or traveller's cheques are accepted by a hotel but coins are not. When handling foreign currency the front office cashier should:

- check the rate of exchange table
- issue a receipt quoting each transaction, guest name, room number and rate of exchange (Figure 12.9)
- arrange for the foreign currency to be banked as soon as possible, on a separate paying-in slip (exchange rates can change frequently)

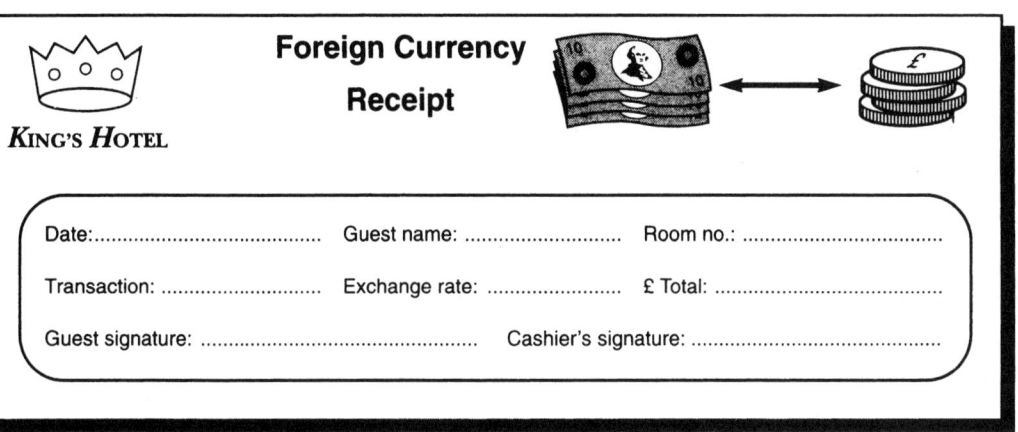

**Figure 12.9** An example of a foreign currency receipt

Hotels which operate computerized systems frequently incorporate the updated exchange rates within the front office program. This allows for easier foreign currency conversion.

### Safe deposit boxes

A hotel is liable for the loss of guests' property while they are staying at the hotel, from midnight on the date of arrival to midnight on the day of departure. If loss is caused by negligence of the hotel or staff, then the hotel can be held fully liable, even if it has its limited liability through displaying the statutory notices from the Hotel Proprietors Act 1956 (Figure 12.10).

---

## NOTICE

## Loss of or Damage to Guests' Property

Under the Hotel Proprietors Act 1956, a hotel proprietor may in certain circumstances be liable to make

good any loss of or damage to a guest's property even though it was not due to any fault of the proprietor or

staff of the hotel.

This liability however –

(a)  extends only to the property of guests who have engaged sleeping accommodation at the hotel.

(b)  is limited to £50 for any one article and a total of £100 in the case of any one guest except in the case

 of property which has been deposited, or offered for deposit, for safe custody.

(c)  does not cover motor cars or other vehicles of any kind or any property left in them, or horse or other

 live animals.

This notice does not constitute an admission either that the Act applies to this hotel or that liability

thereunder attaches to the proprietor of this hotel in any particular case.

---

**Figure 12.10** Excerpt from the Hotel Proprietors Act 1956

It is important to remember that if a guest offered property to the front office cashier for safe-keeping and was refused because the hotel's safe deposit boxes were full, and the property was subsequently stolen, then the hotel might be fully liable for the loss. Only if the property was lost or damaged due to negligence on the part of the guest, an Act of God, or action by the Queen's enemies can a hotel be absolved of liability.

The front office cashier holds a position of considerable trust and is responsible for large sums of money and items of unlimited value. Therefore, it is essential that the cashier is careful and alert when handling safe deposit boxes.

A safe deposit box which has not been surrendered by a guest at the time of check-out can cause considerable inconvenience to a hotel. For this reason boxes are normally offered only to resident guests who are likely to surrender the box at the end of their stay.

Objects which are too large to fit a safe deposit box must also be accepted. The same procedure is followed, but a broad description of the article is also given, e.g. 'received one lady's fur-style coat'. Do not write 'one mink coat' unless you are sure that it is definitely mink. This is because some people use the ploy of getting you to record the article as something that it is not, and then claim that it has been changed.

---

**Activity 8**   (a) To what extent is a hotel liable for losses and damages to the property of hotel guests in the following situations? (Refer to the Hotel Proprietors Act 1956 in order to answer this question.)

- a camera left in the guest's car which has been parked on the hotel property

- a suitcase with belongings (valued at £300) left in the guest-room

- a diamond ring with a declared value of £10,000, which has been offered for deposit, but which was denied because all deposit boxes were full

- a fur coat belonging to a non-resident guest, who hung the coat in the hotel cloakroom herself

(b) Does the provision of an in-room safe comply with the terms of the Hotel Proprietors Act 1956?

---

## Safe Deposit Agreement

**KING'S HOTEL**

Safe box no.: ....................................................    Date: ......................................................................

Guest name: ..................................................    Room no.: ............................................................

The use of this safe deposit box is subject to the rules printed below:

1. Safe deposit boxes are available only to registered guests. If the use of a deposit box is authorized in the name of two or more persons, it is deemed to be under the control of each of them.

2. The King's Hotel is hereby released from any liability whatever arising from the loss of the key or the presentation thereof by a representation other than one authorized herein. Safe deposit keys must be surrendered at the time of check-out. A charge of £50 will be made for a key lost or carried away and not returned.

   * I have this day surrendered my safe deposit box and have removed the contents in good order.

Guest signature: ........................................................................................................................................

**Figure 12.11** An example of a safe deposit agreement

## Safe Deposit Record

**KING'S HOTEL**

Box number: .................................................    Guest name:.........................................................

Room no.:............................    Date: .......................................    Cashier: ..................................

Authorized signature: ...............................................................................................................

Date: ...................................    Time: ..............................................    Guest signature: ........................

Cashier: ....................................................................................................................................

**Figure 12.12** An example of a safe deposit record

## SECURITY

Security may be defined as the protection and conservation of all assets, which include:

- hotel property
- guests' property
- the reputation of the hotel

Hotel security is, therefore, not merely an extension of the police function into the private sector. Security staff in hotels are employed to safeguard the hotel, employees and guests' property.

Hotels have several different types of security problems which the front office staff should be aware of. As previously mentioned, the Hotel Proprietors Act states that hotel management is liable for the safety of guests' property while they are resident. Depositing guests' valuables into safe deposit boxes is one method of security but the security of guests' clothes and luggage in the guest-rooms is also of great importance. Therefore, a well-controlled system of handling guests' keys is essential.

There are two systems for the control of room keys:

- the conventional key system
- the electronic key system

### The conventional key system

When a guest checks in they are usually given a key card by the front desk clerk. In some hotels the card may also be called the key envelope, or hotel passport. You will remember that we discussed the importance of the key card in Chapter 7. In this chapter we will deal with the security aspect of key control.

The following procedures should be followed to ensure security of guest-rooms:

- A hotel will very often issue only one key for each room, even if two guests are sharing.
- If a guest requests a key, their identification should be checked by the front office clerk.
- Guests should be reminded to return their keys at check-out, i.e. hand their keys to the front desk clerk or place them in the key box.

- Duplicate keys, and keys to connecting rooms, should be kept on a separate board and should only be handed out when absolutely necessary.

- The front desk clerk should regularly check that all keys are accounted for and that none are missing.

- If a room key is lost, the hotel must consider changing the door lock to that room.

In the event of a guest locking themself out of a room, an emergency key can be used. Either the assistant manager or executive housekeeper will have access to this key. This key can open all guest-room doors, even those which have been double-locked. Therefore, it is important that this key is highly protected (and should never leave the hotel property). This key may also be known as the grand master key.

Similarly, for guest-room doors which are not double-locked, a master key can be used, but the same control procedures should be followed. The master key should not leave the hotel property, and when not in use must be secured in a designated place of safekeeping. A written record should be maintained of which employees have received a master key.

### The electronic key system

A sophisticated computer-based electronic key system may be used instead of the traditional method to access guest-rooms. This system operates through a master control console at the front desk which is wired to all guest-room locks.

At check-in, a front desk clerk will insert a special key or plastic card, similar to a credit card, into the appropriate slot on the console. The keys have been randomly coded, and this unique code is then transmitted to the guest-room door lock. When the next guest checks in to that room number, a new door lock code will be re-programmed to that room.

The system also monitors the number of times the guest exits and re-enters the room, including the number of times the room attendant enters the room, when using their pass key. This gives an additional dimension to the security of a guest-room. If a person tries to enter using an incorrect key, then the system alerts the security staff.

Security is only effective when all employees participate in a hotel's security effort. Front desk clerks, porters, doormen and parking attendants all play important security roles. Continuous observation of people arriving and departing, and maintaining an awareness of luggage or parcels being left unattended, as well as people acting in a suspicious or strange manner, should be done by all staff.

---

**Activity 9**  (a) Why is it important for hotels to have strict control over guest-room keys?

(b) Explain the procedures that have to be followed in the following cases:

- A guest requests a key for their room.

- A guest locks themself out of their room.

(c) In what ways does an electronic key control system provide better security than the conventional system?

---

## DEALING WITH EMERGENCIES

It is the responsibility of management to develop procedures for responding to emergencies, e.g. fires, floods, electrical failures, medical problems, robberies, or bomb scares. Planning for emergencies is of the utmost importance. In many cases, the front desk will act as the command centre in the event of an emergency. The front office manager should be familiar with the following emergency guidelines.

### *Emergency guidelines*

1. The initial planning for emergencies is normally carried out by an executive planning committee, which usually involves the front office manager. Points to consider include:

- identifying areas of emergency

- identifying who is to be responsible

- deciding what procedure is to be followed

- deciding how that procedure is to be implemented

- deciding when the procedure is to be implemented

2. The front office manager should ensure that all emergency procedures are regularly reviewed with their personnel so that they can respond properly to any emergency situation.

3. Front office personnel should:

- react quickly and efficiently

- remain cool and calm

- avoid panic

- follow standard emergency procedures

4. Training of front office personnel in various emergency procedures is essential to ensure effective control at times of crisis. Such procedures can include:

- first aid

- fire drills

- police, fire, and ambulance procedures

- telephone handling

- security

- documentation necessary for an emergency

- notifying guests of what precautions to take and how to behave in an emergency

For the sake of the protection of property and human life, it is therefore up to each hotel employee, and in particular front office management, to develop skills for dealing with any emergency. They must know the rules and ideally have had practical experience in simulated training sessions. Regular drills and discussions must be used to keep old and new staff members current in their knowledge of emergency procedures.

### Fire safety skills

Because the greatest threat to any hotel is fire, front office staff should be able to demonstrate the following fire safety skills:

- describe fire precaution rules

- describe fire-fighting procedures

- know the exit routes and doors (all parts of the hotel)

- identify fires by types

- identify the different types of fire-fighting equipment

- operate fire-fighting equipment

- inform the fire department

- inform guests

- verify that guests and staff are out of a potential danger zone
- assist in evacuation of guests
- assist the fire brigade

## SUMMARY

The front of house staff, as well as being processing agents, are also the centre of activity for many other services which a guest has come to expect from a hotel.

The mail and information section of the front office may operate as a specialist department on its own or could be part of the reception desk or porter's desk. Either way, the handling of guest mail requires both great care and efficiency. This same efficiency is required when receiving, recording and delivering messages. For many business people the way in which messages are handled can determine whether business deals are made or lost. What to you is just another message is very important to the guest.

Equally important is the telephone department. Its handling of incoming calls and speedy transfer to their correct location again reflects the professionalism expected of every hotel.

The porter very often is the centre of activity should the guest want to book something, collect an item, have their bags moved and so on. It is the duty of the head porter to ensure that they know where their staff are at all times. This is especially so for those staff who have to leave the hotel to perform a job for a guest. If the head porter is unaware of where their staff are, they could find themselves operating a department on their own.

Other tasks and duties performed by the front desk staff include the exchanging of foreign currency and the issuing and control of safe deposit boxes.

This respect for safety and security is part of the responsibility of every member of staff. Security in this instance means looking after the safety of the guest and hotel personnel, and the security of the property of the guest, the staff and the hotel.

In order to ensure that staff are fully aware of the types of emergency and how to handle them, management should encourage all staff to attend programmes on emergency procedures.

# Review and discussion questions

1 You are the front office manager of a small tourist hotel which caters mainly for FITs. You are given the responsibility of designing appropriate guest services for your department. Explain which of the following services you will or will not provide in your hotel. Give reasons for your decisions.

   - local and international direct dialling telephone services in guest-rooms
   - 24-hour local and international telephone services (through operator)
   - mail and information
   - baggage handling
   - hotel transportation
   - escorting guests to guest-rooms
   - an electronic key system
   - bookings for local tours
   - restaurant or theatre reservations
   - safe deposit boxes
   - car hire
   - others (specify)

2 (a) Why is it important for front office personnel to be aware of the Hotel Proprietors Act?

   (b) Besides the Hotel Proprietors Act 1956, what other hotel legislation may affect the operations of a hotel front office?

3 What are the advantages and disadvantages of an in-room safe?

4 Explain what other functions an electronic key can be used for.

# Case Study: *It's Raining! It's Pouring!*

Early one evening, John, Philip and Jill, the Daintree Forest Hotel receptionists, were busy checking in guests and dealing with their everyday reception duties. John, the senior supervisor who had been at the hotel since its opening, was replying to some questions asked by Mr Vidler, one of the hotel's regular guests. Whilst this was happening, Jill was busy preparing tomorrow's arrivals and departures list for the housekeeping department, and at the same time working with Philip, the junior member of staff on duty, rechecking the hotel's room status. The hotel was fully booked for this evening. In fact, at the time it was overbooked by 20 rooms. This was allowing for possible no shows, late cancellations and 6p.m. release bookings. Other hotels in the area were also fully booked for the evening. This was due to a catering exhibition being held in the nearby Convention Centre. The exhibition was very busy today, being the last day. Janet, the front office manager, came into the front office to check if everything was in order and said that she was popping out for a few minutes, to buy her nephew's birthday present. As she went out of the hotel, the telephone on the front desk rang and it was Mrs Rossi, the executive housekeeper, asking why six particular rooms had not been vacated. John checked the room status board, and confirmed the rooms should be empty. He carefully checked which guests were occupying the rooms and found them to be exhibitors at the catering exhibition. He asked Mrs Rossi if their luggage had been packed and was told their belongings were all over the rooms. It was agreed nothing could be done at this stage until the actual guests returned back to the hotel.

The hotel reception desk was directly opposite the hotel front door. As the doors were opening and closing it was becoming apparent to the receptionists that the wind was building up in pressure. The sound of the flag outside the hotel cracking against the pole, and the canopies hitting against the building, could be heard at the reception desk. Also, an emergency bell seemed to be ringing in the distance.

At that moment George, one of the hotel's porters, sauntered across to the reception desk.

'Just heard a cyclone is on its way,' said George. 'Did you know?'

'No,' replied Jill. 'I didn't even know we were scheduled for a cyclone.'

'Never mind,' responded John. 'It's that time of the year.'

Whilst the receptionists and the porter were discussing the weather, Mr Wilson, an American tourist who was staying in the hotel, arrived at the front desk.

'Just heard on my portable radio, very bad weather is coming. Is that serious?' he enquired.

'No,' replied John. 'Its only a thunderstorm. Be over shortly.'

'Is it wise to leave the hotel?' an anxious Mr Wilson asked.

'No problem,' said John. 'Just be careful of the rain.'

Just at that moment, all the lights in the foyer and the reception area went out.

'Where's the torch, John?' asked Jill nervously.

'Bottom right-hand cupboard, near the computer terminal,' replied John.

Jill reached into the cupboard to find the torch. On finding it, she switched the torch on, but found it would not work.

'John! the torch is not working,' cried Jill.

'Try the other one,' responded John. 'Oh no, I lent that one to the engineering department last month.'

Fortunately, as if on cue, the lights came back on. In the meantime, Mr Wilson had disappeared from the reception counter, but was replaced with a Mrs Cox. She was due to check out later that evening, to catch a Cathay Pacific flight to Hong Kong.

'Are flights still scheduled to depart this evening?' enquired Mrs Cox.

'Er . . . probably,' replied Jill.

'Can you check for me please?' asked Mrs Cox.

'Er . . . yes,' an uncertain Jill responded.

Whilst Jill was telephoning the airport, Philip was asking John if it was okay for him to go off duty. His shift had finished 15 minutes previously.

'You go off duty Philip,' said John, looking at his watch. 'Nigel should be in shortly, in fact he is 20 minutes late.'

Meanwhile, many people were entering the hotel, with soaking hats and coats, leaving pools of water along the foyer's marble floor. At the same time, the sound of crashing plant pots could be heard as the hotel's front doors were swinging backwards and forwards.

'Someone's stuck in the lift!' shouted a voice.

'Call engineering immediately, Jill,' said John.

Jill called the engineering department for assistance. This was then followed by the sound of Jill crying in the corner. What no one at the hotel knew was that she became very nervous and tearful during thunderstorms. Unfortunately, many years previously, her father and brother had been driving in the northern part of Australia during a bad storm when a falling tree had hit their car. Both had died instantly. On seeing Jill in a tearful state, John told her to go into the back office for a while.

'Can I stay an extra day?' inquired Mrs Cox. 'It has just been confirmed my flight is cancelled for this evening.'

'Sorry, Mrs Cox. We are fully booked for this evening,' replied John.

At that moment, Nigel walked up to the front desk, stating that a cyclone warning had just been announced on the radio.

### Questions

1. As the front office manager, what steps need to be taken immediately?

2. After the establishment of relative normality, what would you do next?

3. To ensure that these problems would not occur again, what policies, if any, would you investigate and implement?

# *13*

# *Handling corporate and group sales*

## Introduction

In this chapter we are concerned with the work of the sales and public relations departments and how their work integrates with the reservations, front office and other departments.

In Chapter 5, we saw that many reservation requests are directed to the reservations department. These reservation requests are normally from individual guests. In many large hotels, bookings for groups and tours, and incentive and corporate bookings are dealt with by the sales department. This chapter will identify the work of the sales department, and the type of guests they are concerned with.

The final part of the chapter will look at the role of the public relations department and its effect on the hotel, the guest, the public and the hotel employees.

## THE WORK OF THE SALES DEPARTMENT

The sales office promotes the sale of all of the hotel's services. Its staff are trained to maximize the revenue of all outlets, especially accommodation and the food and beverage (F&B) department. The functions of the sales office include:

- promotion of sales of all services and facilities of a hotel

- publicity and sale of special promotion

- coordination of sales activities with all relevant departments

- coordination with the reservations office or front desk over matters relating to group room sales

- awareness of the sales activities of competitors.

In addition, the sales department is the principal section for clients enquiring about sales facilities and services. It is the role of the sales team to identify customers and interest them in the services of a hotel. The sales team is often involved in arranging appointments to meet the general managers of local companies, and in inviting them to view and use the facilities of the hotel. The team may use these opportunities to discuss ways of satisfying their clients' needs for accommodation, banquets, and so on.

The sales team might be organized into particular market segments in order to better sell the hotel product. For example, the team might consist of a corporate sales section and a groups, tours and incentive sales section, as well as a travel agent section.

---

**Activity 1**    If the sales department does not make money directly for the hotel, how does it contribute to its profitability?

---

## SALES TRAINING

Selling is a competitive activity, especially in hotels. It is, therefore, important that a hotel's sales personnel have the appropriate sales training. Sales training starts with a trainee having a full understanding of the product, the facilities and the services offered within the hotel. A full knowledge of a hotel's market and the characteristics of the customers within that market is also necessary. For example, a Japanese tour staying two to three nights for the purpose of shopping and sightseeing would be interested in a hotel package comprising accommodation, breakfast and transport. Alternatively, a company weekend conference would require accommodation, meals and meeting-room facilities.

As well as new trainees, existing sales personnel should be included in continuous sales training programmes. The training programme may include a change in marketing policies and the introduction to new selling techniques and skills and possibly products.

---

**Activity 2**   You are the sales manager of a hotel in your area. What type of package might you offer in order to attract the following types of guests?

- independent business travellers

- a tour group

- local people on a special weekend or short holiday package

---

## CORPORATE SALES

Most hotels wish to have a high percentage of FIT guests. This is because FITs, especially business people, generate the greatest room revenue and their accounts are normally settled by their companies. This type of guest also tends to spend more money and entertain clients using a hotel's facilities.

Because of intense competition within the hotel industry, the sales personnel need to work hard to obtain their required share of the market. In particular, they need to develop good relations with business people (i.e. corporate or company clients). Therefore, it is essential that the sales department maintain good relations with the people in companies who are responsible for booking hotel services.

Many local and international companies will regularly need to accommodate their visitors. In some companies they may have a separate travel department (or a person responsible for corporate visitors), whose main responsibility is to organize airline tickets and hotel bookings. The travel department manager is an important contact for a hotel sales manager. In return for regular bookings from a company, a hotel may offer a corporate room rate, credit arrangements for bill settlement, and tailor-made services for that client.

The corporate market is also the source of group business. Many companies will have hotel conferences, sales training classes, business seminars and annual conventions. Therefore, it is essential that the hotel sales team keep a careful check on these activities in order that they can offer the company the appropriate hotel facilities and services. The booking of accommodation and conference facilities for business purposes is one aspect of a corporate client's activities. Another aspect can include special functions (e.g. the company annual dinner dance and departmental farewell parties) which are social rather than business activities. Since corporate business is important to a hotel's profitability, many sales teams include a salesperson responsible for specific corporate accounts. It is this person's responsibility to establish a good contact with the companies' personnel and business departments, and thus be able to identify a company's exact needs.

Within a hotel, the sales department must liaise closely with the reservations department (for room bookings), and with the front desk (for the smooth handling of all special requests). Special liaison is also required with the guest relations officer so that personal service and recognition are given to important FIT corporate guests. (Further explanation of the duties of the guest relations officer will be given in Chapter 14.)

---

**Activity 3** You are a salesperson in the corporate accounts section of a hotel's sales department. Your responsibilities include two large contracts with the hotel, the Computer Technology Company and American Banking Corporation account. Describe your duties.

---

## GROUP AND TOURS

Group room business is volume business; that is, a sizeable number of rooms are booked, the guests could well arrive on the same day, and possibly at the same time, and all are on the same room rate. Each hotel has its own policy which dictates the minimum number which constitutes a group; for some hotels this might be 10, for others 30.

The main characteristic of a group booking is the uniformity of the arrangements. All group members will arrive and depart either on the same day or within a few days of each other, and the booking details will normally be handled by a tour operator, agent, or organizer.

Group business can vary from company meetings to groups of tourists and incentive tours. Whatever the group type, this source of business has certain common characteristics:

- It is volume business.

- Group bookings can be steered into periods when business is needed, e.g. during the low season.

- There is the opportunity to encourage repeat business.

- There is the opportunity to generate more money, through the use of other revenue-earning departments of the hotel.

Hotel sales executives and tour coordinators who specialize in group sales must establish good relations with local and international conference organizers, tour operators, airlines and travel agents.

Before accepting any group bookings for a hotel, the executive management team (which normally comprises the general manager, rooms division manager, sales manager and financial controller) would have to decide on the sales mix ratio. The sales mix ratio is the acceptable percentage of FIT business in relation to group business. For example, if a sales mix ratio is 60:40, this means that a hotel will accept 60 per cent FIT bookings and 40 per cent group bookings.

There are many factors which may influence this particular sales mix ratio:

- time of year (e.g. low or high season)

- time of week (e.g. weekdays or weekends)

- length of stay (e.g. one or five nights)

- number of rooms required (e.g. one room or 50 rooms)

- facilities to be used (e.g. business or food and beverage services)

- room rate and discounts (e.g. full room rate or group rate)

The sales mix ratio is important to a hotel's business because of its contribution to its finances. For example, GIT bookings normally contribute a higher room occupancy but a lower average room rate, and, therefore the total revenue could well be lower, whilst for FITs, who normally pay a higher average room rate but possibly generate a lower room occupancy percentage, the total room revenue could be higher. Consequently, it is the responsibility of the rooms division manager to balance the sales mix ratio, thereby obtaining the highest possible room revenue and occupancy rates throughout the year.

---

**Activity 4**  A hotel with 200 guest-rooms has the sales mix ratio at 70:30.

(a) From the ratio, what is the main target market of the hotel?

(b) If a request for 100 rooms during the high season is received from a tour operator, should the request be accepted? Why? Why not?

---

## Pricing

Groups and tours usually stay on a reduced rate because of the volume of business they provide. If the booking has been made through a travel agent, normally a commission is paid to the agent for the introduction of the business. This commission is a form of payment made to the travel agent. When quoting a group rate it is important, therefore, that the sales team includes the commission rate within the group price.

---

# Activity 5

(a) What are the benefits to a hotel in accepting group bookings?

(b) If group bookings bring benefits, why do hotels set a sales mix ratio to restrict the percentage of group bookings in business?

---

## Planning

Planning for a group or tour booking may involve many departments. For example:

- the front office for rooms
- food and beverage for meal arrangements
- accounts for bill settlement
- banqueting for functions

When discussing group and tour arrangements, sales staff, reservations clerks and travel agents frequently use the term package'. A package is a combination of services offered to a group set on inclusive rates, i.e. one price for everything. Such a package could include hotel accommodation, transport, restaurant meals, sightseeing tours, and possibly entertainment.

### Booking procedures

Group bookings work on a long lead time and various procedures have to be followed, adhering to specific time schedules.

### 18 months to 24 months before arrival

The sales office will receive an initial enquiry from a tour operator or company organizing a large conference or exhibition. The sales personnel will record the basic requirements and then contact the necessary departments in the hotel to check availability. For example, they might contact the reservations department to check on room availability and the banqueting department to check the availability of function room space.

When deciding whether or not to accept the booking, the sales office will need to address various questions, which may include the following:

- What conditions should be specified in the contract regarding confirmation dates for final numbers, advance deposits, and penalty charges for cancellations?

- What price should be quoted so as to achieve a good profit and yet not too high that we lose the business?

- Is the business the kind wanted by the hotel?

- Are there sufficient rooms available from the sales mix ratio allocation to accept this booking?

Once these questions have been answered, and the details agreed, a contract is signed.

Information normally found in a contract can include:

- number and types of rooms required

- details of food and beverage requirements

- payment details (could include banker's reference)

- amount of deposit required

- price quoted for the group

- details of what the price includes

- payment details for guest extras

- deadline dates for confirmation of final number of rooms

- deadline date for the receipt of the rooming list from organizer

- details of penalty charges for cancelled rooms

The reservations office should estimate the wash factor, i.e. an estimate of the number of rooms the group or tour will cancel (the shrinkage of the tour). As previously mentioned, groups and tours operate on a long lead time, and therefore a hotel must expect that some of the rooms booked 24 months prior to the actual arrival date will be cancelled. An example of the wash factor is shown below.

A hotel has 100 rooms booked by a tour group for next year. The wash factor may be estimated (from past experience) as follows:

12 months before the tour group arrival date = 30 per cent

3 months before the tour group arrival date = 15 per cent

1 month before the tour group arrival date = 2 per cent

This means that rooms can be released for resale from that tour group's allocation as follows:

12 months before 30 rooms = 30 per cent of 100 rooms

3 months before 11 rooms = 15 per cent of 70 rooms

1 month before 1 room = 2 per cent of 59 rooms

Twelve months before the group and tour arrival date, 30 of the 100 rooms originally booked will be cancelled, and a total of 42 rooms will be cancelled by the time the tour actually arrives.


### *One month to three months before arrival*

The group or tour organizer should confirm with the hotel on a specified date the actual number of rooms required. For example, confirmation may be made one month before the date of arrival.

As a protection against last-minute cancellations of rooms, a system of cancellation deadlines is used. This formalizes the arrangements for cancelling rooms, and is written into the initial contract signed by both the hotel and tour or group organizer. The cancellation deadline is normally four weeks prior to the arrival date; however, for very large groups the hotel may require to know the number six or even eight weeks prior to arrival. If the hotel receives any room cancellations after the agreed cancellation deadline (e.g. one month before arrival), the hotel can charge full room rate or an amount specified in the contract.

Prior to arrival, the group or tour organizer will usually send the hotel a list of the guests' names (normally called a rooming list), and their estimated arrival times. The rooming list may also include pre-registration information concerning passport numbers, addresses and the nationalities of the guests. With this information the hotel is able to pre-register all the members of the party prior to their arrival at the hotel, thus speeding up the check-in process.

The sales office will send out a list of groups or tours expected to arrive in the hotel over the next seven-day period to all departments in the hotel.

---

**Activity 6**  (a)  Why is it necessary for a hotel to estimate the wash factor in group bookings?

(b)  (I)  Why do hotels set a cancellation deadline for group bookings?

(ii)  What are the consequences if bookings are cancelled after the deadline for both the hotel and the tour or group?

(iii)  What is a rooming list and why is it useful to a hotel?

---

### Arrival day

The arrival of a group or tour can place great strain upon reception staff, and therefore it is important that advance preparations are made. For example: housekeeping may assist in room allocation; the porters must arrange sufficient staff so as to handle the baggage and the coach parking space; accounts can check billing arrangements; front office can allocate rooms and prepare key cards; and mail and information can ensure that all the keys are available.

A tour coordinator or assistant front office manager or head receptionist will usually greet the tour leader when they arrive. The front desk manager will consider the best method of registering a large group. There are different methods which may be considered:

- If the group requires less than 12 rooms, then a check-in at front desk is normal.

- If the group requires more than 12 rooms, arrange for a separate check-in area (e.g. use a meeting room or separate area of the lobby if there is room).

For some nationwide tours, the members of the party can register and receive all their information and keys actually on the bus. In this case the tour leader acts as an assistant for the hotel as well as an interpreter if necessary.

### Departure day

On the day the group is due to check out, the reception and/or cashier departments have to ensure that the main account has been signed by the tour leader or group organizer, and all extra bills have been paid by the guests. The return of keys needs to be checked, and the baggage cleared before the group departs. If a tour is leaving later than midday, a hospitality room may be provided by the hotel.

---

**Activity 7**     You are the front office manager of a hotel. Your hotel is expecting a tour group of 40 persons all in twin or double rooms to arrive today. Explain the advance preparations you would make for the arrival of the group.

---

## INCENTIVE TOURS

An important sector of the travel business which uses a hotel is the company incentive tour. Incentive tours are awarded by employers to those employees who have reached a quota of sales or who have shown outstanding performance. An incentive award can range from a restaurant meal to a four-week foreign holiday, and the number of participants may range from one person to hundreds of people.

The companies which specialize in creating, promoting and carrying out all the details of an incentive tour on behalf of the employer provide hotels with an excellent source of business. Therefore, it is essential that the sales team are aware of which companies offer incentive schemes to their employees, and that they establish good relations with the company organizers.

Incentive schemes awarded by employers come in varying sizes and requirements, even to the organizing of a 'thank you' banquet for the staff. The best method of acquiring this type of business is to identify company decision-makers, research the business, and then sell direct to the company concerned.

**Activity 8**  Discuss the advantages and disadvantages of accepting incentive business in your hotel.

## THE PUBLIC RELATIONS DEPARTMENT

The purpose of the public relations department is to ensure that guests and the general public receive a clear, attractive impression of the image and service of a hotel. A successful public relations campaign can help to increase hotel revenue by giving messages via the newspapers, Internet, television or radio which are positive and which attract a profitable or identified market to a hotel.

In order to do this, a hotel informs the media of all newsworthy events concerning the hotel. However, since public relations is dependent on the discretion of the media, there are no guarantees that a public relations announcement or press release will actually reach the public. When announcements are considered newsworthy, they hopefully help to create a good impression of the hotel in the mind of the public.

Regular reporting of a hotel in the news media also helps to raise the hotel's profile. That is, when a person thinks of a hotel, they think of your hotel first. Consequently, a continuous flow of positive articles to the media and public is important in a public relations campaign. This can also include sending newsletters to previous guests, listing any forthcoming events of interest, and highlighting features of a hotel.

The public relations department must ensure that the guest relations officers and front office staff are fully briefed on up-to-date press releases. Similarly, it is important that employees are kept well informed on publicity activities. An employee who has no knowledge of the purpose behind a particular publicity campaign is likely to have a detrimental effect on its promotion. Employee relations are, thus, an extremely important part of any public relations effort.

The public relations manager must also be on good terms with local companies, clubs, organizations, and people who use or come into contact with the hotel, e.g. the local tourist board or management association.

Hotel staff are ambassadors for a hotel. When staff talk to guests and outsiders about their hotel, they should speak knowledgeably and positively, reflecting a good image of the property. In their own way, every member of staff is also a member of the public relations team. To encourage the staff in this role the public relations manager should be involved in hotel activities such as retirement presentations, training and scholarship awards, and personal achievements of staff, such as a chef winning a culinary award. All of these events can contribute to increasing a hotel's profile.

You can therefore see that the sales and the public relations department play a vital role in the marketing and selling of a hotel's products, facilities and services and the integration of their role with all departments is extremely important.

**Activity 9** (a) Explain why public relations is important to the successful operation of a hotel.

(b) You are currently working as a front desk clerk. Explain how you and your department could help in promoting the image of your hotel.

## SUMMARY

It is insufficient for hotels to believe that they are so well known that the general public will be queuing at the door to check in. Certainly there are some properties where this is the case, but it is usually because of highly successful public relations on the part of the owners or managers.

In order to ensure that a hotel achieves maximum occupancy, many properties have a sales department. It is the responsibility of this department to sell all the services and facilities which the hotel has to offer. To do this successfully it is important that the staff are knowledgeable about their product, their market and the locale.

The sales department very often is split into specialist sections such as corporate sales, groups and tours and possibly incentive business. All of these specialisms have the chance of being very important to any hotel. Each needs to be handled in a specific way.

A person who very often works with the sales department and front office in assisting the guest is the public relations officer. He or she is responsible for the 'image' of the hotel. In order to survive, a hotel needs customers, and to this end the sales team, receptionists and staff in general attempt to sell the property's facilities and services. However, the public relations (PR) staff create an image of the hotel through the use of the media, such as radio, television, Internet or newspapers. Anything or anyone who is newsworthy and is involved with the hotel the PR officer tries to have featured in the 'press'. This will help to keep the name of the hotel in the mind of the public.

Hotels cannot just rely on repeat business or word of mouth to fill their rooms. There needs to be a pro-active campaign of making businesses and the public aware that they exist.

# Review and discussion questions

1 A request has been received from a tour operator for a group booking for 30 rooms. The group plans to arrive on 10 December and depart on 15 December.

(a) If the hotel has 150 rooms and the sales mix ratio is 70:30, should the request be accepted?

(b) What other factors should the sales department consider before accepting the booking?

(c) Devise a plan of operations for handling the booking by specifying in the table below what has to be done on or by specific dates, and which departments are responsible.

| Date | Actions to be taken | Department |
| --- | --- | --- |
| | | |

2 As a member of the public relations team, design a publicity campaign to celebrate 25 successful years of operation of your hotel.

# Case Study: *Ishikawa Tours*

Ishikawa Tours has booked a Japanese tour of 45 twin rooms, plus one single room for the tour guide, on a room only basis. This is the first time that the hotel has accommodated this tour group and you want everything to go well with them. Your hotel has 200 rooms all with en-suite bathrooms, tea and coffee making facilities, mini-bars and in-house 'pay' movies. It has a 70-seater restaurant and a 100-seater coffee shop where breakfast is usually served. The hotel also has a series of function rooms capable of seating numbers from 20 through to 500.

The group will make its own way to the hotel by coach and are expected to arrive at approximately 1p.m. The group rates of the hotel apply to the twins and the tour guide is given a room FOC. The tour is scheduled to leave at 7a.m. and will be having breakfast on departure.

The tour will be staying for three nights and they will want an Asian-style buffet breakfast each morning and a tour dinner on the third night. Ishikawa will be paying for all accommodation and the breakfasts and the dinner on the final night on a master account; however, all other expenses are the guests' own responsibility.

**With regard to the following scenarios**

**(a) prior to arrival**

**(b) on arrival**

**(c) on departure**

**list the steps that need to be taken by the front office manager to ensure that the Ishikawa tour group is handled efficiently and courteously.**

**Also list the other departments, both of the rooms division and the hotel in general, that need to be informed and why.**

# 14

# Dealing with guests' problems

## Introduction

The front office is concerned with the selling of a hotel's facilities and services to different types of guest. However, there are occasions even in the best-run and best-organized hotels when things go wrong, and it is to the front desk that guests will generally come to raise the problems, and air their feelings.

This chapter is concerned with identifying the different type of problem which guests may encounter, and the procedures that front desk clerks or guest relations officers need to follow in order to deal with them.

## TYPES OF GUEST PROBLEM

Problems tend to be of two kinds; those created by the hotel itself, or those created by external factors outside the control of the hotel. Both types of problem may cause guests to complain (Table 14.1).

**Table 14.1** Some examples of problems that inconvenience the guest

| Cause of problem | Example |
| --- | --- |
| Guest unfamiliar with hotel policies | A guest arrives early in the morning and is told that the room will not be ready until midday<br>The guest arrives at the front desk only to find that their room has been re-let because they did not guarantee the booking, and it was on a 6p.m. release |
| Guest unfamiliar with terminology | A guest books a room and expects two single beds, not a double |
| Hotel is fully booked | The guest does not believe the front desk clerk who tells them that the hotel is fully booked |
| Impolite front desk staff | The guest is ignored when arriving at the front desk<br>A guest telephones a hotel and is kept on hold for a long period of time |
| Errors made by the hotel | A guest books a twin room and is given a double room<br>The guest is overcharged<br>A guest receives slow service<br>A guest does not receive a requested early morning call |
| External | The guest's luggage is lost by an airline<br>A guest is expecting a visitor who has not arrived<br>A guest has mislaid their safe deposit key |

Complaints, therefore, may be considered to be the results of problems that cause upset to guests, and which are of such importance that they have been brought to the attention of the hotel management (e.g. a guest receives slow service).

Regardless of the source of problems, the front desk staff must deal with the situation in an appropriate manner, always bearing in mind that it is the duty of the hotel to make a guest's stay as relaxed and enjoyable as possible.

## Activity 1

Explain the differences between the two following situations:

- A guest has a problem sending a fax after the business centre has closed.
- A guest complains of dirty bed linen.

## SKILLS NECESSARY FOR DEALING WITH PROBLEMS

Front office staff must possess the correct skills for dealing with guest problems.

A front desk clerk should be:

- calm and helpful
- understanding
- tactful and discreet
- empathetic

When dealing with a guest who has a problem, it is important to remember that, as well as social skills, one's appearance and posture are also important. The following check-list summarizes the key procedures to follow when looking after a guest who has a problem, or who wishes to make a complaint.

1.  Stand up straight with your shoulders back, and look the guest in the eye. If at all possible, it is better to stand next to the guest, rather than remaining behind the desk. This is because the desk forms a psychological barrier between yourself and the guest, which can cause the problem to be exaggerated.
2.  Your hands may be lightly clasped, or by your sides. Do not fold your arms, put your hands in your pocket, or jingle keys; this could again exacerbate the problem, or indicate that you are not listening or caring.

3. Use your face to display empathy and confidence in your ability to help the guest.

4. Always behave in a calm and positive manner. Do not show disapproval or disbelief when a guest complains or behaves aggressively. Act as if you are supporting the guest, i.e. try to solve the complaint.

5. Take all complaints seriously. Always make notes about the complaint. The guest then sees that you mean to do something.

6. Always act on the complaint. What seems to be a small thing to you is important to the guest.

7. Try to maintain a sense of humour and do not ever take complaints personally.

Dealing with guest problems or complaints always requires tact and diplomacy. Remember that it is better for a hotel if guests do complain, no matter how small or serious the complaint is. A dissatisfied guest who leaves the hotel angry about their experience can cause bad publicity, particularly through word of mouth. Also remember that not all guests are easy to satisfy because some actually enjoy complaining. In such situations, the front desk clerk, as well as all other relevant staff, should be alerted to pay special attention to this type of guest.

The front office staff should have the confidence in their abilities to receive complaints and to handle problems. Each problem can highlight an area of inefficiency about which management might be unaware. Once it has been brought into the open, action can be taken and a better standard of service may result.

**Activity 2**   Look at the illustration on p. 264. Comment on the attitude and posture of the front desk clerk who is dealing with a guest's problem.

## SOLVING PROBLEMS

In the check-list above, points 5 and 6 referred to the need to note the complaint and to act on it. The following are some guidelines which should be followed when dealing with a guest's problem.

1. Find out and record all the information.

2. Identify the main problem.

3. Use your professionalism to identify different ways of overcoming the problem.

4. Choose a course of action. This may require discussing the alternatives with the guest; if at all possible use the alternative chosen by the guest. This makes the guest feel happier with the solution.

5. Give instructions to relevant staff in order to rectify the problem.

6. Always check that the actions have been carried out, and the problem solved.

7. Re-contact the guest to ensure that they are now happy.

8. Record the problem and the appropriate action taken in the relevant log book. The front office may wish to discuss the problem at handover time. Additionally, the rooms division manager may wish to devise a policy to ensure that the problem will not occur again, or set up procedures for dealing with regular problems which are outside the control of the hotel.

---

**Activity 3** For each of the following problems explain how you would handle the situation. Your answer should include how you would behave and what action you would take.

- Mr Young, a guest, has misplaced his medication which he needs to take regularly. His prescription is back in the United States but he does remember the name and dosage of his medicine.

- It is 11.45a.m. and you are on duty at the front desk when you receive a telephone call from an Australian, Mr Jones. He is calling from the airport. Mr Jones stayed at your hotel the previous night and has left his passport on the table by the bed in his room. His room number was 225.

---

## HANDLING COMPLAINTS

The handling of complaints is a task no one likes to undertake, and, as previously mentioned, very often requires great tact and diplomacy. The emotional mood of the guest can affect the way you, as a member of the front desk team, will handle the complaint. An angry guest is difficult to deal with and the situation must therefore be handled with care. In order to solve their complaint you must calm the guest down, so that you can ascertain exactly what the trouble is.

In general, the following guidelines are applicable to most guests who approach you with complaints.

1. Greet the guest, and maintain good posture and eye contact. This will make the guest feel that you are a capable, responsible person.

2. Do not interrupt the guest. Guests may become frustrated and angry if they cannot finish what they have planned to say.

3. Apologize, even if the hotel is not at fault. By apologizing you are expressing your empathy with the guest's situation, but you are not accepting responsibility.

4. Do not excuse the fault by blaming someone else. The guest will not be interested, and it shows very poor professionalism.

5. Thank the guest for bringing the problem to your attention. Remember, it is always better to handle a complaint and ensure the guest is satisfied, than for the guest to complain to other guests, or leave the hotel dissatisfied and not wanting to return.

6. Classify the guest's complaint, into:

- serious complaints which can be dealt with by the front desk clerk (e.g. a guest whose room has been re-let)

- minor complaints which can be dealt with by the front desk (e.g. a guest who has no bathroom soap)

- complaints which have to be referred to the assistant manager or equivalent (e.g. the hotel has lost a guest's laundry)

- complaints which the front desk clerk can only deal with by offering empathy and limited assistance and guidance (e.g. a guest has left his camera in a taxi)

7. Discuss possible courses of action with the guest, and reach an agreement as to the most suitable solution.

8. Give instructions to other staff regarding the agreed action.

9. Record the complaint and action taken in the front office log book, and report the matter to your supervisor.

10. Speak to the guest later to ensure that appropriate action has been satisfactorily taken.

---

**Activity 4**  For each of the following complaints, explain how you would handle the situation. Your answer should include how you would behave and what actions you would take.

- A guest at the front desk complains that she does not have any towels in her room.

- A guest complains that he did not receive his early morning call and is now late for his flight.

- An angry guest complains that he has been overcharged by the hotel for his accommodation. Although you have already explained to him that his account has been accurately computed, he is still dissatisfied and behaves in a rude and demanding way.

---

## COURSES OF ACTION TO TAKE WHEN HANDLING PROBLEMS

In some cases guests may indicate what action they require in order to resolve their problems. For example, a guest who has lost her luggage may be very pleased when you offer to contact the airline for her. A guest with a noisy neighbour, on the other hand, may request a change of room, while a guest who had late room service may ask for a complimentary meal.

It is often the responsibility of front office staff to decide whether this action is possible and justified. Alternatively, a guest may wait for the staff to offer appropriate alternative action. In this case, it is important for the staff to watch for clues to indicate the guest's desires. For example, front office staff might offer a reduction in price, but the expression on the guest's face would indicate that this was either inappropriate or the amount was sufficient.

Front office staff should avoid applying their own judgements to the situation, or offering solutions too readily. It is sometimes better to wait for the guest to respond to the suggested remedy. Many guests will expect more than the staff can offer. For example, a guest may expect a complimentary room, not just a price reduction. Other guests may have lower expectations. For example, a guest who expects a price reduction and is instead given a complimentary room is likely to be pleased with the offer. The level to which you can offer recompense to the guests depends on the amount of leeway given to the front desk by the hotel management.

It is not usually good policy to reduce the price of a room or meal; this will lose the hotel actual revenue. A more positive and constructive procedure is to provide an extra service.

If a guest is very difficult and will not agree to any course of action, you may then have to refer them to a more senior member of management, or realize that they are in an intractable mood and will not be pacified. In the latter case, take their name and address; a carefully worded letter inviting them to dinner or a complimentary stay on another occasion may be well-received another day, when they are in a better mood.

---

**Activity 5**   What course of action would you recommend in the following situations?

- At 5.30p.m. a guest complains to the front desk that his room has not been cleaned.

- A guest complains she has not received her morning newspaper for two consecutive mornings.

---

## FOLLOW-UP

The front office staff are responsible for the follow-up procedures on a problem, particularly if it is a complaint. This can be done either later the same day, or the following day. The staff member who dealt with the initial complaint should contact the guest and ensure that the problem has been rectified to their satisfaction. For instance, if a call to the housekeeper was promised, call immediately. If a guest complained that their room was not cleaned properly the previous day, they should be contacted the following day. For example:

*Receptionist*:     Good afternoon, Mr Young, this is Amanda on reception who you spoke to yesterday evening. I am calling to inquire if your room has been serviced satisfactorily today?

Learning to deal effectively with problems requires experience on the part of the front office staff. This experience can be helped through planned training sessions and role-playing situations. By anticipating problems, planning and practising responses, and receiving constructive feedback, staff members should be better prepared to deal effectively with guest problems as they arise.

---

**Activity 6**   Explain why it is important that the front desk clerk should follow up on a complaint.

---

**Activity 7**   You are working at the front desk when the following complaint occurs. Explain what you would say and what action you would take.

Two guests have just come from one of the hotel's restaurants, and are complaining to you about their dinner. They have already complained to the restaurant captain about the cold food and slow service, and received no satisfaction. They are now demanding to see the manager; however, the manager is unavailable.

---

## COMMUNICATION SKILLS

Direct and continuous interaction with guests means that good communication skills are essential for front office staff. The following are some examples of phrases and terms to use when talking to guests in different situations.

Apologizing does not always mean you are accepting responsibility. You are sorry a guest has been upset; not because you are at fault. For example:

- I am so sorry you have been troubled.

- I am sorry to have kept you waiting.

Never blame someone else, especially your colleagues. For example, never say 'Oh, that waiter is always careless' or 'Yes, room attendants often forget to put clean towels in the bathroom'. It is better either to pass no comment on fellow staff or to say:

- Oh, it is most unusual for that waiter to be careless.

- I am so sorry, it must have been an oversight by housekeeping.

Do not give excuses; the guest is not interested in or concerned about your problems. Never tell a guest that you are short-staffed, or that the supervisor is away today, as reasons for poor service. Give simple comment such as:

- Thank you for pointing out this problem. I will investigate immediately.

- I will inquire of the manager why you have not experienced our usual good service.

Always summarize the guest's problem, so that they know you understand what the trouble is. For example, say:

- You ordered a meal from room service at 8p.m., and the meal arrived at 8.40p.m. and you wanted a steak and the waiter brought lamb cutlets, so the order was incorrect as well as the fact that you were kept waiting. Is that correct?

## THE ROLE OF THE GUEST RELATIONS OFFICER (GRO)

The main duty of the GRO is to ensure that guests feel welcome, receive personal attention, and enjoy their stay. The GRO may also assist the assistant manager (or duty manager) by handling complaints, welcoming VIPs, and making courtesy calls. Normally a GRO will have a desk in the front lobby of the hotel. They may also have a desk in the assistant manager's office, where they can do their administrative work. Since a GRO is expected to carry out a variety of tasks, many skills must be possessed. These are outlined in the job description shown in Figure 14.1.

## Job Description

Job title:              Guest relations officer

Department:            Front office

Job summary:           To ensure that guests feel welcome and enjoy their stay in the hotel.

Conditions of work:    Refer to Employment Contract and Staff Information Handbook

**Job Description**
- Check all the arrangements for VIP and CIP arrivals.
- Check arrangements for guests with special requests (e.g. handicapped).
- Check that all resident guests are being well looked after (e.g. see that long-stays have flowers and fruits in their rooms).
- Escort VIPs and regular guests from the front desk to their rooms.
- Handle guest complaints when the assistant manager is unavailable.
- Provide courtesy calls to VIPs, sick and long-stay guests (to show that the hotel recognizes their importance and wishes to make their stay as comfortable as possible).
- Attend any social or promotional gatherings the manager may hold.
- Assist sales staff by escorting potential clients around the hotel.
- Provide miscellaneous clerical services where appropriate (e.g. sending guest faxes if the business centre has closed).
- Provide information on hotel's business and retail outlets (e.g. provide information about hotel's restaurants).

**Social skills needed:**
- Very smart appearance.
- Mature and sophisticated manner.
- Natural courtesy.
- Awareness of and sensitivity to different cultural backgrounds of guests.
- Ability to handle all complaints with tact, courtesy and initiative.
- Be fully conversant with the different departments and systems within the hotel.
- Good general knowledge of local and international current affairs, of local geography and of places of interest, as well as knowledge of your own country.

**Figure 14.1** Job description for a guest relations officer

Guest relations is a very important aspect of the service of a hotel. While the majority of guests in a hotel are pleasant, unassuming, understanding, and a joy to serve, there are demanding guests who offer a challenge to all the hotel staff, and the way they are handled can have a lasting effect on both the guests and the hotel. If guests can be made to feel comfortable and satisfied then they will be more likely to return to the hotel. Remember that the GRO and the front office staff all play a very important role in the guest's stay. The helpful and friendly service provided to the guest creates a favourable impression of the hotel and it is this favourable impression which is essential to ensure that the guest views the hotel sufficiently highly that they will want to return, and will tell their friends or colleagues to stay with you.

---

**Activity 8** You are the rooms division manager of the King's Hotel and have recommended to the general manager that a guest relations officer should be employed. Discuss the scope and degree of responsibility you consider it appropriate for your guest relations officer to have.

---

## SUMMARY

However professional or efficient a hotel may be, all will be worth nothing if its staff are not willing to deal with or not capable of dealing with the guest when things do not run according to plan.

Guest problems arise from two sources: things going wrong at the hotel, and something going wrong but outside the control of the hotel. For the guest, it is often not immediately possible to discern where the problem has originated, and their frustration and annoyance are vented at the front desk. Your ability at handling such a situation can help make the guest a friend of the hotel for life or chase them away for ever.

Front office staff need to be calm, courteous and helpful as well as understanding what the guest is going through or why he or she is behaving the way that they are.

All of these attributes can be learned and practised, and with practice comes the knowledge that you are a highly effective, socially skilled member of the hotel staff.

To help any member of the hotel staff cope with difficult or complaining guests there is a set of procedures which will help you to diffuse the situation, as well as eventually redeeming the hotel in the guest's eyes. Apart from explaining how to investigate what has gone wrong, the rectification of the problem, if at all possible, and ensuring that the guest is happy after the incident, this chapter has emphasized the need for clear and concise communication.

Finally, we explored the role of the guest relations officer, and their use to large hotel properties.

## Discussion and review questions

1  Explain, with the aid of a flow-chart, the procedures for handling guest complaints. When you construct your flow-chart, pay special attention to areas where an alternative course of action may be required (e.g. a guest may or may not be satisfied with your suggestions).

2  In what ways are guest complaints

(a)  beneficial to a hotel?

(b)  harmful to a hotel?

3  Suggest what a front desk clerk should say to a guest in the following situations:

–  A guest is kept waiting at the front desk.

–  A guest complains that there is no soap in the bathroom.

–  A guest demands to talk to the manager, who is unavailable.

4  As a front office manager, how would you design a complaints-handling training programme for a new receptionist in your hotel?

## Case Study: *The Customer is Always Right: or Are They?*

The Bella Vista Hotel is one of the most famous five star properties in the country. It attracts visitors from all over the world and the hotel staff regularly caters for movie stars, royalty, presidents, national and international dignitaries.

Mrs. Etteridge the executive housekeeper received a copy of a letter that had been sent to the general manager.

Room 4803 – Bella Vista Hotel

*General Manager*
*Bella Vista Hotel*
*June 11th*

*Dear Sir,*

*We have been staying in your hotel for the last two and a half months and are absolutely appalled and disgusted at the way in which you have totally ignored us.*

*We are attached to a Dutch international company and have travelled the world for the last thirty years, but* never *have we stayed in a hotel where we have been made to feel so unwelcome.*

*For the last six weeks we have had to put up with a maid who is brusque, excessively rude, never says 'Good evening' and always slams the door hard when she is finished. It has left my husband and me speechless. During the whole of our stay, soap has* never *been put out, but the old ones left until they are impossible to use any more. Three bags are meant to be left for dry cleaning, laundry and pressing. Rarely does this happen. On the occasions when I have asked for a extra bag for dry cleaning in addition to the laundry, I have been told they were unavailable. For two solid weeks I stared at the same two apples left in the fruit bowl. When I asked if we might have a little more variety I was told that most fruits were out of season. Unbelievable. (However, Private Dining would arrange for extra fruit to be sent up to us: doubtless at an extra expense to ourselves.) This happened for three days then nothing – the bowl has been empty for two days.*

*We have come to your country to live – it is a difficult enough experience moving to another country but you have made it more so. This is by no means our first visit. On this occasion we particularly selected your hotel, and it has turned out to be a grave mistake.*

*We are certainly not in the habit of complaining but I cannot emphasize strongly enough how utterly offended we feel. That after two and a half months the only courtesy you have shown us is one bottle of wine and two bath robes which we received in the first few weeks of our stay. I could go on but true to form there is no more stationery in the desk – it has never been replenished since we came here.*

*It goes without saying that if you choose to ignore your guests and their welfare we would never recommend your hotel to anyone.*

*Yours faithfully,*
*Sarah van den Born*

## Questions

1. **What would you do if you were the rooms division manager?**

2. How would you deal with the customer?

3. Are there ever any circumstances when the guest may be wrong?

4. In the space provided below, now draft a letter you would send to Mrs van den Born.

# 15
# *Yield management*

## Introduction

Rooms division managers have many problems to wrestle with, such as staff productivity and morale and also rooms and revenue maximization. That is making the very best use of the product that they have, namely bedrooms. We must remember that hotel bedrooms are a highly perishable commodity; that is, bedrooms unsold on any given night cannot be reused or be stored for possible future use, and this is why rooms managers try to ensure that they fill their hotel bedrooms each night.

The perishability of such a service product is not solely associated with the accommodation industry, the same parameters are also associated with the transport industry.

---

**Activity 1**  List as many reasons as you can why the transport and hotel industries can be said to be similar

The principles of yield/revenue management had their origins in the airline industry, but have also taken hold widely throughout the rest of the travel and tourism industries. The majority of major lodging corporations, airlines, cruise lines and a fast growing number of tour operators, car rental and passenger railway firms are practising more or less sophisticated yield/revenue management methods and maintain stock control systems.

---

## A YIELD MANAGEMENT SCENARIO

A customer phones the hotel reservations to book a cheap rated room for Monday night through to Wednesday.

*The question that is raised is: does the reservations department take this booking or not?*

If this were the last single room available then reservations would not like to sell this room at a cheap rate. However, what if reservations knew that there was a likelihood that they could sell the room for a longer period of time, for example, until Friday? Then there was a greater chance that the hotel would gain more revenue by selling the room for a longer period of time but at a lesser rate, than selling the room for one or two nights at rack-rate.

*How does the reservations manager know how many bookings to take for what types of product (room types/rates) for what arrival and departure dates?*
*This is yield management in the hotel industry.*

Although yield management is seen as a relatively new term initially coined by the airline industry, the underlying concept of revenue maximization is not. The basic idea is that during periods of high demand for hotel rooms the price is set at the highest rate so as to maximize revenue and at times of lower demand the rates are set so as to encourage occupancy.

**Activity 2**  (a) List ways by which a hotel can maximize its rooms occupancy.

(b) List ways by which a hotel can maximize its revenue.

(c) Explain how the F&B element of the hospitality industry could use yield management.

Apart from the variety of discount packages being offered by hotels to entice the prospective guest into the hotel during periods of low occupancy, the front office manager has to balance the rooms being sold during high occupancy periods. This is so as to ensure that a 'full house' is achieved with the best average daily rooms' rate achievable.

Yield management, whether manual or computerized, endeavours to maximize revenue by adjusting prices to suit market demand. Although this American theory has proved beneficial to both the airline and hotel industry, present day yield management systems have been very slow in gaining total acceptance within the European and Australian hotel industries.

## A YIELD MANAGEMENT DEFINITION

'Yield management' or 'revenue management' (as it is mainly called in the United States business environment) is a revenue enhancing technique appropriate to many service industries. To be able to utilize this technique properly the hotel has to undertake the following procedures or practices, overbooking, duration and itinerary control and market segment pricing (price differentiation plus fencing). The results from these practices are then subjected to detailed analysis.

### Overbooking

The reason for taking more reservations than we have rooms available has been explained in Chapter 7, however the reason for it being a necessity in yield management is to ensure that the best market mix of customers is achieved. But it must be remembered at all times that overbooking is in breach of contract and must be managed with extreme care.

### Duration and itinerary control

Duration and itinerary control is simply a longwinded way of saying that the reservations department and the front office manager constantly monitor the length of stay of the various people who book rooms and at the same time they monitor the types of room that they book. This is so that a pattern can be built up as to the average length of stay of what type of guest in what type of room and at what time during the week or month. This information on its own may be interesting but will not have a great deal of significance. But combined with all of the other historical data it will help give the rooms division management a very clear picture of their operation.

### Market segment pricing

This once again is a complicated way of saying that the hotel has a variety of different rooms' prices for different segments of the market.

---

**Activity 3**  Using an earlier chapter of the book list the various market segments that a hotel encourages staying in their hotel.

---

The 'fencing' element of this strategy means that each of these market segments has a finite or limited number of spaces available. It is this idea of 'fencing' the various rates that makes yield management slightly different from previous rooms and revenue maximization techniques. Instead of taking as many of any category of guest as requests a room the hotel decides how many rooms to open not for that week but for that one single day.

## WHEN IS THE USE OF YM APPROPRIATE?

The objective of the intelligent use of yield management concepts and principles is to increase bottom line profitability in hotels that have the following characteristics:

- Demand for the hotel can be divided into distinct market segments.

- Each of these segments are prepared to pay different amounts of money for their room.

- The capacity supply is relatively fixed and it is costly or impracticable to add or subtract room supply in the short term. That is that the hotel has a fixed number of rooms and that it is not really feasible to instantly add extra rooms.

- The room supply is perishable and cannot be stored to be sold at a later date.

- The marginal cost of selling an additional room is low.

- The request for a room is ordered in advance of its use.

- Demand for the room fluctuates and cannot be predicted with a high degree of certainty.

- The physically (not commercially) identical product can be sold to different market segments for different booking conditions.

---

**Activity 4**    (a)   For each of the dot points above give a relevant example of explanation.

                 (b)   Find out from a hotel local to you what their marginal cost of selling a room is.

---

## SYSTEMS AND STRUCTURES IN PLACE FOR YIELD/REVENUE MANAGEMENT

Yield management tends to operate within a hotel that has a mix of market segments with variable rack rates, the property should ideally have over fifty rooms and a computerized reservation/management information system. However, such a limitation of property size has now been shown not to be necessarily true, similarly whilst a computerized system is very beneficial it is not mandatory.

## YIELD MANAGEMENT FORMULA

Yield management works by using a very simple formula, and that is:

$$\text{Yield} = \frac{\text{revenue realized}}{\text{revenue potential}}$$

The revenue realized is a variable amount, whilst the revenue potential is fixed. Revenue potential is calculated by multiplying the number of rooms by the actual rack rate. For example: a hotel has 100 rooms of which 80 are doubles at £70 per room and 20 are singles at £50 per room. The revenue potential would be £6,600. That is derived from the following calculation $80 \times £70 = £5,600$ plus $20 \times £50 = £1000$.

**Activity 5** (a) For the past week the King's Hotel has taken the following amount of revenue from its rooms: Monday £12,629; Tuesday £16,782; Wednesday £22,542; Thursday £19,083; Friday £13,652; Saturday £9,086; Sunday £5,420. Using the King's Hotel room detail and rack rates (see page 31) give the yield percentage for each day.

(b) Now compare the yield percentage against the following occupancy percentage for the same period. What comments can you make?

Monday 50 per cent; Tuesday 69 per cent; Wednesday 100 per cent; Thursday 80 per cent; Friday 64 per cent; Saturday 78 per cent; Sunday 25 per cent.

## TOOLS AND STRATEGIES

Yield management emphasizes the achievement of high rates on high demand days and high occupancy when demand is low. The focus of yield management is to maximize revenue EVERY DAY – not just for seasons or periods.

The underpinning framework of yield management consists of four steps:

1. Forecasting

2. Systems and procedures

3. Strategies and tactics

4. Feedback.

### Forecasting

Forecasting is the key to effective yield management. Forecasting must be done on a regular basis, a minimum of once a week during normal occupancy periods and possibly daily during high demand periods, and must encompass more than 30- or 60-day projections. In order to make accurate forecasts a variety of information is required.

The information sources available to the yield management team are: historical data – both recent and past years are required on the number of bookings, the type, e.g. group or tour, transient, airline, corporate and so on; also information regarding the number of cancellations, walk-ins, no-shows, overstays and understays, and on what days these occurred. This information will give the team details on lead times, wash factors, high and low demand periods, from which the team will formulate the rates to be offered.

---

**Activity 6**    In groups, discuss why the above data is necessary for the accurate forecasting of rooms occupancy, and the maximization of revenue.

---

Other factors need to be considered when undertaking forecasting, such as

- weather conditions, both locally and nationally

- events in local area

- competitor's activities

- airlines' schedules and services

- limitations of the property

- strategies of the property

- internal promotions

- internal policies on overbooking

- consumer behaviour

Not all the above factors are controllable but they will affect the demand upon a hotel's facilities and the subsequent pricing strategies and decisions.

Yield management is only a management decision tool and even if the forecasts are 'off', the decisions made will be better than if they were made on the basis of no forecast at all.

### Systems and procedures

A computerized system aids the communication of forecast information from the yield management team to relevant departments of a property and in some cases between properties and booking agencies or central reservation systems. A computerized system allows 24-hour input of information and link up to enable efficient circulation of current information. The yield management team and/or analysts can, in some cases, enter the system directly and make phantom bookings. This is done so as to close a rate level in order to stop any reservations clerk or booking agencies selling any more rooms at that particular rate.

The information from the yield management team regarding the various rate levels per number of rooms is input into the computer system. The customer makes a telephone inquiry and the reservations clerk, working from the VDU screen, first looks at the days required and then checks the room availability. The reservation clerk, using basic up-selling skills (see Strategies and tactics below), will always offer the highest priced room and work down, in an attempt to not lose any potential revenue.

However the system needs to be flexible in order to accommodate the 'regular' customer who will expect a continuation of their corporate or 'special' rate. This flexibility is necessary to maintain goodwill especially for the long-term customer. It is vital that the hotel must remember to retain a human side in yield management. The system cannot take over the role of the manager and many situations may still require to be handled on a case by case basis.

### Strategies and tactics

The two main aims of the yield management are as follows:

1. On high demand days maximize average room rate to increase revenue.

2. On low demand days maximize occupancy and average room rate.

On high demand days the team will plan for transient reservations (a guest that is not part of a group booking). They will determine the correct mix of market segments so as to sell out at highest rates possible, e.g., the 'walk in' businessman who will pay the highest rate for the privilege of walking in off the street at the last minute and be able to book a room. Once the mix of market segments has been decided the team will assign a number of rooms to each segment of the mix.

## A ROOM ASSIGNMENT SCENARIO

A hotel has 100 rooms, and allocates the following numbers of rooms to each market segment:

Rate levels

|  |  |
|---|---|
| No. 1 (highest) | 100 rooms |
| No. 2 | 50 rooms |
| No. 3 | 40 rooms |
| No. 4 (lowest) | 30 rooms |

This means that at all times a 100 per cent of the rooms will be held for rack rate guests. However, in reality a hotel will always have a number of guests on corporate or special rates. Thus the practicality of the situation may dictate that 80 per cent of rooms are ALWAYS kept for rack rate guests, leaving 20 per cent for necessary discounted rates. Similarly the rate levels reflect that only 30 per cent of the rooms will be ever be available for the cheapest of rates.

The operating procedure is simple. The reservations clerk will monitor the pick-up of each room category as they progress through the lead-time to the day of arrival. If they find, unexpectedly, that the high rate categories are filling up faster than anticipated this would mean that they would close out the lower rates.

Thus this strategy restricts low profit categories such as sports teams or mass tours. The YM team may also require minimum stays to prevent the early departure factor. Also it helps the hotel to fill on down-times such as weekends. For example, a minimum two nights stay is required as long as one night is a Saturday or Sunday.

The team will also plan for group bookings that fall on high demand days. First of all, the hotel will only sell to groups who are willing to pay higher rates and provide high occupancy per room. A tactic that is often used is to only sell to a group who book meeting space and hospitality suites as well as their accommodation, thus encouraging the guests to stay in-house for meals to use the bar and other facilities. For more price sensitive groups, the YM team will attempt to allocate their booking in low demand dates, this is particularly relevant for local clients who want to book function space for a dinner dance or meeting and who wish to have overnight accommodation.

## SALES STRATEGIES

It was mentioned earlier that the reservations department is expected to sell the highest rated rooms first. This means to always quote rack-rate. However, it is acknowledged that for many reservations staff this form of hard sell is difficult, accordingly reservations staff are encouraged to undertake an alternative approach known as 'Up-selling'. The reservations clerks may offer a standard room first and then offer a more luxurious room at a slightly higher price or offer 'extras' for a minimum cost. For example, an upgrade of an £80.00 per night standard could be sold by stating that for a slight increase in price, i.e. £95.00 the guest can have a deluxe room, whilst for only £110 per night breakfast is included. The customer may be offered an upgraded room at a lower rate than normal, however, it is good practice to inform the customer that it is a 'once-off' deal, a gesture of goodwill, so the customer does not expect that rate every time they book. The benefit of this practice is that the hotel gets a higher average room rate and at the same time gives the guest the opportunity of staying in a better room, with the possibility that they would like the room sufficiently to continue to book that grade of room.

## FEEDBACK

Feedback enables the team to judge the accuracy of their forecasts and form the subsequent months' and years' historical data. More importantly it gives the team an indication of the responsiveness of the organization's reservation system to their strategies and also the effectiveness of their strategies in response to market demand. The monitoring of denials (the guest cannot stay because there are no rooms available) and conversions (the guest who enquires about a room and is persuaded to reserve that room) helps this effort. Feedback allows everyone involved in yield management to keep updated on strategies and information as well as acting as a mechanism for praise and assessing individual or departmental performance. These are the structures and basic systems of yield management, but to implement them in a hotel requires a yield management team.

## THE YIELD MANAGEMENT TEAM

Before an effective yield management system can be put into place and used it is necessary to have an operations team. They will be the driving force behind the successful implementation of yield management and will be the group of people who regularly meet to forecast the forthcoming business of the hotel.

The yield management team will typically consist of the rooms division manager, the sales manager and the reservations manager. This does not mean that anyone else is excluded, but for a speedier and more effective decision making progress it is wise not to make the management team too big. In some hotels the general manager likes to be involved or the front office manager may take the place of the reservations department. However the original three would tend to make the best team. The rooms division manager has the overall control of the department with targets for maximizing both occupancy and revenue. The sales department must be a part for it is they who go out on a daily basis to sell the hotel's bedrooms, and whilst they are fully aware of the need to maximize revenue their primary thrust is to get bodies into the hotel. Thus by working with the forecast team it ensures that the sales and marketing staff are fully informed as to the peaks and troughs of the hotel's business. The last but probably the most important member of the team is the reservations department. The reservations manager is the person who has a complete understanding of all of the hotel's bookings, the future booking patterns and the past histories of the hotel's arrivals and occupancies, and who is most up to date with bookings.

The role of the yield management team is fourfold:

1. To predict demand

2. To assign rooms to transient reservations

3. To open or close rates as seen fit

4. To conduct feedback sessions.

The principal role of the team is to predict the demand for rooms into the foreseeable future. It is insufficient to simply take last year's figures and adjust by an agreed percentage figure. The question that now has to be asked is 'What would be our mix of market segment if we were to maximize yield?'

It is now generally accepted that what was a successful formula for filling bedrooms a few years ago is now wrong for today's hotel market mix. Thus it is up to the team to constantly remind each other of the fact that neither the customer nor their expectations remain static. By trying to predict demand the team assesses what has happened in the past; the time of year, the weather, any exceptional circumstances which surrounded bookings for then and so on. They then look into the future for any similar occurrences that could affect, either positively or negatively, the booking of hotel rooms. Whilst no one can accurately predict what the future may hold, it is still better to conduct such predictions and to make management decisions with limited information than with no information at all.

Once a fair estimate has been made of the room requirements for both the near and distant future, the team then has to allocate the right amount of room inventory, i.e. number of rooms, to the various market segments. This is done by discussing, reasoning and deciding what groups will arrive; their room requirements; what will be the volume of corporate rate business; how many walk-ins will arrive, etc. All of these imponderables are examined and with them, the historical data which management has amassed. The yield management team decides which classes or levels of rates to open or close.

Another aspect of the yield management team's work is to conduct feedback sessions. These sessions are necessary to help judge whether or not the forecasts have been accurate and effective. Feedback acts as a measure of responsiveness in terms of systems, strategies and the management of revenue and occupancy. It also acts as a measure of staff performance.

It is necessary for the yield management team to constantly strive to have the most up to date information and to react quickly to the subtle changes in the accommodation business. It is no longer sufficient to believe that a good overbooking policy is enough to ensure a full house. Unless all of the available data is used then the rooms division manager can end up with a 100 per cent room occupancy but with a revenue yield that is considerably less.

## TRAINING DEVELOPMENT AND ORGANIZATION CULTURE

A yield management system creates a formalized and efficient procedure for manipulating rates to optimize both market demand and revenue. This presents the individual property manager and the organization with change; that is a change in both staff attitude and working procedures. An integral part of this management of change process will require managers, reservation clerks and booking agents to be trained. The training process would consist of education in new computerized systems, yield management policies and customer enlightenment programmes. For example, reservation clerks will need to be trained to say 'NO' to low rates and learn to 'hold out' for the higher rates of late corporate business and the techniques of up-selling.

The organization may also undergo a culture change in its approach to using yield management. The system actively encourages managers to be proactive in their decision-making, planning and communicating strategies to both staff and booking agencies.

## THE CUSTOMER

Yield management is a system that is entirely objective in its approach. That is, it places the needs of the customer secondary to those of the hotel. Yield management systems want to maximize both the occupancy and the revenue of the hotel, and to do this the yield management team opens and closes room categories at their will and not in accordance with what the customer wants.

For many years the prospective hotel guest has become used to bargaining for their room rates or at least expecting that a room at the rate which they normally pay will be available. The hotel has been seen by their customers as being simply providers of room and bed space. The idea that they are highly organized establishments where the sole purpose for the owners is to make money does not appear to be a part of the hotel guest's thought pattern.

Yield management has turned this aspect of hotel operation on its head. What the system now tells the customer is that we have certain rooms set aside at certain price categories, and once the cheaper categories fill you will have to pay more. The initial fear of hoteliers is that prospective guests may choose not to stay with one hotel because of its perceived inflexibility and intransigency over room rates.

The attitude of the general public towards the practice of yield management by the hotel industry is that hotels are not like aeroplanes (the originators of YM) in that they cannot move, and therefore hoteliers will sell their rooms at any price. Customers seem to be resigned to the fact that airlines charge different prices depending on how far ahead a ticket is bought and what restrictions are met, but it is dubious as to whether hotel customers will accept this pricing method. The airline industry comprises a small number of major competitors, and customers seldom have much choice. Hotels, on the other hand, have numerous competitors. If customers don't like having to pay different prices for the same room, they may decide to patronize the competition. Likewise, customers may believe it's unfair to pay a higher price for a room than someone who reserved it a few weeks earlier.

Thus hoteliers may face a customer-education problem. Time will tell whether the hotel industry's newly found cavalier attitude will be maintained, or whether it will revert back to the 'old ways'.

## THE FUTURE NOW

Yield management will run most successfully for any hotelier, providing they follow the concepts as described in the previous sections. Even the original idea that yield management will not be successful for hotels of less than 50 rooms has been shown to be completely untrue. Yield management will work for any hotelier who operates a manual operation or computerized system, provided they are prepared to commit the time and effort. In all cases such effort will be shown to make a substantial financial difference.

However, for those properties that are determined to fully maximize their room space, there are now software packages on the market that will do much of the decision making for the hotel management. It has to be said that they do tend to be expensive, but in most cases the increase in the annual rooms revenue would probably cover the purchase cost.

## WHAT IS A YIELD MANAGEMENT SOFTWARE SYSTEM?

A yield management software system is a powerful decision-making tool that automatically makes yield management judgements to determine the rate availability by length of stay to maximize overall revenues. Such software analyses raw data collected from in-house property management systems, and identifies certain booking patterns, categorizes all the information and prepares forecasting models in the form of straightforward reports.

Quite simply a yield/revenue management system:

- Monitors and manages risk automatically
- Identifies dates that have low demand and/or revenue
- Provides optimal length of stay control
- Manages risk of overbooking
- Automatically highlights abnormal market behaviour
- Allows events to be entered before they occur
- Creates flexible reports for marketing programme evaluation
- Minimizes data that must be reviewed
- Determines total transient and group demand displaced by a potential group arrival
- Helps determine group availability and rates.

## HOW DOES THE YIELD REVENUE MANAGEMENT SYSTEM WORK?

### Forecasting

The forecasting element of the system prepares its forecasts by using:

- Demand patterns
- Special events databases
- On-books information and the
- Results of any user demand changes.

Based on this data the software forecasts transient demands based on historical bookings and folio data. The system will forecast no-show and cancellation patterns, demand and uncertainty in demand, according to market segments, room type, day of the week, length of stay and booking lead-time. These transient forecasts are then fed into the opportunity cost optimization aspect of the system.

### Analysis

When a hotel adopts a fully computerized yield management system an

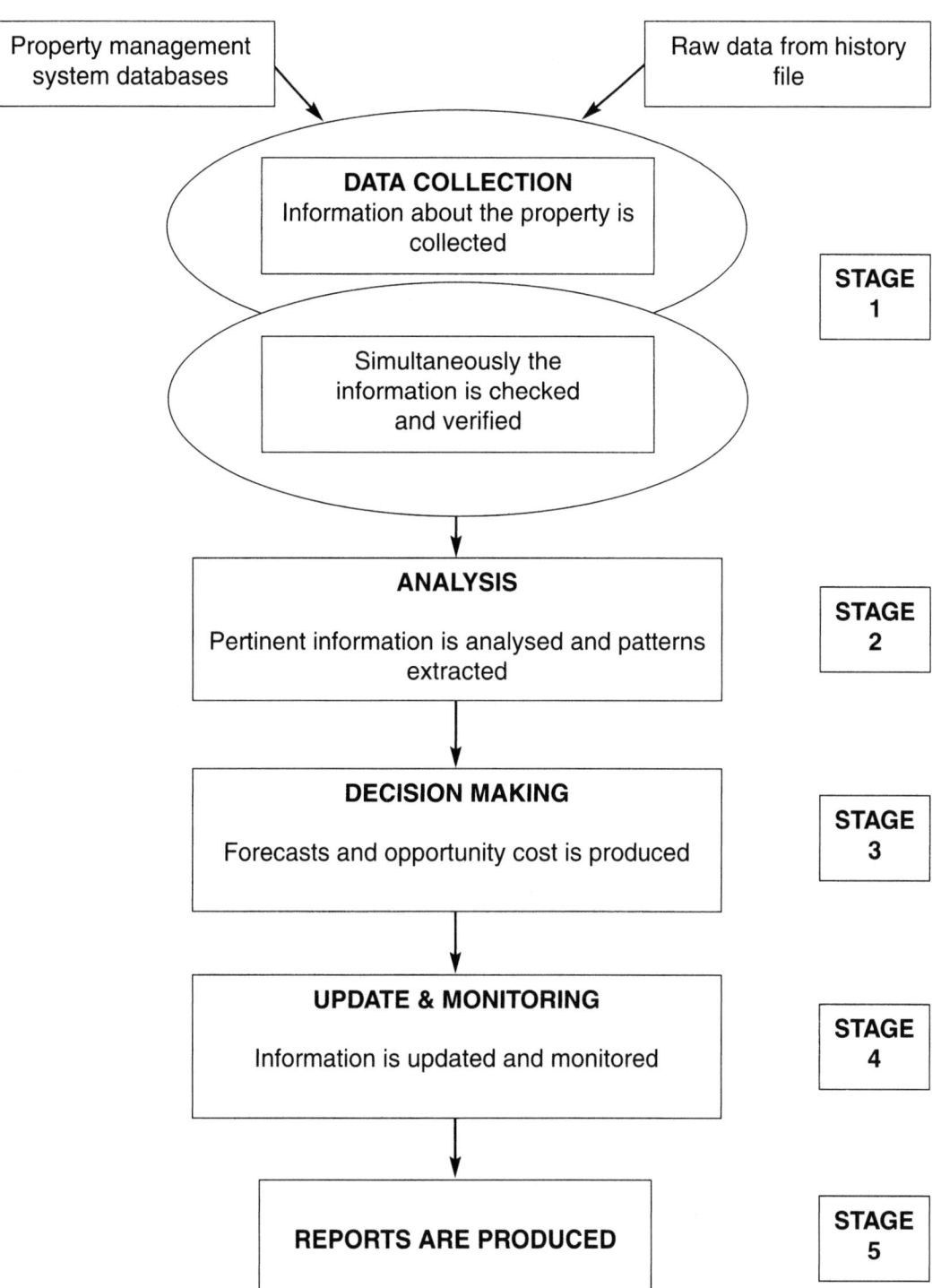

**Figure 15.1** Yield management process

initial analysis of the property is conducted. After the data has been collected it is analysed for patterns and exceptions. These patterns and exceptions are then searched during the nightly processing activity. In running the nightly activity the system looks for:

1. Booking lead times.

2. Demand patterns such as average length of stay, no-shows, day of the week and seasonality.

3. Special events where for any set of dates there is significantly different:

   - Occupancy patterns

   - Market segment patterns and

   - Booking lead-time patterns.

4. Hotel booking patterns, where bookings are sorted into suitable forecasting groups. (Market segments and rates are translated into rate categories, as with rate fencing.)

The system also operates history databases, which keep track of all the detailed and summary information needed for forecasting as well as a monitoring system that surveys forecasts, whether system generated or manually input, for significant deviations of actual bookings from anticipated levels. Most systems also operate two other operations. Firstly is the overbooking system that allows 'overbooking' to make up for the no-shows, cancellations or early departures, whilst at the same time freeing rooms for additional guests. The second operation is the group evaluation system. This helps the property place and evaluate group demand. It provides the property manager with a tool to evaluate the group based on profitability, placement, displaced total demand and fair market rate.

As can be seen in Figure 15.1, the process of the latest software packages is very simple in its operation. It follows the procedures mentioned earlier, but unlike those it does it with a far greater depth of analysis than can normally be expected from a purely manual decision-making base.

Thus it can be seen that the use and development of yield management in the hotel industry has been enhanced greatly over the past few years. Initially seen as another fad, yield management has now been accepted as one of the major ways forward for the maximization of both space and revenue – which, after all, is the primary function and role of any discerning rooms division manager.

## SUMMARY

In this chapter we have looked at two very important aspects of the rooms management function of front office operations. The first part of the chapter looked at the use of yield management as a method of maximizing a hotel room's revenue as well as its space. It was seen that it was not sensible to sell a hotel bedroom for any price, despite how hard the sales department of a hotel may try to convince you. The role of the sales department is to show that they have all of the rooms, or at least as many as they can get, full. The rooms division manager had another agenda, and one that was more important to the company and its shareholders: to maximize the revenue achieved from a hotel bedroom. To do this required the appropriate front office staff to be vigilant about external constraints and trends, competition, in-house promotions, the effects of the weather, and so on. Based on all of this information they were then able to decide the extent to which they could insist on full rack rates rather than offer discounts of one sort or another. Whilst a form of rooms management had been available for many years, the use of the computer in hotels has had a profound effect.

In fact the effect of electronics has changed hotel operations in many ways. We explored this when we investigated the origins of the hotel computer and the reasons for and benefits of computerizing a hotel front desk and reservations. We had already found how important it was to use computers in the management of a hotel's rooms yield, but computers give management more statistical data faster, to enable them to make better informed decisions.

Finally a brief excursion was made into the possibilities created by the future advancement of computer technology.

# Review and discussion questions

1   Yield management is a method that can help a firm sell the right inventory unit to the right customer at the right time and for the right price. Discuss this statement in its application, using relevant examples from the hotel industry.

2   Yield management is only of relevance to large corporate hotels in North America. Discuss this statement.

3   Yield management is a revenue maximization technique that aims to increase net yield through the predicted allocation of available bedroom

capacity to pre-determined market segments and optimum price. Discuss this statement with relevance to the hotel industry.

4 Discuss how forecasting plays an important role in the implementation of yield management.

5 Yield management systems are forecast in the 'future' in terms of reservation management in the industry. Discuss the difficulties of implementing a yield management system in a hotel.

6 Assess the benefits and problems which can occur when implementing a yield management system in the rooms division department.

# 16

# *The electronic front office*

## Introduction

In today's modern hotel, computerization is becoming more and more important for the efficient and effective operation of the front office. Data are collected from all sources of the front office operation, i.e. from the time a guest makes a reservation to the time they actually check out of the hotel. The hotel records data, not just for the benefit of the guest, but also for the benefit of the hotel, especially in the analysis of data for the purposes of sales, marketing and finance. For example, the adoption of an overbooking policy requires data on previous guest stays and their status, trends, number of no-shows, non-guaranteed bookings and possible late cancellations. The use of computers can assist front office management with their short- and long-term planning of such strategies and policies.

It should be noted that this chapter is not intended to teach you how to use a computer in a front office department, but rather to understand the uses of computers and the benefits and problems associated with them.

## THE ELECTRONIC FRONT OFFICE

The development of the computerized hotel has taken place alongside that of the computer itself. Originally, hotels operated manual systems covering such matters as the control of the occupancy of their rooms (conventional or density charts), the recording of guest expenditure within the hotel (the posting of hand-written dockets to a tabular ledger) and the eventual departure of the guest (a handwritten bill and receipt).

With the improvement in both reliability and size of the adding machine, many companies, but most notably Sweda and NCR, designed and operated the mechanical billing machine. This piece of equipment was really a number of adding machines interlinked, all under one casing. However, mechanical billing machines were still reliant on the operator to hit the correct keys, and punch in the correct amounts, i.e. *accurately* transcribe information from the dockets to the keys of the machine.

With the advent of the transistor and the printed circuit board, hotels quickly started to use the electronic billing machines. Once again, the principles were the same as for a manual system, but with the added advantage that a limited memory was available. This meant that the machine held in a memory the final balance of all the guest accounts. This was a great step forward because one of the major problems of balancing the front desk folios was the occurrence of 'pick-up errors', which occurred when the receptionists inadvertently transcribed the last balance of the guest account incorrectly.

As developments in the technology of electronics and computerization gained pace so too did the developments in the use of computers in the hotel industry. What we see today is the logical progression of information and accounting systems from an entirely manual method of operation to an electronic method. Despite the change in systems methods, the basic principles are still the same. However, what we see today is a system which, apart from performing basic operations, is capable of automatically generating information, posting charges to guests' accounts and balancing its own functions. This does not mean that the receptionist or cashier is no longer necessary, but rather that they are relieved of some of the boring and repetitive work which is part of the day-to-day operation of every hotel front office.

An example of how things have changed is shown by the guest bill in Figures 16.1, 16.2 and 16.3.

First we see the bill with its charges as it would appear on a manual tabular ledger. The bill is handwritten, and every transaction is performed by the receptionist(s) on duty. At the end of each shift, and especially at the end of each day, the receptionist has to balance their work. Any alterations to the bill mean that the receptionist has to delete or 'white-out' the change.

| DATE | | | | | | | | | | | | |
|---|---|---|---|---|---|---|---|---|---|---|---|---|
| Brought forward | | | | | | | | | | | | |
| Apartment | | | | | | | | | | | | |
| Breakfast | | | | | | | | | | | | |
| Early Morning Tea/Coffee | | | | | | | | | | | | |
| Newspapers | | | | | | | | | | | | |
| Telephone | | | | | | | | | | | | |
| Paid Out | | | | | | | | | | | | |
| Laundry | | | | | | | | | | | | |
| Sundries | | | | | | | | | | | | |
| Lunch | | | | | | | | | | | | |
| Dinner | | | | | | | | | | | | |
| Wines & Spirits | | | | | | | | | | | | |
| | | | | | | | | | | | | |
| | | | | | | | | | | | | |
| DAILY TOTAL | | | | | | | | | | | | |
| Service Charge | | | | | | | | | | | | |
| | | | | | | | | | | | | |
| GRAND TOTAL | | | | | | | | | | | | |
| Less: Cash Received | | | | | | | | | | | | |
| Deposit | | | | | | | | | | | | |
| Carried Forward | | | | | | | | | | | | |

King's Hotel

Address: South Coast Road, Dover, Kent.
Telephone: (0527) 723 6788
Fax: (0527) 745 6345
E-mail: kingsotel@hotemail.com.uk

M _____ Room No: _____

VISITORS ARE REQUESTED TO VACATE THEIR ROOMS BY 12 NOON
ON THE DAY OF DEPARTURE.
ACCOUNTS DUE ON PRESENTATION. **PLEASE LEAVE YOUR KEY.**

**Figure 16.1** Example of a manual tab bill

With an electronic billing system the built-in memory of the last balance of the guest bill ensures that there are no 'pick-up' errors, and no overprinting of transactions. The electronic system also has an increased range of alpha-numeric characters. This means that a better description of the origins of the charges can be given. Not only does the bill look professional, but it is also easier to read and understand.

A computerized bill has no limitations as to the alpha-numeric characters which it can print, so the bill can be quite explicit as to the

| Amount: | | | Date | Ref. | No. | Code |
|---|---|---|---|---|---|---|
| Room no.: | 120 | | 12/12 | 001 | Rm | 85.00 |
| Rate: | 85 | | | ... | Tl | 85.00 |
| | | | 12/12 | 002 | Tel | 3.20 |
| No. in party: | 1 | | | | Bev | 4.20 |
| Name: | Jones | | | | Tel | 4.50 |
| Address: | 35 Main Street, Illogan, Cornwall | | | | Rest | 12.60 |
| | | | | | Wine | 3.60 |
| Terms: | | | | ... | Tl | 113.10 |
| Date of arr.: | 12/12/99 | | | | | |
| Date of dep.: | 13/12/99 | | | | | |

**Figure 16.2** Example of an electronic bill

origins of each charge. Because the charges can be sent directly to the guest's bill from any of the hotel's outlets, and the computer holds everything in its memory, when a guest bill is requested it is printed out neatly and precisely. Errors can be removed before the final bill is printed.

## Activity 1

On p. 298 is a chart showing the development of the three main billing systems. Complete the chart using the criteria given. Note that some of the elements have already been filled in for you.

## REASONS FOR HAVING AN ELECTRONIC FRONT OFFICE

The electronic front office is expensive, and to justify its cost it must offer substantial benefits both to the hotel and its guests. Many jobs in the front office are suited for the use of a computer because of their

| | | | | | Address: | South Coast Road, Dover, Kent. |
| | | | | | Telephone: | (0527) 723 6788 |
| | | KING'S HOTEL | | | Fax: | (0527) 745 6345 |
| | | | | | E-mail: | kingsotel@hotemail.com.uk |

Arrival:      12/12/99
Departure:    13/12/99
No. in party: 1
Rate:         85.00

| Account no. | Date | Room no. | Description | Amount | |
|---|---|---|---|---|---|
| 1200 | 12/12 | 120 | Restaurant | 23.90 | 23.90 |
| 1324 | 12/12 | 120 | Dickens Bar | 1.10 | 25.00 |
| 1256 | 12/12 | 120 | Room Serv. | 6.50 | 31.50 |
| 1342 | 12/12 | 120 | Telephone | 4.40 | 35.90 |
| 1145 | 12/12 | 120 | Room | 95.00 | 130.90 |
| | 12/12 | 120 | Adjust. room | -10.00 | 120.90 |
| 1453 | 12/12 | 120 | Paid out | 15.00 | 135.90 |
| 1325 | 13/12 | 120 | Visa | 135.90 | 0 |

All charges include VAT and service charge.

**Figure 16.3** Example of a computer-generated bill

clerical, repetitive, data manipulation and number calculating nature. They can include: the processing of reservations and registering of guests; the updating of room status; posting guests' charges; settling folios; updating of guest history; and generating relevant reports for use by department heads and management.

Despite the large amount of information, computers work with great speed and accuracy. The benefit for the front office is that information is current, is accurate and is made available more quickly. For example, for reservations it improves forecasting; it gives room status availability; a guest's history is easier to obtain; it enhances direct and up-to-date guest billing; it provides automatic telephone billing; and, for accommodation budgeting, past data are easily accessible.

Computerizing front office operations can also have other benefits, including streamlining of paper and data, improving the control over the front office operations, reducing unnecessary costs, particularly labour costs, by automating jobs that are clerical and often repetitive, as well as improving the service to the guest.

|  | Tabular | Electronic | Computer |
|---|---|---|---|
| Economy | Cheap to operate | ? | ? |
| Time | ? | Quick to use, no need to pick up balances | ? |
| Neatness | ? | ? | Very neat, with printing facilities |
| Accuracy | ? | ? | ? |
| Balance | Slow to balance | ? | ? |
| Analysis | ? | ? | Quick; enter code and dept |
| Checks and copies | ? | Copies of all bills, audit rolls | ? |
| Control | ? | ? | ? |

**Activity 1**: chart to be completed

Computer systems can also help reduce the front office problems of long check-out time. The use of guest facilities, e.g. mini-bars, in-house movies, telephones, restaurant and bars, can be instantaneously billed to the appropriate room numbers. Guest folios can be remotely inspected by the guests on their television screen prior to check-out.

Many problems over the years, between housekeeping and the front desk, have arisen over the point at which a room becomes ready for letting. The advantage of a computer system is that the housekeeping can be linked to the same system, so that when rooms have been serviced or are vacant this information is readily available to the front office department. No time is wasted on telephone calls and trying to find the housekeeper. Room status information is instantly available between housekeeping and the front office.

An electronic front office does not mean that it operates in isolation. On the contrary, the front office now has the ability to work directly with many or all of the other departments within the hotel. Departments such as housekeeping, restaurants, bars or a health club all have access to the information normally held at the front desk. This ability to call up front desk information is known as being interfaced with the front desk.

We will now investigate the jobs and tasks most commonly served by the electronic front office.

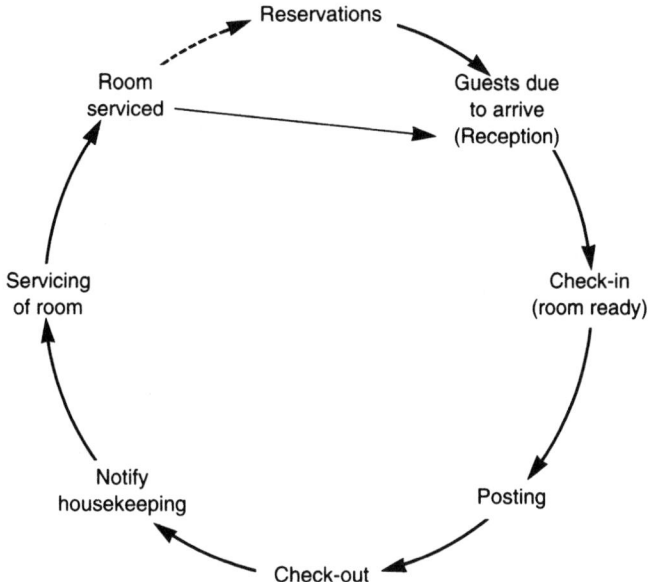

**Figure 16.4** Room status information between front office and housekeeping

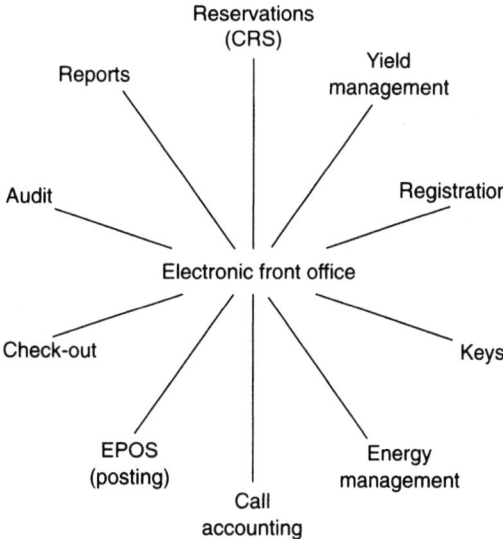

**Figure 16.5** Jobs and tasks served by the electronic front office

## RESERVATIONS

The reservation system is capable of taking the information on a forth-coming room booking for either an individual or a tour or group, and matching it against the existing data held in the computer. This is done almost instantaneously, and, provided that the room status is correct within the system, it is completely accurate. The matching process does not simply see whether that type of room is available on that date, but will also look at room location, facilities, rates or any other parameters you wish to enter against a room. Once the booking has been made, all of the information, along with any special requests, is kept in the memory of the computer for anything up to three years.

The front office manager can access the reservation system to obtain a variety of information which would be helpful to them in their role, e.g. information concerning credit card guaranteed reservations, last-minute cancelled bookings, deposits for rooms, blocked-out rooms, estimated times of arrivals or departures, VIP and CIP lists, and projected occupancy forecasts.

The CRS (central reservation system) may also be a part of the internal house reservation system. This permits the guest of one hotel to know the availability of rooms in a sister hotel, either in the same country or internationally. For example, a guest staying at the Holiday Inn, London, could know within minutes whether or not the Holiday Inn Crowne Plaza in Beijing can accommodate them.

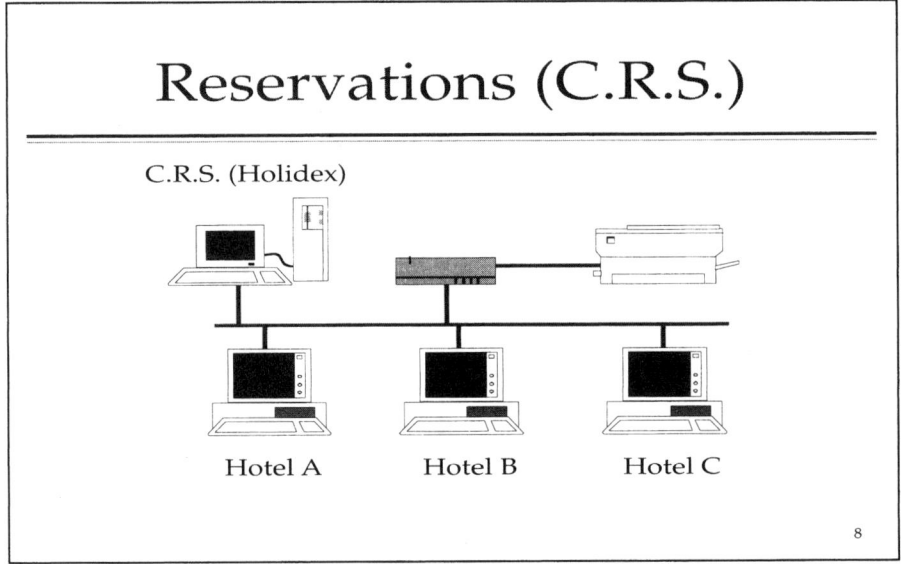

**Figure 16.6** Example of reservations through CRS

### Reservations and the customer

With the growth of technology, the computer, especially through the Internet, and e-mail have become powerful tools for today's customers. The customer, through seamless connectivity, can access, through the Internet, a global distribution system which links directly the reservation systems of hotels, airlines, car rentals and travel agency companies on a worldwide basis. The customer can sit at home and book his/her airline tickets, car rental and reservation in most parts of the world. Most large hotel companies are now on the Internet which makes it much easier for the customer to check marketing information, room availability, room rates and, through the increase in security passwords, to generate a booking using a credit card. Figure 16.7 illustrates how this process can be achieved, through the Internet, global distribution system, central reservation system and, finally, to the individual hotel reservation system. Therefore the role of the reservation clerk is changing and they have to become more computer-literate and able to handle more bookings via the Internet/e-mail and to ensure the information on the Internet is relevant and updated.

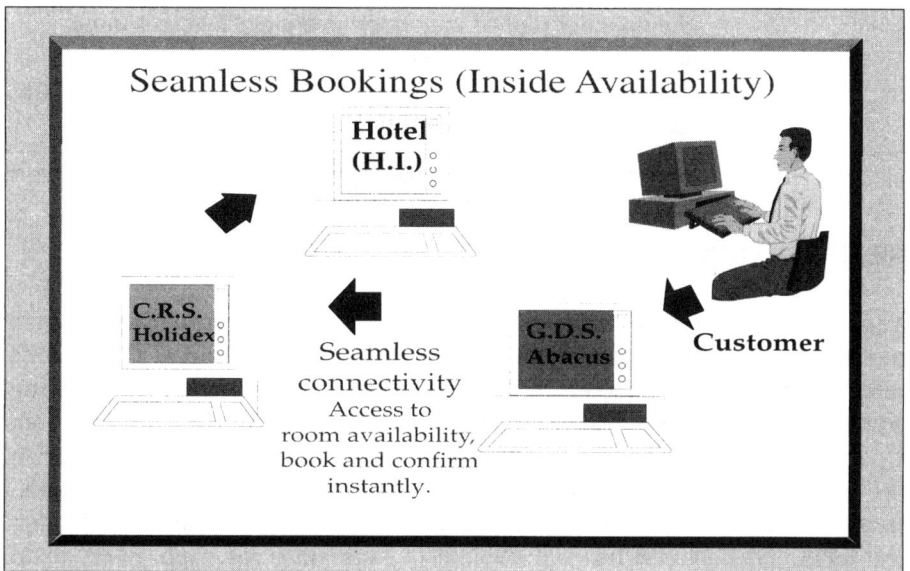

**Figure 16.7** Example of seamless bookings

## YIELD MANAGEMENT

Yield management is a room management technique which has been adapted from airlines to suit the hotel industry. Its main purpose is to maximize room occupancy while at the same time realizing the best average room rate.

A computerized yield management system enables the reservations clerk to make the best choices as to what rooms to take and at what price. The system gives the ability to instantly analyse the profit potential of each booking. This is done by adjusting the room rate to suit the need for rooms at any particular time.

So that an accurate assessment of room needs can be made, all historical guest information, low and high demand periods, availability of room rates and sources of business are all computerized. This information, along with knowledge of local activities, can assist the sales and booking clerks to see at a glance all of the 'What if . . .' possibilities, not just for the day-to-day operation, but well into the future.

**Activity 2**  Given the following request for rooms, what information would you want from the computer to add to your own knowledge to decide whether or not to accept it?

You are a 170-roomed city centre hotel near to a major airport. Horizon Airlines has requested 50 single rooms in the quietest part of your hotel every night from 1 June through to 15 November. Because of the volume of business they are giving you, they have requested a 60 per cent discount on room rate.

## REGISTRATION

The computerized front office can be seen to come very much into its own at the point when a guest checks into a hotel. Because all of the guest's information has been taken by the reservations clerk when the booking was made, all that the receptionist has to do is call up that information. Upon the arrival of the guest the receptionist calls on the system to print the guest's registration card, confirms all of the details with the guest, confirms the method of payment, and then simply gets the guest to sign the form. This procedure will obviously save time for each guest upon check-in, and in turn reduce the queues which tend to form at busy times.

Whether the room booking was made direct to the hotel or via a central reservations office does not matter. The information is held in the computer system, and can be accessed by the hotel at any time.

Even at the front desk, technology has developed. A remote check-in system called 'the roaming front desk' has been introduced. It is a portable computer, hand held, with a small printer and a magnetic card swipe, and is interfaced to the hotel property management system. A customer can use a touch-screen keypad to download reservation details and to check in from any remote location. The system has signature capability and credit card recognition, and prints a registration form for customer use.

Also, the use of the multi-functional travel/'smart card' is becoming more popular. A smart card can include many functions, such as:

- Hotel booking information

- Credit card details

- Passport details

- Customer photograph

- Ticketing and boarding information

- Storage of biometric identifier (hand geometry) – used for check-in/check-out and immigration clearance

- Access on plane 'smart phones'

- Storage of hotel loyalty/frequent flier points

Many hotels which run a computerized system now have the electronic room key system linked with the front desk computer. Once the guest has checked into the hotel, and the receptionist has allocated a room and processed the arrival, a paper or plastic room key is automatically printed. Simultaneously the lock configuration of the allocated room is changed to suit the unique key. This means that upon check-out or should the guest inadvertently lose their key, the lock is reprogrammed, and that any lost keys or keys belonging to previous guests will not be able to be used. This, therefore, ensures a far greater element of room and guest security.

## ENERGY MANAGEMENT

An energy management system (EMS) is a system which is designed to control automatically the operation of mechanical equipment in a hotel, so as to achieve the optimum savings on utilities such as gas and electricity. This system determines when equipment such as heating, air conditioning and ventilation can be turned on or off, or regulated up or down. An example would be the control of lighting and central heating or air conditioning of a guest's room. When the guest enters the room they insert their key into a special socket located next to the door. This notifies the energy system to activate all power to that room, which in turn means that the room lights can be turned on and the room ventilation system works. When the guest leaves the room, the system will automatically shut down after a short delay period, thus saving on electricity that would be wasted if room lights were left on, and saving gas or oil from heating a room which is not in use.

It is important that the front office staff notify the guest upon arrival that the hotel has an energy management system. They must also explain that the electricity and room ventilation system have to be operated by inserting the key into the slot by the door.

## CALL ACCOUNTING SYSTEM

A call accounting system (CAS) can also be interfaced to the hotel's main front office computer or it may operate as a stand-alone system. A call accounting system handles, as the name implies, all local and international telephone calls and automatically charges all of the appropriate costs to the guest's folio.

The main advantages of this system include the following: the guest can call direct from their room without having to go through the hotel operator; it enhances guest services and guest satisfaction, by offering an instantaneous and private telephone link; the system automatically records the call details in their fullest extent, thereby ensuring that possible customer complaints are reduced; the accuracy of processing telephone charges is greatly increased through the use of a call accounting system.

Because the CAS reduces the need for operator intervention, the hotel telephone department can utilize the time of its staff more efficiently and at the same time offer the guest a better service.

---

**Activity 3**
(a) List the reasons why a call accounting system benefits the hotel guest.

(b) How does a call accounting system benefit the work of the hotel switchboard operator?

---

## ELECTRONIC POINT-OF-SALE (EPOS) SYSTEMS

Another interface to the front office system is that of an electronic point-of-sale system. This is made up of a number of computerized cash registers, better known as terminals, commonly found in the food and beverage departments of a hotel.

The interface of the food and beverage EPOS system allows an instantaneous and automatic transfer of charges to the guest's account at the front desk. For example, a guest can have breakfast and the charges incurred will have been posted to their account before they actually leave the restaurant or coffee shop.

Similarly, the EPOS system can work in the lounge areas, and bars, as shown in Figure 16.8.

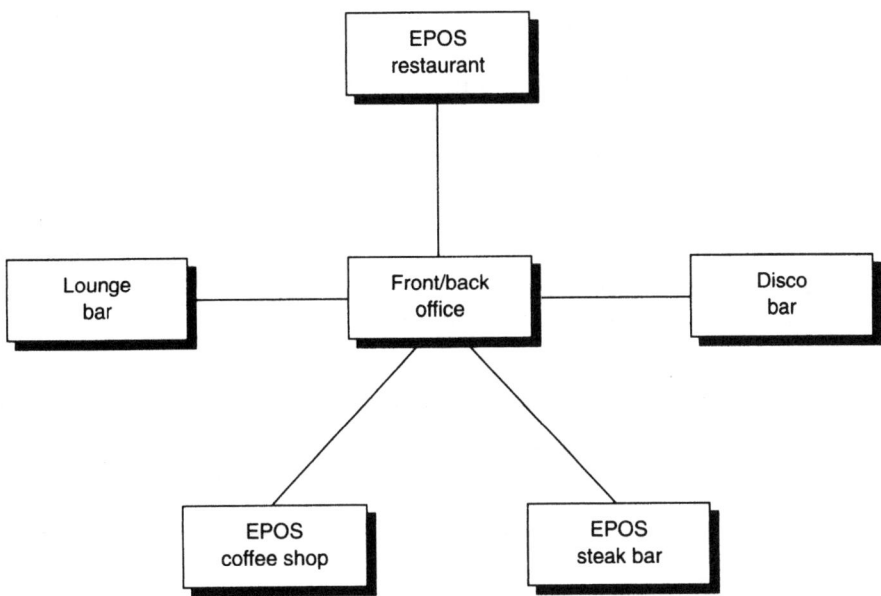

**Figure 16.8** Electronic point of sale's interface with the front office

## CHECK-OUT

The hotel computer system greatly helps to reduce the drudgery of the guest check-out procedures. It prints, in a matter of seconds, an accurate, neat and complete guest folio, unlike a semi-automated system, which may show charges from other guests, reversed charges, and over-printing, all of which reduce the image of the hotel, as well as making the bill difficult for the guest to read.

The computerized system also helps to reduce the check-out queue, which is a common complaint found in many hotels. The system does so by speeding up the settlement process by offering such facilities as an automatic foreign currency conversion, a constant monitoring of house and credit limits, and an automatic verification of company account status.

A fully automatic 'in-room' check-out system directly linked to an on-line credit card computer system offers prompt service to the guest. The guest can simply call up their account to date on their television screen. If, at the end of the guest's stay, the bill is accepted as being correct, then all the guest has to do is to ensure that they have their method of payment and the appropriate amount ready when they check out at the front desk. Alternatively, should the guest be paying by credit card or sending their account to the company, they can sign an 'express check-out' card which is in their room, acknowledging that they agree with the bill, and simply place it in the sealed box provided at reception.

This check-out system has now been extended with the use of a computer-synthesized voice response. The guest-room telephone is interfaced to the front office computer system, and by a simple telephone call the guest can provide information as to their special requests, as well as give directions as to their check-out procedure.

At the point of check-out the cashier can ascertain whether or not the guest would like another booking at the hotel for a later date, or a booking at a sister hotel, thus giving the guest an increased service, and at the same time helping to increase hotel occupancy. Transfers to city ledger are electronically made at this time.

**Activity 4**    In what ways can a computerized check-out system improve the image of the hotel to a guest?

## AUDIT

As mentioned in Chapter 9, the work of the audit clerk, which is very often conducted through the night, is labour-intensive. It requires posted entries to be verified, accounts to be balanced, the cash flow to be checked, any room discrepancies to be resolved as well as acting as a front desk clerk.

The front office computer greatly simplifies the audit procedure, by self-balancing. This means that the computer automatically checks that the correct amount has been posted to the correct room, that the totals for the various customer service outlets cross-balance with the amounts paid into reception as cash or credit, and that the actual room status input by housekeeping matches the front desk room status. From all of these audit procedures come the reports which are required by management and operational supervisors.

## REPORTING

One of the major features of a front office computer system is the ability to retrieve and print relevant reports for management, other departments and other sections of the front office department, such as housekeeping, cashiers, mail and information, reservations and so on. The amount and type of reporting can vary considerably; for example, the housekeeping may require an up-to-date list of all the day's check-ins and check-outs, or the front office manager may require an hourly report of the room status from the front desk or even current status from the

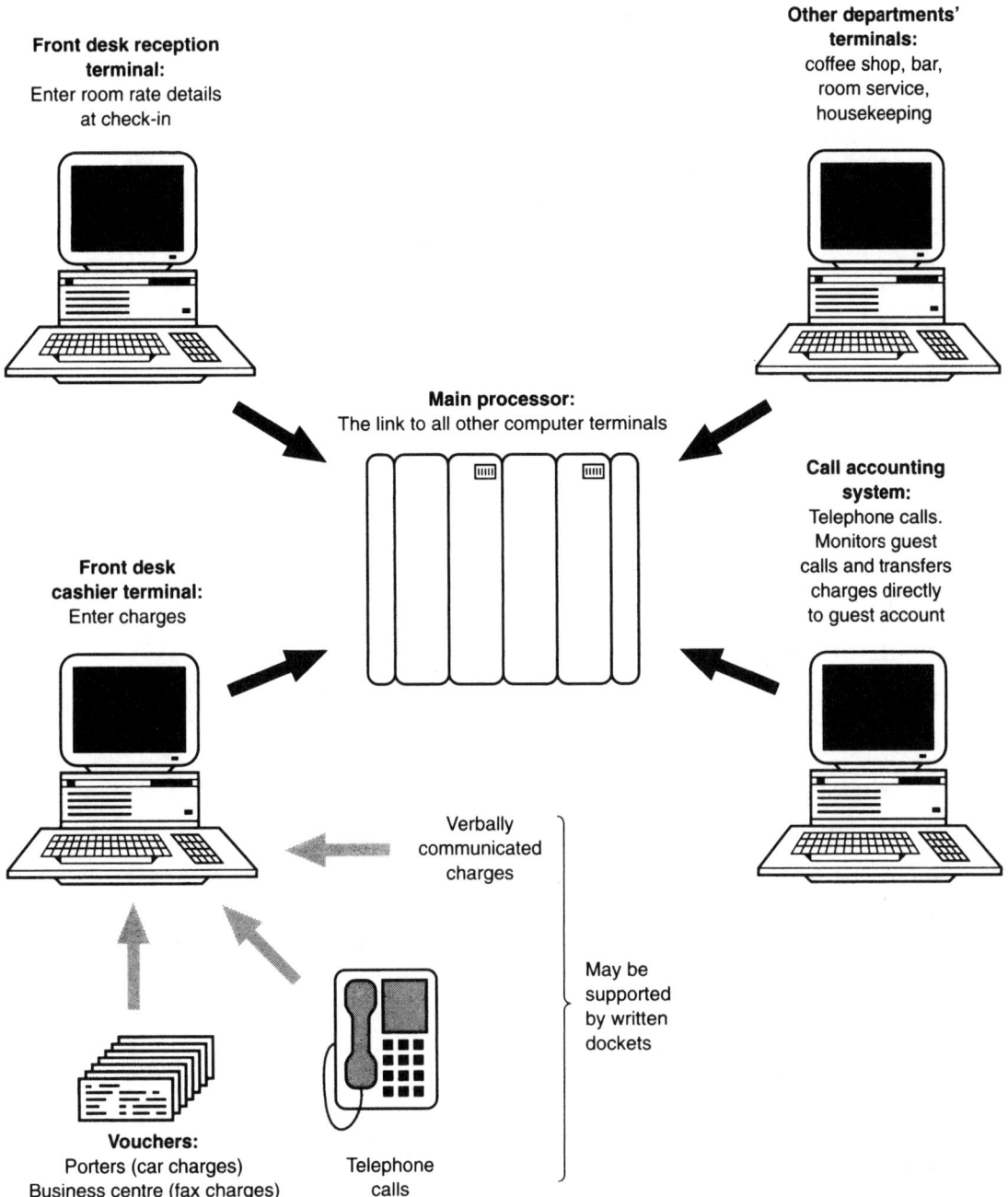

**Figure 16.9** A computer-based front office accounting system

housekeeping department. The hotel manager may require particular statistical information, perhaps on room occupancy, average room rate, bed occupancy, average sleeper room rate, average guest expenditure, and cash and credit takings for the day. All this information can be obtained using the appropriate report program through the front office system.

As well as obtaining reports on a daily basis, data can be collected and reports produced on a monthly, yearly or when-required basis.

The report program on a front office computer system enables management to have an accurate idea of the current state of affairs of the hotel's operation. Other relevant reports can include the following:

- No-show report
- Hotel statistic report
- Advance ledger deposit
- Today's arrival report
- Today's departure report
- In-house guest list
- Guest ledger report
- VIP report
- Rate discrepancies
- Geographic statistics report
- Housekeeping report
- Night audit report
- Credit check report
- Cashier's report

Many other reports, peculiar to an individual hotel, can be programmed to be printed, based upon the needs of the individual management requirements.

## DATA PROTECTION ACT 1984

It should be noted that since November 1987, under the Data Protection Act 1984, 'all individuals are entitled to be given details of personal information concerning them held by a Data User'. This would include guest histories as well as staff records, but hotels are able to apply for exemption.

## TOMORROW'S ELECTRONIC FRONT OFFICE

With the continual decrease in the costs of setting up a front office computerized system, more and more hotels are using them. However, in almost direct proportion to the reduction in costs is the advancement of the facilities and tasks which a computer can now perform. As mentioned earlier, some hotels now have voice-operated systems. Soon to follow is biometric computer operation, in which the computer will recognize the guest's physical characteristics, such as their hand-print. This could then replace the need for guest-room keys.

Check-in systems are also being updated. A guest can check in to a hotel without necessarily contacting the front desk. They initiate the self-registration process by inserting their credit card into a terminal situated in the hotel lobby, and then enter their particular details. This terminal can be interfaced into the front desk room assignment program, which would then automatically allocate an appropriate room and a relevant rate, and program the room lock to accept only that guest.

As well as improving check-in and check-out procedures for the benefit of the guest, many other technological services can be provided. These include: electronic indicators informing the front desk when a guest is not in the room, so that servicing and turndown service can be provided without interrupting the guest; in-room computers linked to external computer information services, such as airline schedules, entertainment guides, stock market reports, local restaurant guides, and cable television; and in-room beverage service systems. This type of system is capable of monitoring all sales transactions, as well as determining the necessary inventory replenishment quantity.

The interactive television-based services are also enhancing their technology to include such functions as language selection, room status and repair report, conference audio/video relay services, personal welcome message, voicemail, wake-up services, guest questionnaires, digital television, Internet/intranet/e-mail services, CD/DVD-ROM, promotional movies and tele-shopping. The hotel product is changing in the guest bedroom to allow for such developments. Also, it is becoming what the customer expects.

To stay ahead of the competition, more and more hotels are concentrating on data mining, also known as 'warehousing'. This is where hotel companies centralize their guest history records. Previously, individual hotels kept a record of their customers. Now, this information is being centralized. This means that any hotel within that company can have access to the customer details. Therefore, the receptionist can recognize the customer's needs prior to their arrival and keep track of their preferences.

The possible uses to which the computer can be put are as varied as the imagination of the computer experts. Technology is undergoing continuous change, and it is therefore vitally important that the professional front office employee keeps fully up-to-date.

**Activity 5** Using your imagination, give examples of the future potential of computers in the hotel industry.

## SUMMARY

In this chapter we have been concerned with identifying the uses and benefits of a front office computer system. We first investigated the origins of the hotel computer, and explored the reasons for and benefits of computerizing a hotel front desk, such as eliminating repetitive clerical tasks. Some of these tasks included the processing of reservations, updating of room status, posting guests' charges and preparing relevant reports for management. A computer system also increases and enhances the availability of statistical data, thus enabling better management decisions through faster and more accurate information.

We then looked at the effects of the electronic front office on reservations, yield management, check-in, energy management, EPOS, checkout, auditing and management reporting. These areas were expanded so as to look at the benefits which would be gained by both the guest and the hotel.

Finally, a brief excursion was made into the possibilities created by the future advancement of computer technology.

# Review and discussion questions

1  State the advantages and disadvantages of using a computerized system in the front office.

2  Explain why some people may be frightened by computer systems.

3  Discuss what other areas in a hotel can be interfaced into the front office system, explaining their usage and benefits.

4  How do the reports printed by the computer help management run their hotel more efficiently?

5  'Computers can enhance customer service.' Discuss this statement.

6  If you were asked to investigate the advisability or otherwise of computerizing a small hotel, which areas would you begin with and why?

# Glossary of terms

**ABTA**  Association of British Travel Agents.

**Adjoining rooms**  Two or more rooms side by side without a connecting door between them.

**Affiliate reservation system**  Hotel reservation system in which all hotels within the same hotel chain participate.

**AH&MA**  American Hotel and Motel Association.

**Airline rate**  A reduced rate offered to airline crew and personnel.

**À la carte**  Individual dishes on a menu individually priced.

**American plan**  All meals are included with the accommodation, i.e. breakfast, lunch, dinner and sometimes afternoon tea. Also known as **en pension** or **full board**.

**Arrival and departure lists**  Lists of expected arrivals and departures for a particular day, normally prepared and distributed the evening before to all relevant departments.

**Average room rate**  The average income generated from each room.

**Back-of-the house**  Service areas in which the staff have little or no direct guest contact, e.g. personnel, accounting and purchasing departments.

**Back to back**  Heavy check-out and check-in on the same day, relating to tours and groups. As one tour leaves another arrives.

| | |
|---|---|
| **Blacklist** | A list authorized by the hotel management of the names of all persons not welcome in the hotel. |
| **Block booking** | Term used for a reservation for several people at the same time, normally on the same rate, e.g. tours, groups or conference delegates. |
| **Budget hotels** | Provide cheaper and more basic guest-rooms, often with limited food and beverage services. |
| **Cancellation** | A term meaning that a guest with a booking cancels the room in time for the room to be re-let. |
| **Cash sale** | When goods are sold for cash. Also known as **chance** and **walk-in business**. |
| **Cashier's office** | Office separated from that of front office where payment of guests' accounts, foreign currency and safe deposits are made. |
| **Chance guest** | Customer who arrives at the hotel with no previous booking made. Also known as a **walk-in guest**. |
| **Charge voucher** | A bill or docket showing the details of the amounts to be charged to a guest's account, e.g. drinks in the bar. |
| **Check-in** | The procedure of registration as well as a name given to a guest who arrives at the hotel and registers. |
| **Check-out** | The procedure of settling the hotel account on departure of a guest as well as a name given to a guest who settles the account and leaves the hotel. |
| **CIP** | Commercially important person. A person who has influence over a large amount of business. |
| **City accounts** | Records of financial transactions between the hotel and non-resident guests. |
| **Closed dates** | Particular dates on which the hotel is fully booked. |
| **Commercial hotel** | Hotel which mainly caters for business people. |
| **Commission** | Payment or discount made to a travel agent or company for the introduction of the business. |
| **Communicating rooms** | Rooms side by side with a door between, allowing access to each room without the use of a public corridor. Also known as **connecting rooms**. |

| | |
|---|---|
| **Concierge** | See **Porter's desk**. |
| **Confirmed booking** | Written or verbal confirmation by a hotel that a booking has been accepted. |
| **Continental plan** | This rate includes breakfast as well as the accommodation. Also known as **room and breakfast**. |
| **Contract** | A legally binding agreement between two parties. |
| **Conventional chart** | An availability chart showing room numbers, type of room, guest's name and length of stay. Normally used in the reservation departments of smaller hotels. |
| **Corporate rate** | An agreed rate charged for executive personnel from businesses and corporations, normally regular guests. |
| **Credit card** | Issued to persons by a credit card company or bank; allows the holder to charge amounts and pay at a later date. Examples are Visa and American Express. |
| **Curtailment** | Means that a booking has been made for longer than the guest actually requires the room. Also known as **understay**. |
| **Day let** | A room let during the day for business use. |
| **Deadline** | The final date by which a provisional booking must be confirmed to the hotel. |
| **Density chart** | An availability chart commonly used in large hotels, displaying the total number and type of rooms available each night. Used in the reservation office. |
| **Deposit** | Payment received in advance to guarantee a booking; it does not constitute a contract. |
| **Disbursement** | See **VPO**. |
| **Dishonoured cheque** | Cheque returned by the bank, usually when an error has been made. |
| **Double-bedded room** | A room for two persons with one large bed, normally 4'6''. In American terminology this can also mean the same as a **twin**. |
| **Double occupancy** | Room occupied by two persons. |
| **Drawee** | Bank on which a cheque is drawn. |
| **Drawer** | Normally the person who signs a cheque. |

| | |
|---|---|
| **Early departure** | Means when a guest leaves prior to the original departure date. Also known as **curtailment** and **understay**. |
| **EMT** | Early morning tea (can include coffee). |
| **European plan** | Room-only rate, no meals included. |
| **Executive floors** | Rooms provided, especially to business people, on a separate floor which also provides separate check-in desks, meeting-room space, business centre facilities and sometimes separate lounge and bar areas. |
| **FIT** | Free (foreign) independent traveller. International traveller, normally requiring accommodation only. |
| **Float** | An amount of money entrusted to the cashier for the purpose of giving change and making small payments. |
| **Floor limit** | A maximum amount a hotel can accept on a credit card. Also known as **sanction limit**. |
| **Folio** | Guest bill on which all charges are recorded. Also known as **guest account**. |
| **Foyer** | See **Lobby**. |
| **Front desk** | Area of the front office where a guest registers, where keys are possibly kept and where information can be obtained. |
| **Full-service hotel** | Provides a wide selection of guest services in addition to accommodation, such as food and beverage, room service, laundry services, etc. |
| **GIT** | Group inclusive tour. A package tour. |
| **Group rate** | Specific room rate for group, agreed by hotel and group in advance. Also known as **flat rate**. |
| **Guaranteed booking** | Reservation held overnight as payment has been made to hold the room whether or not the guest arrives. |
| **High season** | Peak season of a hotel; prices are normally at their highest. |
| **Hospitality industry** | A collective term for businesses providing accommodation and/or food and beverages to people who are away from home. |
| **Hotel diary** | A book which records all the guest's details under date of arrival order. |

| | |
|---|---|
| **Hotel register** | A system used when guests are checking into the hotel to record personal details of that guest. Some of this information is required by law. |
| **House count** | Number of rooms let on a particular day. |
| **Housekeeping department** | Responsible for the management of guest-rooms and the cleanliness of all public areas of a hotel. |
| **Imprinter** | Machine used to imprint details from a credit card onto the sales voucher. |
| **Incidental account** | Charges which are the guest's own responsibility and are not paid for by a company or travel agent. |
| **Inspected** | Room has been thoroughly checked by a supervisor or housekeeper. |
| **Interleading rooms** | See **Communicating rooms**. Also known as **interconnecting rooms** |
| **Key card** | Card issued to the guest on registration. It displays room number, name, rate and other relevant details. Used when the guest requests the key. |
| **Lead time** | Time period from when a booking was made to the time a guest checks into the hotel. |
| **Lobby** | Entrance hall of the hotel; same as **foyer**. |
| **Lost property book** | Book kept by the housekeeper; records all lost property found in the hotel. |
| **Low season** | Quietest period at the hotel; prices are normally at their lowest. |
| **Luggage book** | Book kept by concierge, records all the dealings concerning guests' luggage, e.g. number of articles handled, by whom, and from or to where they were taken. |
| **Mail advice note** | A form notifying a guest that a letter or parcel is awaiting collection. |
| **Management accounts** | Expense accounts or allowances given by some hotels to the hotel management. |
| **Master bill** | The main account on which charges have been recorded to a company or particular guest. Charges not recorded on the main account are normally posted on an **incidental account**. |

| | |
|---|---|
| **Modified American plan** | The rate includes room, breakfast and one meal, usually dinner. Also known as **demi-pension** and **half board**. |
| **No-show** | Person who has made a reservation and does not arrive on a particular day. |
| **Non-affiliate reservation system** | A subscription system which is designed to connect independently operated hotels. |
| **Non-profit-making business** | Business which is not run specifically to make a profit, e.g. private clubs, institutional or welfare catering. |
| **Open** | Term meaning rooms are available for letting. |
| **Out of order** | Rooms not available for letting, e.g. rooms being repaired or redecorated. |
| **Overbooking** | Term meaning to accept more rooms than there are available. This is done to ensure 100 per cent occupancy, allowing for cancellations, no-shows and early departures. |
| **Payee** | Person to whom a cheque is made payable. |
| **Porter's desk** | Area situated in the front of house in which porters, bellboys and doormen carry out their duties. Also known as **concierge**. |
| **Posting** | Term used for entering charges onto a guest's account. |
| **Prepayment** | An amount paid in advance of services rendered. |
| **Pre-registration** | Registration details provided in advance of a guest's stay, e.g. a tour or group. |
| **Profit-making business** | A business set up with the intention to earn a profit, e.g. commercial restaurants and hotels. |
| **Rack rate** | Current rate charged for each room as established by the hotel management. |
| **Reception office** | Section of the front office dealing with check-ins and room status. |
| **Release time** | Booking held for a guest for a particular time; if they do not arrive, room can be re-let to another guest. |
| **Reservation form** | Form used to record all the guest's details when accepting a booking. |

| | |
|---|---|
| **Reservation office** | Section of the front office where all reservations are dealt with on behalf of the guests. |
| **Revenue management** | See **Yield management**. |
| **Room occupancy percentage** | Refers to the actual number of rooms let as a percentage: Rooms sold/Total rooms available $\times$ 100 per cent. |
| **Room state/ status** | Indicates whether a room is occupied, vacant or reserved at any given time. |
| **Safe deposit** | A facility offered to guests for the storage of valuable property. |
| **Self-catering hotel** | Provides no other service besides basic accommodation. |
| **Shoulder period** | A price offered between high and low season. |
| **Single** | Room for one person. |
| **SITs** | Special interest tours. People who normally visit a place once. |
| **Skip** | See **Walk-out**. |
| **Sleeper** | A person occupying sleeping accommodation in the hotel. |
| **SPATTS** | Special attention guests. |
| **Standard room rack rate** | Standard rate for the room, normally without meals, discounts or reductions. |
| **Stay-on** | A guest who makes a booking for more than one night; also refers to the second and subsequent nights of the guest's stay. |
| **Stay-over** | A guest who was expected to check out and now wishes to stay an extra night or nights. |
| **Table d'hôte** | A set menu at a set price. |
| **Tours** | A party of people staying at the hotel for the same period. Also known as **GIT**s. |
| **Travel agent** | An agent who reserves accommodation and activities at the hotel on behalf of the guest, and who normally charges a commission. |

| | |
|---|---|
| **Twin** | One room with two separate beds. |
| **VIP** | Very important person. |
| **VPO** | Visitors paid out. When the hotel cashier will pay out on behalf of the guest, e.g. flowers, theatre tickets. Also known as disbursement. |
| **Walking a guest** | The relocating in another hotel (owing to lack of available rooms) of guests who hold a confirmed or a guaranteed reservation. |
| **Walk-in** | See **Chance guest**. |
| **Walk-out** | A person who leaves the hotel without paying their account. Also known as a **skip**. |
| **Wash factor** | The number of rooms which are reduced during the period of lead time. This is forecast as a percentage by the front office manager; normally applies to GIT bookings. |
| **Whitney system** | A patented system incorporating all guest details from the time a guest makes a reservation through to departure. The system may be used in part or as a complete system. |
| **Yield management** | A room and revenue maximization technique. Also known as revenue management. |
| **Z-bed** | A portable bed which can be folded up for easy storage. |

# Index